Belief, Language, and Experience

BELIEF,
LANGUAGE,
AND
EXPERIENCE

RODNEY NEEDHAM

Fellow of Merton College, Oxford

BASIL BLACKWELL · OXFORD

ISBN 0 631 14430 7

Printed in Great Britain by
Western Printing Services Ltd, Bristol
and bound at the Kemp Hall Bindery, Oxford

To the memory of
LUCIEN LÉVY-BRUHL
(1857–1938)
and of

LUDWIG WITTGENSTEIN
(1889–1951)

Contents

Acknowledgements

The epigraph, from T. S. Eliot's 'East Coker', is reprinted from *Four Quartets* (London, 1945) by kind permission of Messrs. Faber & Faber, London, and Messrs. Harcourt Brace Jovanovich, Inc., New York. The numerous quotations from the works of Wittgenstein are made by leave of Messrs. Basil Blackwell & Mott, Ltd., and Ludwig Wittgenstein's literary executors.

So here I am, in the middle way, having had twenty years—
Twenty years largely wasted, . . .—
Trying to learn to use words, and every attempt
Is a wholly new start, and a different kind of failure
Because one has only learnt to get the better of words
For the thing one no longer has to say, or the way in which
One is no longer disposed to say it. And so each venture
Is a new beginning, a raid on the inarticulate
With shabby equipment always deteriorating. . . .

T. S. ELIOT

Preface

I

This investigation is an attempt, from a comparative standpoint, to answer Wittgenstein's question: 'Is belief an experience?' More largely, the issue is whether a capacity for belief constitutes a natural resemblance among men such as must form part of any account of human powers.

The result is less simple to characterize. Although I am by academic title and employment a social anthropologist, this work is not an ordinary anthropological monograph. Some of my colleagues may well think that it is not really social anthropology but more an exercise in philosophy. It is quite likely, for that matter, to be dismissed in certain quarters as what I have been assured is 'airy . . . metaphysical nonsense', not at all the solid stuff of legal cases, decision-making, or struggles for political advantage. Certainly it propounds no sociological generalizations, establishes no empirical correlations, and says very little directly about the organization of groups and the regulation of social life. In these respects perhaps the more rigid or pragmatical critics in the profession might have a point, for in everyday terms my ultimate concern is indeed philosophical rather than anthropological. But this also is to put a too exclusive and disjunctive cast on the inquiry, for it is not conventionally philosophical either but is more recalcitrant to definition.

What kind of an undertaking it actually is may be indicated by the very difficulties encountered in the search for an informative sub-title. Some of the descriptions considered were: A Revisionary Essay in Comparative Epistemology; An Anthropological Essay on the Philosophy of Mind; Comparative Ethnography and Cognitive Philosophy. But none of these, at any rate, would serve. I decidedly did not want 'Anthropology' on the title page, for the word not only had little useful meaning but would put off many of the potential readers whom I wanted to get at. 'Philosophy' sounded too grand, or presumptuous, and obscured the predominantly empirical aspect of the argument. 'Epistemology' was closer but too narrow and eventually misleading, for it was not strictly knowledge that was in question but belief. Moreover, even phrases so comprehensive as these were not nearly wide enough, for I wanted to engage the attention of theologians and linguists and psychologists as well, and I could not cater for them all in a line. So in the end I dispensed with a formal sub-title, and this discursion has taken its place.

The burden of it all is that I have tried to tackle an issue which transcends the conventional boundaries of academic subjects and which has to do with fundamental premises of any humane discipline. While it is true that I think of this line of inquiry as belonging to an empirical philosophy, which is how I conceive the social anthropology that stems from the Enlightenment, I wish to offer this essay to anyone, of whatever occupation or persuasion, who is seriously interested in the interpretation of human experience. It is not about anthropology but about man, not science but life.

II

The investigation was begun, in January 1968, as a tribute to Professor E. E. Evans-Pritchard, and the resultant paper was to have been a contribution to a Festschrift in his honour (Beidelman 1971). But as soon as I had embarked on more intent reading, and had begun to discern what the problems were, it became obvious that the task was far too extensive and intricate for that purpose.

I therefore greatly enlarged the preliminary drafts and set about the work on an appropriate scale. The main course of the inquiry was then worked out, and the greater part of this book written, in the spring and early summer of 1968. This much formed the basis of a course of lectures delivered at the University of Oxford in the Michaelmas Term of that year and in Hilary Term 1969. The pressure of academic duties, however, combined with other commitments, forced the abandonment of any further writing for an entire year, until two short periods in the long vacation of 1969. In its extended and almost complete version the work was presented as lectures at Oxford in the Hilary and Trinity Terms of 1970.

I am conscious that these circumstances may have impaired the coherence of the exposition, and that the interruptions to its composition have reduced the impetus of the argument. Ideally perhaps

I ought to try to rewrite the book, but I find that after the extremely intense application which brought it to its present form, and then the lengthy distraction from the problem, I no longer feel capable of useful thought about the topic. With the encouragement that the investigation is at least of an unusual kind, and in the hope that it may lead to some revision of ideas about human nature, I therefore present the results of the analysis so far as the original impulsion was able to carry it.[1]

During the period in which the book was written, towards the end of 1969, there appeared to my alarm a long treatise by Professor H. H. Price, under the title *Belief*. After the first dejection, however, I discovered that his premises, intention, and method were distinct from mine, and that there was still some point in going on with my own study. The greatest divergence, and that which most decisively marked the separate characters of the two investigations, was that Price nowhere made any mention of Wittgenstein. Also, his book was in part, and in evident inspiration, an apologia of Christian belief, whereas mine was not. I respectfully acknowledge, nevertheless, that it would have been far easier for me to see what the

[1] The award of a Senior Foreign Scientist Fellowship by the National Science Foundation, at the kind instance of the University of California at Riverside, afforded me in the academic year 1970–71 the time at last to type the manuscript and the opportunity to re-write much of chapter 10. I am grateful to these bodies for support and hospitality, and to the University of Oxford for the period of sabbatical leave that allowed me to enjoy these advantages.

For generous aid in the form of a personal grant, at a turning point in the preparation of this work, I am indebted also to Dr. Lita Osmundsen and the Wenner–Gren Foundation for Anthropological Research. I much appreciate their substantial trust, the liberty this afforded me, and their readiness to underwrite researches apparently so much removed from conventional anthropology.

Most of the argument of the book was read out to my graduate class at Riverside, afforded me in the academic year 1970–71 the time at last to type mittently typing. But this very resumption of work on the topic, after yet a further lapse of time, served once more to emphasize that the argument, after an illustrious precedent, was 'written by incoherent Parcels; and after long Intervals of neglect, resum'd again, as ... Occasions permitted'. I can only say that I well recognize that belief, language, and experience are not fit subjects for occasional treatment. In these circumstances I trust I shall not be misunderstood, or be wrongly suspected to vaunt my minor investigation with an obliquely immodest comparison, if I echo another prefatory note (Wittgenstein 1953: x) that carries a peculiar poignancy: 'I should have liked to produce a good book. This has not come about; but the time is past in which I could improve it.'

situation was, and then to go more efficiently for what was essential to my less orthodox concerns, if I had earlier enjoyed the advantage of his learned and reflective disquisition.[2] I should like, indeed, as an ideal counsel, to advise the reader that it would be a great advantage to read that book, written as it is by a most accomplished professional philosopher, before turning to the divagatious difficulties of my inexpert speculations.

Since the references to the sources that I have employed are rather numerous, abbreviated citations have been run into the text within parentheses and the full particulars have been consolidated in the bibliography. This, although topically quite comprehensive, has been kept down to manageable proportions: no pretence has been made at covering the literature on so vast a subject, and only works mentioned have been listed.[3]

III

In this undertaking, as in many others over the past twenty years and more, I have in the first place been under constant obligation to the magnificent resources and inspiring ambience of the Bodleian Library, Oxford, and to the ready efficiency of its staff.

Among my academic colleagues the following have my special thanks for consenting to read the manuscript and for their painstaking and helpful comments: Professor T. O. Beidelman, Professor Max Black, Dr. J. K. Campbell, Dr. James J. Fox, Professor Alasdair MacIntyre, and Dr. P. G. Rivière. If I happen not to have responded adequately to every question or doubt that some of them raised, I have none the less greatly profited by having had to consider whether my argument could, in its essentials, withstand the points of criticism to which they thought it might be vulnerable. These lines are

---

[2] At about the same stage in the elaboration of my ideas I was given a book with an even more unnerving title, *Language, Persons, and Belief* (High 1967), which is expressly a study of Wittgenstein's thought on these topics. I can only regret, however, that I have not found myself able to derive any comparable profit from that essay. At least, I think I am right in saying that it does not forestall or controvert my own arguments.

A recent paper with the promising title 'Understanding Alien Belief-Systems' (Peel 1969) does not, as it turns out, touch on the problem that I present here.

[3] A number of further titles are to be found in the bibliography to Griffiths (1967).

short recognition of their assistance and encouragement, but they stand for my very warm appreciation of all they did on my behalf.

My most profound and lasting debt of gratitude is to Professor Francis Korn. Her gentle companionship sustained me throughout the formation of the argument, the clarity of her fine intelligence provided me with an exquisite critical direction, and amid many distractions and troublesome occasions her kindness gave me peace of mind in an exigent task.

MERTON COLLEGE, OXFORD   R. N.

B

I

Introduction

I

The minor circumstances in which this investigation began are relevant, for they explain the initial concern, bring the issue into a recognizable focus, and prefigure the empirical and translational characteristics of the argument.

Like most ethnographers, I suppose, I was dreaming one night that I was trying to converse with people whom I had once studied, in this case the Penan of the interior of Borneo. As often happens in these imaginary re-encounters, I found myself in a grammatical difficulty and was awoken by the distress of this setback, dejected at my inability any longer to compose correct and intelligible utterances in Penan. The particular proposition that dragged me from my uneasy sleep was 'I believe in God'. I could not think how[1] a Penan would make such a statement, and this worry led me to other aspects of the question. It was certain that the Penan spoke of the existence of a spiritual personage named Peselong;[1] his attributes were well agreed, and these gave him an absolute pre-eminence in the universe to which in the English language the designation 'God' was appropriate. But the Penan had no formal creed, and so far as I knew they had no other conventional means for expressing belief in their god. Nevertheless, I had been accustomed to say, to myself at any rate, that they believed in a supreme god, that they believed that their god was distinguished by certain features, that they believed he possessed certain powers, and so on in the same idiom. Yet now it suddenly appeared that I had no linguistic evidence at all to this effect. Not only this, but I realized that I could not confidently describe their attitude to God, whether this was belief or anything else, by any of the psychological verbs usually found apt in such situations. In fact, as I had glumly to conclude, I just did not know

[1] Pa Sělong to the neighbouring Kenyah, best described by Elshout (1923: 49).

what was their psychic attitude toward the personage in whom I had assumed they believed.

The obvious question then was whether the reports of other ethnographers were much better founded, and what evidence these really had that their subjects believed anything. Clearly, it was one thing to report the received ideas to which a people subscribed, but it was quite another matter to say what was their inner state (belief, for instance) when they expressed or entertained such ideas. If, however, an ethnographer said that people believed something when he did not actually know what was going on inside them, or if he simply reported nothing of their usual psychic states in association with presumed articles of belief, then surely his account of them must, it occurred to me, be very defective in quite fundamental regards.

These were some of the considerations which led eventually to the inquiry that is embodied in this book. They also called into question the premises, activities, and aims of social anthropology as a humane discipline.

II

So far as the term 'anthropology' has a patent sense, it ought to denote the discipline that determines the characteristics of man; but in the course of its development the emphasis of the subject has generally been placed instead on the environments in which man has his being. Social anthropology has devoted attention almost exclusively to social forms, both ideological and behavioural, but scarcely at all to the intrinsic forms of human nature. The variability of collective representations has been constantly stressed, and has for that matter sometimes been taken as the very justification of the academic subject; but anthropologists have commonly written as though the essential faculties of man himself, namely the capacities with which mankind has devised and responded to social forms of ideation, were constant and already known. It is true that early in this century Lévy-Bruhl caused a great stir by proposing, as he did at first (see chap. 9 below), that there was a distinct type of 'primitive mentality' which differed logically from the modes of thought of educated Europeans, but this radical proposition had in the main little revisionary effect on the thinking of anthropologists. Nearly all of them rejected the notion, and they did so, moreover, precipi-

tately and with a degree of bias and distortion which served in itself
to exhibit their conviction that the common intellectual nature of
man was intuitively understood and had already been pragmatically
established.

It has seemed to me that these presumptions are not well founded,
and that the essential capacities of man have yet to be empirically
determined by comparative investigation. One presumed capacity,
which by the frequency with which it is cited claims a special
attention, is that of belief. That men can be said to believe, without
qualification and irrespective of their cultural formation, is an implicit premise in anthropological writings of the most varied kinds,
from abstract and generalizing disquisitions to the most particular
of ethnographical reports. Thus, under the former heading, Cassirer
states that 'in mythical imagination there is always implied an act of
belief', that without the belief in the reality of its object myth would
lose its ground, and that such belief is an 'intrinsic and necessary
condition' of the mythical mode of apprehension (Cassirer 1944: 75;
original emphasis). From the contrasted point of view, a modern
ethnographer, in a very fine and revealing study of cargo cults in the
southern Madang district of eastern New Guinea (Lawrence 1964),
rests his account fundamentally and constantly on the explicit
premise that the peoples whose ideas he examines believe the collective representations that he reports of them: 'The Ngaing believed
that their world was brought into being by their deities' (16);
'all these peoples believed in a creator god' (21); 'the Garia believed
that the natural environment, human beings, and their culture were
created by deities' (25); 'the natives believed that they could obtain
cargo [i.e., wealth in the form of European manufactured goods]
largely by ritual' (235); and so on repeatedly. Lawrence's entire
analysis of the cargo cults is itself organized according to his understanding that 'the ... natives' interpretation of contact history took
the form of five separate cargo beliefs' (63), and he defines the
interpretative focus of his book as 'the belief structure' (273) subscribed to by the peoples in question. He does not find it necessary,
however, to specify what he means by belief or how it is known
that men in New Guinea believe what they say. The tacit assumption, rather, is that this common psychological category in the
English language denotes a common human capacity which can
immediately be ascribed to all men.

3

III

Ethnographical literature in general is replete with allusions to belief, and the notion is so well accepted that it has even become a standard term of description.

Usually, however, ethnographers provide no rules for the interpretation of their reports about belief, and they appear to take it for granted that 'belief' is a word of as little ambiguity as 'spear' or 'cow'. Yet a little reflection on the ordinary use of the word in current English (a matter that we shall take up in chap. 4) must show that this is not so; and in that case we are confronted with a further source of difficulty. Not only have we to try to grasp, in English, an ethnographer's understanding of an alien concept or inner state that he conveys as belief, but we have also to try to work out (and without the guidance of clues comparable to the explicit apparatus of the sociological description) just what he himself, in that cultural setting, may understand by this English word. This poses particular problems of interpretation, for there is certainly no conventional definition of belief that is enjoined upon anthropologists, or professionally recommended, or tacitly agreed to.

Works of instruction in social anthropology typically refer to beliefs with as little qualification as do the ethnographers. *Notes and Queries*, the guide to field research issued by the Royal Anthropological Institute, devotes a substantial chapter to 'Ritual and Belief', but it takes a comprehension of the latter word entirely as given. 'No people so far studied,' it begins, 'have been found to be without belief in supernatural powers of some kind.' Beliefs that presume the existence of spiritual beings, the chapter continues, are commonly described as religious, whereas beliefs that presuppose the necessary existence of such beings are called magical. The point is stressed that there is a lack of professional agreement on the use of the terms 'religion' and 'magic', but no attention at all is paid to the underlying difficulty in attaching these labels to what are distinguished as 'two classes of beliefs'. Throughout this account of a central topic of investigation beliefs are repeatedly referred to, but the definition of the concept is nowhere questioned (Royal Anthropological Institute 1951, chap. 7).

Similarly, a conventional pedagogical work, announced as an

introduction to the aims and achievements of social anthropology (Beattie 1964), touches again and again on beliefs, in connection with sanctions and with ritual, but it treats the notion of belief itself as understood. Social anthropologists, it declares, study 'belief systems' as 'systems in their own right,' but even the chapter devoted expressly to 'Beliefs and Values' does not consider what is really at issue. The author states that 'ritual and religious sanctions owe their effectiveness mainly to the systems of belief in which they are incorporated,' but he still does not think to explain, or suggest, what this blunt assertion is about (29, 40, 173). Admitted, he is by no means alone in this attitude, but in this regard his textbook serves all the better as a current illustration of the lack of any technical or agreed anthropological definition of so fundamental a matter.

IV

There are certain more radical and unresolved grounds of difficulty in construing ethnographical statements referring to belief.

If they are assertions about the inner states of individuals, as by common usage they would normally be taken to be, then, so far as my acquaintance with the literature goes, no evidence of such states, as distinct from the collective representations that are thus recorded, is ever presented. In this case we really have no empirical occasion to accept such belief-statements as exact and substantiated reports about other peoples. If, on the other hand, such statements refer only to the collective representations that prevail in particular cultures, then according to the standard acceptation of belief as a psychic phenomenon the ethnographer's reports are misleadingly phrased. Leach writes, in this connection, that 'when an ethnographer reports that "members of the X tribe believe that..." he is giving a description of an orthodoxy, a dogma, something which is true of a culture as a whole' (Leach 1967: 40). In this case, the special psychological differentia of belief is either assumed to inhere in the orthodoxies that are subscribed to by a given people, or this distinctive feature is eliminated from the ethnographical use of belief-statements. But the assumption is unjustified, because people do not necessarily believe what their culture trains them to say; and the ascription of belief is also unjustified if the psychological reference is elided, for then there is no distinction between an

5

article of belief and the supposed capacity for belief which gives the verbal description its force.

Leach, again, makes it a point of method to override these difficulties by declaring: 'A very large part of the anthropological literature on religion concerns itself almost wholly with a discussion of the content of belief and of the rationality or otherwise of that content. Most such arguments seem to me to be scholastic nonsense' (Leach 1954: 13). 'To ask questions about the content of belief which are not contained in the content of ritual is nonsense. . . . Ritual action and belief are alike to be understood as forms of symbolic statement about the social order' (14). This is an admirably plain and forthright position, and there is indeed no doubt that traditional ideas about spiritual beings and forces can sometimes be interpreted by reference to the institutions of the societies in which they are current. But by this view of the matter ethnographical accounts of 'beliefs' are not even to be assumed to report the inner states of individuals. They are instead reports about collective representations, and these themselves are taken to be oblique statements about the social order.

There may well be methodical advantages in adopting this analytical procedure, but there seems to be no real compensation for depriving the notion of belief of its properly individual and psychic connotation. There is no point, that is, in speaking of collective representations, or dogma which are true of a culture as a whole, as 'beliefs' if it is not implied that the individual human beings who compose the social aggregate in question actually and severally believe them. Something that is believed by nobody is not a belief; and if we are to accept that collective representations are believed, we have to be provided with evidence that individuals believe. In this case, we are not dealing with the overt organization of society but with the recognition of an inner state which can pertain only to individual men.

The practical inference, therefore, is obvious: an ethnographer should never describe the utterances of another people as expressing their beliefs unless he is assured, and can demonstrate, that the individuals in question believe what they say. If he has not this assurance, then he ought not to employ a term which entails that he does possess that demonstrable knowledge of individual states. He should instead specify more accurately, by the accepted canons of the English language, what exactly he is reporting; e.g., received ideas, dogma, orthodoxies, general notions, typical expressions,

6

rationalizations, or whatever. But such a rectification of the ethnographer's vocabulary, desirable though it is in itself, would do nothing to resolve the radical difficulty in construing belief-statements; for the rectification itself implies that it is feasible to recognize the state of belief, and the real problem is to justify this implication.

Hume, in 1739, found that 'This act of the mind [viz., belief] has never yet been explain'd by any philosopher' (1888: 97 n.);[2] and he later concluded, after much arduous thought applied to the topic, that 'this operation of the mind, which forms the belief of any matter of fact, seems hitherto to have been one of the greatest mysteries of philosophy' (628). Nearly two hundred years afterwards, Bertrand Russell in turn was still compelled to the admission that 'Belief . . . is the central problem in the analysis of mind' (1921: 231); and although he thought he could distinguish subjectively certain sensations attached to varieties of belief, he expressly conceded that even so he did not profess to be able to analyse such sensations (250). The phenomenology of belief has certainly not much advanced since Russell reported this impasse, and it is a puzzle therefore to conjecture by what means ordinary ethnographers are to discern and demonstrate the beliefs of members of alien civilizations.

This is the problem that I have taken up in the present essay. The reader may well think that it is unconscionably ambitious that a social anthropologist should seek to penetrate what remains one of the greatest mysteries of human understanding; but I can only relate, now that the work is done, how the problem presented itself, the directions in which the inquiry led, and the predicaments in which any investigator is likely to find himself. I am as little confident of the outcome as the most dubious reader may expect, but if only social anthropologists will tackle with me the obstacles that I have encountered, if not go so far as to accept my method or my explications, I think their conception of human capacities, and hence their ethnographical observations and reports, may profit from the excursion.

[2] The pagination of the Selby–Bigge edition (Oxford: Clarendon Press, 1888) of the *Treatise* is cited throughout.

V

The order of the chapters that follow is very close to that in which their subjects were taken up, so that they compose a record, which may have a methodological interest, of how the investigation was pursued. There were, however, certain constant and very powerful theoretical influences which guided me throughout, and it may help the reader to adjust his anticipations if I briefly state what these were and how they came to be accorded such prominence in the argument.

An initial inspiration was supplied, by way of my early education at Oxford under Evans-Pritchard, by Lucien Lévy-Bruhl. The general debt to him is made clear in chap. 9. For the present, I need only mention that he was the first in an 'anthropological' tradition to raise as a comparative problem, though with another intent, the question of the line of demarcation between belief and experience.[3]

Then there was Hume, 'the most ingenious of all the skeptics,'[4] whose repeated attentions to the notion of belief, which he could not account for and could not leave alone, brought out the opacity and the problematical nature of this commonplace category of everyday discourse and psychological report. The clarity and the modest directness of Hume's writings have had an invigorating effect on the formulation of my own ideas on the topic, and I gratefully assign to the example of that great man a main part of any merit that my arguments may be thought to possess.

Another exemplar was Wittgenstein, a genius of a quite different temper. His influence, like his prose, has been enigmatic and subtle, but so profound and long-sustained that a special note of biographical acknowledgement is called for if the reader is to come to terms with the motive and the approach that characterize this inquiry. After I had read the *Tractatus Logico-Philosophicus* when an undergraduate, doubtless without understanding anything of its real import, a philosopher friend (Mrs. E. Daitz) at Oxford lent me one of the copies of *The Blue Book* which at that time were in

[3] Lévy-Bruhl 1938: 125–30. It is Lévy-Bruhl's statement of this relationship, incidentally, which has provided the title of the present monograph (see chap. 9 below, sec. VII).

[4] Kant 1787: 692.

private and jealous circulation. I cannot think that I really under-stood much of this either, but it had the stirring effect that when the *Philosophical Investigations* appeared in print (1953) I at once acquired a copy. Since then—and this is the present relevance of a somewhat extended personal gloss—whenever I have been faced with a problem of a conceptual kind my first recourse has been to turn to this work in order to see whether Wittgenstein had anything to say about it. When I took up the question of belief I realized that his observations on the topic were of ultimate importance, and the latter portion of the present monograph will show the radical direction that they gave to my own investigation. It is impossible, though, to say now what earlier influence they had, and hence how original are the related propositions in my ana-lysis. All I can say, on this score, is that my main work among the Penan was carried out in 1951–2, before the publication of *Philosophical Investigations*, and that when I returned to Borneo in 1958 I still had not understood that there was a problem about ethnographical ascriptions of belief. What seems rather to have happened is that, under the pressure of trying to interpret Penan experience, I slowly and arduously worked my own way through the grounds of puzzlement until I had arrived at a point where I could at last appreciate what Wittgenstein had written. I wish to be this scrupulous in rendering an intellectual account because, whereas my debt to Wittgenstein is incalculable, I may not maintain that anything I have written here is to be taken as an exact exegesis of his views on belief. I have found myself directing something of his style of scrutiny to the issue, but I am well prepared by the character of Wittgensteinian studies[5] to see my application of his insights called very much into question. Even then, however, I should be genuinely satisfied if I could only think that I had at least turned some other minds toward a direct acquaintance with the extraordinary qualities of Wittgenstein's alembicated thoughts.

There are, too, some more particular acknowledgements to be paid to two works which have had an exemplary importance. Van Dorssen's admirably scholarly work on the derivatives of the root אמן in the Hebrew of the Old Testament (Dorssen 1951) has proved a pattern of semasiological investigation. If only ethnographers, including in the first place myself, had ever made such conceptual studies through the languages of surviving peoples it would have

---

[5] See, for example, the variant interpretations collected in Pitcher (1968).

9

been possible to make a far more convincing analysis of belief than I have managed here. Hampshire's *Thought and Action* (1959) has had an influence of a less direct kind, though my admiration for that elegant and fundamental disquisition is shown by the numerous points at which I resort to it. Its intrinsic qualities apart, a main interest that it possesses is that it approaches, from a philosophical starting point, the kind of problem that I go after from the basis of social anthropology, and that it is guided by humane concerns such as I wish to encourage in my own profession.

Finally, I take a comparable pleasure in mentioning that engrossing work *Mencius on the Mind*, by I. A. Richards (1932). While not so much a pattern for my inquiry, it anticipates incisively some of my own dominant concerns. There are many places where Richards makes points, with regard to the understanding of logical and psychological concepts in one tradition (that of China), which I press for in a future comparative discipline that should in principle comprehend all modes of thought and experience. Though I happen to cite his work only occasionally, there are many theoretical conjunctions which deserve a more sustained reference: e.g., 'Western psychology has unduly refrained from examining and criticizing its own basic hypotheses' (81); 'if [our] language and tradition professed a different set of psychic functions we might be conducting our minds otherwise' (82); 'can we maintain two systems of thinking in our minds without reciprocal infection and yet in some way mediate between them?' (87); 'one of the first conditions for genuine comparisons would seem to be ability to use logical apparatus *tentatively*' (90); 'what is needed . . . is greater imaginative resource in a double venture—in imagining other purposes than our own and other structures for the thought that serves them' (92). I should also single out his note on 'the writings of the Durkheim school' (78, n. 2), the influence of Lévy-Bruhl in his allusions to 'participation' (76) and the distinction made in *Les Fonctions mentales* between senses and gestures (98, n. 1), and his proposal for a comparative dictionary of 'the ranges . . . of partially equivalent words in other languages—'primitive' and 'developed'; Maori, Chinese, and Pali, for example' (95, n. 1). Under some aspects, too, my own study might well be taken as an exercise in what Richards, in the chapter 'Towards a Technique for Comparative Studies' (chap. 4, esp. pp. 92–3), terms 'multiple definition'.

VI

I have found the investigation exciting, and perhaps the reader will be similarly exercised by the intense intellectual challenge of the problem. But I must declare that I have also found the development of the argument exceedingly difficult, indeed the most difficult thing I have ever tried to do. There is a type of problem so extreme in character that to work on it is accompanied, as Wittgenstein remarked, by 'a slight dizziness' (1953, sec. 412); and Waismann has also reported that anyone who broods on such a matter 'will soon be overcome by a kind of giddiness . . . as though a bottomless abyss opened before him' (1965: 17). To think at the requisite pitch is indeed to be caught in what Waismann exactly terms a 'desperate situation'. Something of this vertiginous affliction is probably inseparable from any serious attempt to think radically about the connections between language and experience; and perhaps the reader should be adverted that in the present inquiry my own desperation may have left its marks on the exposition of what is already an issue that makes hard demands.

It may be, also, that other features of the argument will be found variously dissatisfying. My chief ground for concern is one that is present in most writings on social anthropology, but this time to a very unusual degree. The analysis depends in part on evidences drawn from extremely variegated fields of inquiry such as theology, philology, and epistemology which are the subjects of long-established branches of exact scholarship, and in adducing such materials I can claim no professional expertness. A theologian, philologist, or philosopher will doubtless find much to qualify or expand, if not to discount, at points in the demonstration where he has a special and authoritative knowledge; and he may thence feel tempted to extend his dissatisfaction to the argument as a whole. I can only aver that I have been particularly conscious of this source of possible weakness, that I have diligently sought good advice, and that I have had to rely on those authorities which I have found most relevant to my problem.

A related expository difficulty is that anyone with an advanced knowledge of one or another topic, e.g., Hebrew or classical Greek, will be bored or exasperated by the rudimentary narration of facts or views which to him are elementary or obvious, but this also is inevitable. The social anthropologist will certainly not feel instructed to be told yet once more of the importance of cattle to the Nuer; but a philosopher is not likely to know much about this evidence, and will appreciate the demonstration of its relevance to matters that he does know about. Conversely, no philosopher will need to be told again, and by me, what were the characteristic views of Hume or Kant; but it is to be expected that the anthropological reader will find even my cursory statements of their theories to be unfamiliar and helpful.

There is, too, a contrary ground for complaint, namely that the investigation does not go deeply enough into any one of the constituent topics, e.g., the 'Sapir-Whorf' hypothesis or the psychology of the emotions, and this charge also I should have to admit. Indeed, I appreciate most acutely that a monograph could be written about each of any number of propositions and topics in my argument, but there are practical limits to what can be done in one exploratory essay.

Naturally, I cannot ask for indulgence on any of these scores, but there are two pleas that I can nevertheless permit myself in order to forestall certain major differences of opinion which are likely to arise. Not that I wish to introduce any idea of an intellectual confrontation, for there is no hint of theoretical discord in this book but instead only a demonstration of the need for better collaboration. Yet in the circumstances it is in fact still to be expected that both the topic itself and my treatment of it will occasion large divergencies of thought, and it is these that I should like to try in advance to mitigate.

The first plea is addressed to dissentient colleagues in social anthropology. They may not much like so protracted an investigation into the grounds of a concept in the philosophy of mind, or the critical redirection of anthropological effort that I urge in thinking about human experience; but I should like to ask them to consider, as they form their opinion of the argument, whether they think they can really make serious inquiries in other civilizations unless they first ask themselves such fundamental questions, about the representation of human nature, as are posed here. That they accept or do not accept my conclusions is far less important than that they should recognize a problem.

The second adjuration is addressed to philosophers. I can well apprehend that some among them may find it objectionable in academic principle that a topic falling so squarely within their professional field should be taken up by the practitioner of another discipline. I should like to ask them, however, to consider that I should not have done so if I had found that their own skilful disquisitions on belief had dealt effectively with the perplexities that attend a comparative purview of man's inner capacities. Perhaps it may mollify philosophical objectors, also, if I can persuade them that I am not trying to encroach on their privileged role as arbiters of abstraction: my special task belongs rather to a search for 'descriptions of the natural history of meanings' (Richards 1932: 127). If it be accepted, moreover, that a philosopher is distinguished above all by 'the way he tries to carry every idea to its logical conclusion' (Waismann 1965: 42), then a further demarcation between our respective concerns is that my ambition is not so ultimate but that I am looking in the main for the empirical grounds of a cultural concept. And, in any event, I am supported in this matter by Kant's encouraging query (1787: 859), which he certainly did not intend rhetorically: 'Do you really desire that knowledge which concerns all men shall surpass common understanding and be revealed to you only by philosophers?'

Disclaimers done with, then, I now attempt what seems to me 'a wholly new start' in the analysis of belief; and if it turns out that the venture does not in every way succeed, as I must expect will indeed be thought, at least it will still be 'a different kind of failure.'

2

Problem

'Nuer religion is ultimately an interior state.' When the social and cultural features of the religion have been abstracted, we are told, what is left is a relationship that transcends all forms; but the ethnographer cannot give any clear account of what for the Nuer is the nature of this spiritual relationship. To do so is difficult, partly because Nuer religious conceptions are not concepts but imaginative constructions, and these relate to an intuitive apprehension, a spiritual experience; and, again, the anthropologist cannot say for certain what this experience is.

These are the main conclusions to Evans-Pritchard's work on Nuer religion (1956: 321-2), and their very uncertainty and obscurity, after so long and detailed an ethnographic account, bring a conviction that one has indeed been led to a confrontation with the ultimate reality of Nuer religion. Much has been made clear, in the course of a detailed factual description of religious conceptions and usages, but in the end we are left with an interior state which neither the Nuer nor the ethnographer can well explain. At this point, Evans-Pritchard suggests, the theologian takes over from the anthropologist, and with these words the eminent ethnographer brings to a close his great study of the Nuer people.

It seems to me, however, that this situation poses instead a radical issue of a truly anthropological kind, and that we ought not to be quite so ready to hand over to the theologians. Certainly they can provide very useful aid in the interpretation of mystical doctrines, but the issue is far more basic and general than their own traditional concerns usually allow for. On the other hand, the descriptive practices of anthropologists have been altogether too general, and their unreflective presumptions in the study of religious conceptions have often vitiated their analyses and hindered the development of comparative research. Both the theologians and the anthropologists have tended, each party in its own fashion, to take too much for granted; for the most part they have not been sufficiently critical of their own concepts, and they have not therefore come properly to terms with the mystical ideas of other peoples. In the Nuer case specifically, both the ethnographer and the theologian would agree that the ultimate reality for the people themselves is an interior state; but I wish to argue that it is precisely the reality of a distinct interior state that is the real question.

Let us therefore concentrate on the Nuer example, for here we are unusually well supplied with reliable ethnographic and linguistic evidences which lay the grounds for an exact analysis.

II

How can we try to understand 'an interior state' of a kind that an ethnographer firmly defines as religious or spiritual?

Evans-Pritchard states that among the Nuer this state is 'externalized in rites' (322). These overt acts can be accurately described, plotted, sound-recorded, and photographed, but such procedures do not of course yield the meaning or the experience of the rites for those who take part in them. In the Nuer situation, 'the significance of the objects, actions, and events lies not in themselves but in what they mean to those who experience them as participants or assistants'. This meaning depends finally, we are told, upon 'an awareness of God'; but experiences of this kind are not easily communicated even when people are ready to communicate them and have, as do the Nuer, 'a sophisticated vocabulary' in which to do so. Nevertheless, it is only through people's statements about their apprehensions, intuitions, awareness, and other subtle modes of experience that we can hope to understand anything at all precise about such interior states.

The translation of the verbal categories which an alien people employ in statements about their cultural universe, especially in the sphere conventionally denoted as that of religion, is a focus of notorious and inescapable difficulty, and the varied attempts to convey the significance of religious concepts have been highly instructive. An Indonesianist may recall in the first place such admirable works as Verheijen's intensive and exemplary study of the conception of the supreme being among the Manggarai of Flores (1951), or Lambooy's paper on the understanding of the concept

15

of *marapu*, a governing idea in the religion of eastern Sumba (1937). There is the converse difficulty, too, when missionaries attempt to translate biblical or theological terms into other languages, and these ventures are comparably instructive. Good examples are to be found, again in the Indonesian area, in such papers as those of Onvlee on the translation of 'holy' into Sumbanese (1938), Middel-koop on the rendering of the Hebrew *nachash*, serpent, into Timorese (1956), or the symposium edited by Swellengrebel on the translation of 'Holy Spirit' into languages of Indonesia and New Guinea (1941).

Naturally enough, it is missionaries who have most constantly and explicitly had to deal with questions of these complementary kinds. Koper has published a thorough survey of various aspects of missionary Bible translations (1956), Nida has pre-eminently devoted the most practical and useful attention to the intricacy of Bible translation (see, e.g., 1964), and the engrossing files of *The Bible Translator* have kept the issue a very live and public one. Scholars in academic disciplines have also faced the same intrinsic difficulties, e.g., in the religious sphere still, Gonda's excellent notes on ancient Indian religious terminology (1961); in literary studies, a collection of expert papers has been brought together by Brower in a book on translation (1959); and, more widely, Mounin has published an extensive examination of the theoretical problems of translation (1963). Finally, and very prominently, there has been published a great deal on the Sapir–Whorf hypothesis that linguistic forms determine to some degree our perceptions, concepts, and modes of thought (see, e.g., Whorf 1956; Hoijer 1954; Henle 1958).

The problematical character of any translation is the object of unremitting attention, indeed, on the part of all those, missionaries, academics, or men of letters, whose business it is to reflect on concepts and their expression in language. The topic is in fact of such generally recognized importance that no more than this very brief introduction is necessary in order to indicate the setting of the present investigation. But the prolonged and diversified attention paid to translation makes it only the more remarkable that the question that we are taking up here has not anywhere, so far as I can discover, been explicitly dealt with.

III

Against this background, let us turn back toward the spiritual interior state of the Nuer. Evans-Pritchard reports that a study of Nuer religion is 'a study of what they consider to be the nature of Spirit and of man's relation to it'; the term *kwoth*, spirit, is 'the key to their . . . philosophy'. He himself found it a long and formidable task to grasp this concept and, even more, to present his conclusions (1956: vi). But the difficulty in comprehending the interior state of the Nuer resides only secondarily in the conceptual ambiguities of the concept of spirit as expressed in the word *kwoth*. The first and most consequential difficulty is posed by the Nuer language itself, both phonetically and in its grammatical complexity.

On the phonetic score, consider this statement of the matter by Nida (1955: 55–6):

The Nuer language has fourteen basic vowels, seven of which may be described as noncentralized and the others as correspondingly centralized. However, these fourteen vowels are completely separate entities as far as the Nuer speaker is concerned. Each of these fourteen vowels may have any one of three phonemic lengths: extra short, normal, and extra long. There are many words which differ in meaning only on the basis of such phonemic length. But there is still a further consideration in dealing with the vowel structure, namely, the breathiness or nonbreathiness, which likewise gives rise to numerous minimal pairs, that is, words which have totally different meanings depending on whether the vowel has a breathy or nonbreathy quality. For example, the only difference between words meaning 'bird' and 'one who thatches a house' is the breathiness of the vowel. Very slight differences of vowel quality, breathiness, and length . . . give a series of words meaning 'chin', 'life', 'hazy sky', and 'bead'. Failure to make proper distinctions in length can produce innumerable ambiguities, in which the series 'relative', 'whip of hippo hide', and 'dried fish' is only one.

But vowel qualities, length and breathiness are not the only factors. There are at least three levels of tone in Nuer and a number of glides. This makes the phonemic structure much more complicated, for a difference of tone is the distinguishing mark for many sets of words, e.g., (1) 'bird' and 'song', (2) 'relative' and 'relatives' and (3) 'leopard' and 'fish scale'.

In the Nilotic languages, moreover, 'the basic tones of the words change constantly in the different syntactic positions'. The sum effect of these possibilities of phonemic variation is worse than formidable:

If we add up the theoretical possibilities for the nucleus of any syllable, we arrive at a figure of 252 different sets of contrasts. We must multiply 14 vowel qualities first by three phonemic lengths, then by breathy vs. nonbreathy quality, and finally by at least three registers of tone. But this total of 252 possibilities is still not all. We must also consider some of the very complex diphthongs, which likewise have phonemic lengths and produce confusion in such pairs as (1) 'fish' and 'ant' and (2) 'egg' and 'horns'.

Nuer is 'a language which makes so many fine distinctions and ... has such short words, thus giving rise to hundreds of nearly similar terms,' that the 'extreme complexity of the phonemic structure' must be a nightmare for even the most gifted ethnographer. It is all very well to concede, with Nida, that in terms of information theory 'one could say that Nuer is a very efficient language in that a great deal of meaning is carried by a highly differentiated consonant, vowel and tonal structure'; but for an investigator trying to get at an interior state, as expressed through this variety and counterpoint of sounds, such an efficiency must be utterly disheartening.

As for the syntactic complexities, these are similarly extreme and must occasion the greatest difficulties in any investigation. Crazzolara's Nuer grammar (1933) does not include a summary statement of these difficulties, conveniently comparable with Nida's account of the phonemics, but by any reading of this work the grammatical complexity of the Nuer language is also quite daunting. A point of special importance in analysing Nuer statements of the relationship between man and Spirit is, furthermore, that 'the relational particles, conjunctions and prepositions have exceptionally wide areas of meaning', and this feature results in 'considerable ambiguity and obscurity in unfamiliar contexts' (Nida 1955: 59).

This, then, is the linguistic medium through which ethnographical inquiries have to be made, and it needs no argument that such complexities of sound and form must interpose a refractory screen between the foreign investigator and the interior states, let alone a 'spiritual' state, of those who employ this language to express the subtle singularities of their own modes of experience.

Moreover, a yet further difficulty relates, as Evans-Pritchard observes, not to Nuer words (such as *kwoth*) but to our own. Comparative religion has failed, he thinks, to build up 'an adequate and agreed-upon terminology', so that even communication (and also, it may be added, analysis) is difficult. 'If I speak of "spear" or "cow" everybody will have pretty much the same idea of what I speak of, but this is not so when I speak of "Spirit", "soul", "sin", and so forth' (1956: vi). A convincing illustration of the conditions of effective communication by the ethnographer, in one prominent and observable realm of experience, is provided by the Nuer cattle vocabulary.

The Nuer are famous anthropologically for their great interest in their cattle, and for the 'enormous number' of words and phrases in their language about cattle and the tasks of herding and dairy-work. Pre-eminent among this 'vast assortment' of expressions are the terms by which the Nuer describe the appearance of cattle, chiefly by reference to their colours; there are 'several hundred' recognized colour permutations, and besides this vast vocabulary, which refers to colours, distribution of colours, and colour associations, there are also many words denoting the shape of cattle horns, adding considerably to the complexity and precision of the classification. In addition, the ears of cattle are often cut in different shapes, and it is possible to describe the beasts by reference to these incisions as well. A further range of permutations, finally, is created by prefixes which denote the sex or age of an animal. These various sets of criteria thus make up 'a galaxy of words in the arrangement of which a thesaurus of some magnitude might be composed' (Evans-Pritchard 1940: 41–8; cf. Kiggen 1948; 333–4 s.v. *yang*, 340 s.v. *tung*).[1] Evans Pritchard emphasizes that 'this intricate and voluminous vocabulary' is not technical and departmental but is employed by everyone and in manifold situations of ordinary social life. 'It is not possible to discuss with Nuer their daily affairs, social connections, ritual acts, or, indeed, any subject, without reference to cattle which are the core round which daily life is organized and the medium through which social and mystical relations are expressed.'

The special vocabulary reflects a dominant interest of the Nuer, and their language, 'by compelling reference to cattle, whatever be the subject of speech, continually focuses attention on them and makes them the superlative value of Nuer life' (Evans-Pritchard

[1] In the citations of Kiggen's dictionary, and also in other quotations in Nuer that will follow, a simplified orthography is employed: ng=ŋ; $\grave{e}$=ɛ; o=ɔ; gh=ɣ; and the retroflex t is not marked. These economies have no effect on the points of linguistic argument.

1940: 48). A non-Nuer can in principle master this vocabulary, discern the discriminatory features, and learn the principles and uses of the classification of cattle. When, therefore, not only the ethnographer but also a Nuer employs the word for (a particular kind of) 'cow', a precise communication with an outsider can indeed be effected. If a beast is described as *jak* (Evans-Pritchard 1940: 42), or as *kuac* (Kiggen 1948: 334), or by any other of the 'hundreds of . . . combinations' of classificatory features (Kiggen 1948: 334), then the observer can indeed have 'pretty much the same idea' of what is spoken of. That is, he is supplied with a detailed denotation of a physical object in the environment which he can observe and distinguish and discuss. There is then some practical possibility that the connotations which the beast has for the Nuer (as indicated by cattle-names, miming, poetic idiom, and so on) will supply some comprehension of the interior state that is experienced by them with regard to their cattle. Evans-Pritchard writes, indeed, of their 'love' of cattle and their 'desire' to acquire them, of their 'devotion' to the herdsman's art, and of how they 'contentedly' watch their beasts. To judge by Kiggen's dictionary, the sentiments indicated by such English words could similarly be identified through the Nuer language, and in this respect as well a useful communication of experience could thus be effected between a Nuer and an outsider. We can perceive, in Nuer terms at any rate, the object of the Nuer's attitude, and through his statements we can hope to appreciate, to a considerable extent at least, his state of mind in relation to that object.

But what about the interior state of a Nuer in relation to *kwoth*, spirit? What is denoted in this case is not, for the ethnographer, an object in the environment; and the word *kwoth* cannot be said to denote empirically anything but the state of mind (if that) which is associated with the verbal concept. In what English terms, then, could we expect to be able to define this state? It is plainly asserted by the ethnographer to pertain to 'religion'; and this means, according to the dictionary, that what is thereby implied is 'a belief in . . . a divine ruling power'.[2] The opening words of the Christian confession of faith, the Creed, define the 'interior state' of the adherent by the declaration, 'I believe in God . . .'. This element of *belief* is certainly, in English and for someone educated in the Christian tradition, the definitive feature of a religious attitude.

[2] *Shorter Oxford English Dictionary*, 3rd ed. rev. with addenda (Oxford: Clarendon Press, 1962), s.v. 'Religion', sense 3.

In social anthropology the definition of religion conventionally includes belief as an indispensable component: e.g., Durkheim defines it as 'a unified system of beliefs and practices' (1915: 47); Radcliffe-Brown thinks that the most satisfactory definition of religion is that it consists of 'a belief in a great moral force or power' (1922: 405); and Geertz, in an elaborate redefinition of religion, even has it that religious performances are 'not only models *of* what they [the participants] believe, but also models *for* the believing of it' (1966: 29). More generally, though still with a religious implication, Mauss is reported to have said that a sociological explanation is done 'when you have seen *what* it is that people believe and think, and *who* are the people who believe and think it' (cited in Dumont 1964: 99). The standard acceptation of belief as the distinctive feature of religion is commonly expressed also by ethnographers in their accounts of exotic religions; e.g., Verheijen sets out the intention of his monograph on Manggarai religion as to describe 'the present-day, living belief concerning the Supreme Being' (1951: 4); Elshout reports that 'a belief in immaterial beings' is a constant element in the religious ceremonies of the Kenyah of central Borneo, and that this belief is for the Kenyah themselves the most important part of the rites (1923: 35); and Geddes asserts that the Land Dayak of Sarawak 'believe . . . that every object . . . has in it a kind of force' which he translates as 'soul' (1957: xxiv).

An extended and typical example of anthropological usage is provided by Radcliffe-Brown's study of the Andaman Islanders, in which it is reported that they 'believe in . . . a class of supernatural beings', 'believe that the noise of whistling would attract spirits', 'believe that the spirits feed on the flesh of dead men and women' (1922: 136, 139, 140), and so on repeatedly. Such definite and characteristic statements can readily be paralleled in many other ethnographic accounts of exotic religions, in which one commonly reads that certain peoples believe that God is bisexual, believe that God created the world in a certain fashion, believe that there are spirits in trees, believe that spirits cause illness, believe that offences against the ancestors will bring calamity, believe that wrong-doing will be mystically punished, believe that the next world has particular features, etc. Among the many peoples to whom the faculty of belief is thus ascribed are the Nuer.

IV

Crazzolara, in his study of the religion of the Nuer (1953),[3] opens his section on the attributes of the supreme being with the statement: 'What is at issue is to establish what in general the Nuer people believe [*glauben*] about God, what they ascribe to him, and what they expect of him' (62). The account that follows this declaration is not in fact couched literally in terms of belief, but the tacit premise to all of the statements made about God and other spirits is nevertheless that the Nuer believe in them.

There is also explicit evidence in Kiggen's dictionary. The crucial entry (1948: 174) runs as follows:

Liaghè ... v. tr. & intr.; believe, have faith.
Liaghne ruai ƙuoth = we believe the word of God. *Èn liagh ruaièmè pale* = don't believe this thing.

Ruai means 'business, case, word, tidings, story', and is glossed with '*Ruai ƙuoth* = religion' (281). The recorded evidence is thus perfectly clear, and on this literal basis we might directly conclude that the Nuer themselves, in their own tongue, phrase their relationship to God as one of belief. When, therefore, we ask ourselves what is that interior state which the Nuer experience with regard to *ƙwoth*, the answer seems to be—as the conventional definition of religion would in any case predispose one to assume—that they believe in their god. The various attributes which they ascribe to God, and the idioms in which they figuratively phrase their relationship to him, are all qualifications of the fundamental premise of their belief in him.

This seems indeed an acceptable enough conclusion, but there is contrary evidence. With this the real question presents itself. Evans-Pritchard reports an everyday affirmation among the Nuer, on occasions when they are faced with some difficulty to be overcome or some problem to be solved: *ƙwoth a thin*, 'God is present'. This phrase, Evans-Pritchard stresses, does not mean 'There is a God' (1956: 9):

[3] It is to be regretted that this authoritative work has been so much neglected, doubtless because it is written in German and also perhaps because of the form and place of its publication, and that it has been quite overshadowed by later writings on the Nuer. Given the prominence of this society in social anthropology, an English translation, which would greatly facilitate comparative studies of Nuer institutions, is a most desirable project.

That would be for Nuer a pointless remark. God's existence is taken for granted by everybody. Consequently when we say, as we can do, that all Nuer have faith in God, the word 'faith' must be understood in the Old Testament sense of 'trust' (Nuer *ngath*) and not in the modern sense of 'belief' which the concept came to have under Greek and Latin influences. There is in any case, I think, no word in the Nuer language which could stand for 'I believe'.

With these characteristically reflective observations the issue is squarely posed. On the one hand, Crazzolara's monograph and Kiggen's dictionary refer explicitly to a Nuer concept of belief; and a distinct word is recorded as the Nuer expression of that concept. On the other hand, Evans-Pritchard emphasizes that the ascription of faith to the Nuer, though possible, calls for special qualification and is not to be represented as belief; and he thinks that there is no Nuer word to express belief.

There is some uncertainty, however, about the precise terms in which Evans-Pritchard intends to press this interpretative confront-ation. Although he cites Kiggen's dictionary at a number of other places in his work on Nuer religion, he does not do so in this instance; in particular, he does not examine the word *liagh*, and he makes no reference to the information in the dictionary which he so plainly contradicts. Other published sources on the Nuer language are not decisive on the question of a word for belief: Huffman has the circumlocutions *ngac- momo ke loc* (know this with heart) and *ngath ke loc* (trust with heart) for 'to believe' (1931: 5), but he does not list *liagh* or any other single word for the notion (cf. Huffman 1929); and Stigand's vocabulary does not include the word *liagh* or any equivalent for 'to believe' (1923). Let us nevertheless consider some of the possible reasons for the trenchant discrepancy between the missionaries and the ethnographer.

Since Evans-Pritchard published his account of Nuer religion after the appearance of the works of the missionaries, and surely with full knowledge of them, it could be assumed that he was claiming for his linguistic report, in this particular, an authority which their writings lacked. Yet this is difficult to accept, for he was rather less than a year among the Nuer, whereas they had a combined experi-ence, impressively attested to by the dictionary itself, covering a far longer period.[4] It is certainly conceivable that a professional social

---

[4] The dictionary published by the late Fr. Kiggen is the product of the combined labours of a whole body of missionary workers over a span of forty years. It is based on the copious notes of Fr. Crazzolara, who is

anthropologist might have discerned features of Nuer society which his missionary predecessors had missed; but in the matter of religious belief, as expressed in an uncommonly intricate language, the inference is not plausible.

The very fact that the question relates to religious belief suggests the possibility that the Christian convictions, and the proselytizing intentions, of the missionaries might have predisposed them to impute to the Nuer a concept that the latter did not exactly possess. This possibility cannot be assessed on the information available, and we can only keep it in mind as we proceed. But there is in any case a converse possibility, namely that the religious concerns of the missionaries actually helped them to discover a subtle concept which observers with other interests might not so readily have come across.[5]

If, however, we take it that there is no indigenous term, in current Nuer usage, the meaning of which Evans-Pritchard at any rate would agree to render as 'believe', what could be the reason for this lack of a verbal concept which is regarded conventionally as essential to a religion?

Is it perhaps that Nuer thought is relatively crude, and that their system of ideas about Spirit simply does not provide for the recognition of the presumptive fact that they believe? The Meru of Kenya, for example, may be in much this kind of situation. 'The idea of God for the Meru is not a very clear one: they take for granted the presence of God in the world, something self-evident, that one does not discuss: He is there, that is all' (Bernardi 1959: 123). From a report of this nature it might be inferred that such a matter-of-fact and uncritical conception of God does not pose to the consciousness of the Meru the possibility, or the degree, of dubiety which would occasion the notion of belief. There might be

described by one of the collaborators in the preparation of the dictionary as 'the greatest authority on the Nuer language.' These were complemented and ordered by the extended investigations of Fr. F. Spakauskas, who lived seventeen years among the Nuer, and of Fr. Kiggen himself, who was six years in Nuerland. (I am indebted for this information to a personal communication, dated 12 March 1968, from the Revd. Fr. F. Spakauskas.)

[5] It is a public fact of relevance to this inquiry (cf. Evans-Pritchard 1956: vii) that between Professor Evans-Pritchard's field studies of the Nuer and the publication of *Nuer Religion* he became converted to the Roman Catholic faith. His religious views, however different they may formerly have been, thus came to correspond doctrinally with those of Fr. Crazzolara and of other priests who had worked among the Nuer. The discrepancy between his report and theirs cannot therefore be ascribed to divergent convictions about religion or about the attitude of the worshipper.

no point, that is, in providing lexically for the assertion 'I believe in God' when God's existence and presence are so taken for granted that no other possibility is either given in Meru collective ideation or occasioned in individual thought. Now this, as we have seen, is the position among the Nuer also: 'God's existence is taken for granted by everybody.' The expression *kwoth a thin*, God is present, means for the Nuer 'that they do not know what to do but God is here with them and will help them' (Evans-Pritchard 1956: 9). To say that God is present, therefore, is not to utter a dubitable proposition, but is instead to invoke an undoubted presence as a constant source of strength. In this case also the inference might suggest itself that the traditional forms of thought were too undeveloped and shallow to make place for a critical notion like that of belief. But this is assuredly not the case, for, as Evans-Pritchard is at pains to emphasize, 'their religious thought is remarkably sensitive, refined, and intelligent' and it is also 'highly complex' (1956: 311).

V

There is another major factor which might possibly account for the hypothetical lack of a word for belief, namely that the Nuer language is not sufficiently discriminating, in the sphere of human capacities, to register such a concept.

On the contrary, the psychological vocabulary of the Nuer is admirably elaborate. They are famous enough for their classification of cattle, but their classification of interior states is also extensive and minutely particularized. If we leave out of account the many words which denote acts that clearly manifest certain dispositions, such as 'boasting', and then retain from Kiggen's dictionary the terms denoting more private psychical conditions, we can easily compile an impressive list.

The Nuer, by means of distinct single words furnished by their language, can say of an individual that he is: inattentive, selfish, complacent, timid, sincere, slightly angry, thoughtful, jealous, shy, benevolent, bored, hypocritical, lovesick, thoughtless, kindly disposed, prejudiced, broken-hearted, irritable, unafraid, bewildered, absent-minded. They can say that he feels: sorrow, disgust, surprise, fear, suspicion, rancour, doubt, pity, shame, compassion. He can be said to be: discouraged, remorseful, perplexed, upset, disappointed, satisfied, nervous, lustful, sorry, worried, repentant, happy, embarrassed, sick at heart. He may also: despise, sympathize, think back, change his mind, hope, pretend, covet, hate, respect, think, trust, know, hesitate, put his heart into something, envy, remember, learn, honour, forget, long for, keep his temper, have bad thoughts, think of, disapprove, detest, force himself to do something.

This is by any reckoning a most respectable and revealing psychological thesaurus. Indeed, this classification may well be thought of greater significance for social anthropology, as a humane study, than the famous cattle vocabulary. It is a catalogue of inner states and dispositions which both reflects and encourages a highly discriminating conception of the psyche. By means of these terms (and doubtless others so far unreported) the Nuer are enabled to make observations of their fellows and by inference to ascribe to them a wide and complex range of sentiments, attitudes, and mental operations. They can also reflect analytically upon their own private states, and can frame by analogy a systematic conception of the interior capabilities and tendencies of the human being.

What this delicately accreted conception may be can perhaps be better seen by an examination of certain words which appear from Kiggen's translations to be related, in Nuer psychology, to *liaghè*, believe.

I must declare at once that I well recognize the dangers in resorting to linguistic evidence taken from the dictionary of a language that one does not understand. Such hazards are especially obvious, anyway, in the case of a tongue so complicated by tonal and syntactic inflection as is that of the Nuer. However, I have made no semantic connections between words that are merely orthographically similar, and I have attempted no interpretations of my own. The words listed have been selected solely on the basis of the English equivalents and the glosses, and I think these renderings can safely be relied upon to make my point.[6]

The following, at any rate, are Nuer words which may apparently be considered as forming a set in which *liaghè* is also a member:

[6] Professor Evans-Pritchard has latterly published the view that a social anthropologist who is ignorant of the Nuer language should not venture to express any opinion on the meaning of Nuer statements (1970: 110). I must say that this strikes me as an extreme objection which if admitted would ultimately put an end to the subject as a comparative discipline. In any case, there are degrees of ignorance, and the opinion of Fr. Crazzolara, for instance, could well lend another direction to this criticism.

butè, to think, trust, believe; e.g., 'I thought you would come' (48);

dhoongè, to think, trust, believe, hope; e.g., 'I trust you will come' (92);

luèngè, to agree, consent, obey; e.g., 'believe what I say' (189);

ngaadhè, to hope, trust, wait; e.g., 'I waited for you yesterday'; 'let us trust in God' (219);

nhoghè (ro), to be clear, acknowledge, (with *ro*) to trust; e.g., 'do you acknowledge (confess) your fault?'; 'he confessed his mistake'; 'repeat this word that it may be clear'; 'you cannot trust that boy, he is a thief' (215);

nyèthè, to follow the example of another; e.g. 'let us follow (obey) the word of God'; 'don't follow his example' (239);

ruaatè, to trust, believe, think; e.g., 'he trusts in his friend, but doesn't know he is not his friend'; 'he thinks that his friend is there' (282);

thèghè, to esteem highly, honour, revere, adore; e.g., 'we always adore God'; 'esteem your mother-in-law highly'; 'hold the customs of the people in esteem'; 'do not adore strange gods' (309);

waanè, to imagine, think, suspect, impute; e.g., 'I think he will come tomorrow' (322).

A number of lessons emerge from this collocation. The first is the confirmation of the previous impression that Nuer is a subtle language; for example, the English word 'trust' appears in the translations as the equivalent of five separate Nuer words, and it can reasonably be supposed that for the Nuer these words stand for different modes of the typical attitude to which the English word generally refers.

Secondly, while for someone who does not know the Nuer language, and has not experienced the culture with which it is associated, it is impossible to comprehend the special significances of the Nuer words in question, it seems that the Nuer psychological vocabulary is particularly well elaborated with regard to the congeries of dispositions to which the English notion of belief is usually assigned.

Thirdly, the definitions bring out the kind of uncertainty that is inseparable from relying on the renditions that happen to have been adopted by the compiler of the dictionary.[7] For instance, in each of those explications in which 'trust' features, this word is combined differently with other words that are not always conventionally

---

[7] It is worth noting, in this connection, that Fr. Crazzolara's original notes for a Nuer dictionary, which formed the basis of that brought out by Fr. Kiggen (cf. n. 4 above), were written in 'German short-hand' (Kiggen 1948: 6).

equivalent.[8] Although one can see the possible interconnection between dispositions such as 'trust' and 'hope' (s.v. *ngaadhè*), and
between 'trust' and 'think' (s.v. *ruaatè*), there is not such a patent
connection between 'hope' and 'think'.

Finally, although it may be possible to determine a standard or
basic sense of 'trust', the English word 'believe' appears in the
translations under very disparate idiomatic guises, viz., think, trust,
hope, agree, consent, and obey; and to these several equivalents may
be added, moreover, such further interpretations as expect, wish,
suppose, and so on.

Nevertheless, the conclusion seems plain enough that the Nuer
language is well adapted to the specification of interior states, and
that it possesses a number of words for the expression of varieties of
belief.

VI

Further evidence is to be found in a recent collection of passages
from the Gospels translated into Nuer, in which 'believe' is consistently translated by *ngath* (Sergi 1968).

A decisive instance is the rendering of John 11: 25–7, verses which
are not only some of the most moving in the New Testament but
are also doctrinally so important as to guarantee that a clerical translator will have devoted an extreme and reverent care to their precise
rendition into the Nuer language. In the following phrases of the
Authorized Version the passage runs as follows:

Jesus said unto her, I am the resurrection and the life: he that believeth
in me, though he were dead, yet shall he live: And whosoever liveth and
believeth in me shall never die. Believest thou this? She saith unto him,
Yea, Lord: I believe that thou art the Christ, the Son of God, which
should come into the world.

Here, next, is the translation into Nuer (Sergi 1968: 170), with the
equivalents to the various grammatical forms of 'believe' set in
italics:

[8] An incidental point of interest is that whereas 'to identify psychological
states the Nilotic languages make considerable use of words meaning either
"heart" or "liver" (Nida, 1955: 59), the psychological verbs listed above are
not so compounded. See Kiggen (1948: 180), s.v. *Loc*, heart or mind; cf.
Huffman (1931), heart, *loc* (29), liver, *cweny* (35).

Co Yesu je jiogh, Han kany rar kene tek, jen ram *ngathe* gha cange me
ce liu, be tek, ke me jen me tek ke *ngatha*, ke gha ce de liu. Jin ci mè
ngath? Cue we, E jen kuar, ghan *ngatha* je i è jin Kristo Gat Kuoth,
min ci ben hoa.

According to this most definite evidence, then, it would certainly
appear that a verbal concept of belief does exist in Nuer, namely in
the form of *ngath*. This, it will be recalled, is the word that the
dictionary (s.v. *ngaadhè*) renders as 'to hope, trust, wait', and which
Evans-Pritchard distinguishes as 'faith', in a sense which he associ-
ates with the Old Testament, from the concept of belief.[9]

It will be noted that the Nuer word adopted in this place is not
liagh(è), even though this is actually the entry in the dictionary
which is most literally and directly given, without any supplemen-
tary meanings or variant glosses, as the equivalent of 'believe'.
In another clerical translation, however, namely in the Nuer version
of the Apostles' Creed, it is this word that is employed and not
ngath. The opening words, 'I believe in God the Father ...' are
translated as 'Liagha Kot Gwan ...'; and the concluding declaration
of belief in the Holy Ghost is likewise translated with *liagh*
(Crazzolara 1934a; 1934b).[10] It may be that an increasingly profound
command of the Nuer language, over the twenty-four years between
the translations of the Creed and the Gospel, is the reason for the
different words chosen in each to stand for 'believe'; but whatever
the explanation the point is still made that a verbal concept of belief
appears indeed to be found among the Nuer.

This conclusion is supported by unpublished evidence which I
trust I may now properly adduce. In a private communication,
which he kindly permits me to quote, Fr. Crazzolara writes that
lyagh is the 'right' word for 'to believe, have faith'.[11] Fr. Spakaus-

[9] In connection with the distinction between belief and faith, it may be
noted that the *New English Bible* uses both terms in the translation of the
verses from John: 'If a man has faith in me ... Do you believe this?' The
response is, 'I ... believe' (1961: 172–3). The French translation of the
Jerusalem Bible has 'Qui croit en moi ... Crois-tu cela?' and gives Martha's
reply in the same verbal form, 'Je crois ...' (*La Sainte Bible*, 1961: 1415).

[10] I am very grateful to the Revd. Fr. Stefano Santandrea for his kindness
in making careful transcriptions, from the scarce copies in the possession of
the Verona Fathers at Rome, of both versions of the Creed in Nuer (personal
communication, 5 June 1968).

The translator of the printed versions cited is not named, but the
probability is that they are the work of Fr. Crazzolara, to whom they have
therefore been tentatively attributed in the bibliography.

[11] I owe a special debt of gratitude to Fr. Crazzolara for his authoritative
response (17 May 1968), and for his permission to quote from his letter.

kas, who was, it will be remembered, seventeen years among the Nuer, similarly writes: 'I think you can safely accept "liagh" as being the Nuer word for "belief" and "to believe", and this in the sense in which it is usually accepted in English.'[12] Finally, Mr. Daniel Bangot Kier, a Nuer who at the time when he responded to my query was an undergraduate at the University of York, has written that *liagh* (or *liak*) is certainly one of the words that can be used to express belief, as in *gän liaghä (liakä) Kuoth*, I believe in God. He explains *liagh* more widely, however, as meaning also 'to praise, glorify', as in *gän liakä jè*, I praise him, and 'to be proud', as in *gän liakä ro*, I am proud. Alternatively, there is the word *ngath*, as in *gän ngathä Kuoth*, I believe in God. The phrase 'we believe the word of God' can equally be rendered as *liaghnè ruai Kuoth* or as *ngathnè ruai(c) Kuoth*. In addition, there is a third word, *pal* (or *paal*), which can express belief. 'But the best word is *ngath*.'[13]

VII

We have been trying to determine how we can understand the interior state of an alien people with regard to their god. Received ideas, professional usage, and linguistic materials have all combined to lead us to conceive this state as one of belief, and our task is then to seek particular evidence of this specific state.

Here we encounter a grave occasion of difficulty in the form of conflicting reports by serious and trustworthy observers. The missionary linguists and the ethnographer agree in ascribing to the Nuer the attitude of 'faith', but they disagree about whether this is describable as belief; they agree that *ngath* can denote the attitude in question, but they disagree about the existence of a distinct word (such as *liagh*) which can stand for 'believe'.[14]

[12] Personal communication (12 March 1968). I wish to thank Fr. Spakauskas, not only for this precise opinion but also for a valuable insight into the conditions in which Fr. Kiggen's dictionary was prepared and for the interest of his own views on the question of belief among the Nuer.

[13] Personal communication (31 May 1968). I owe my contact with Mr. Bangot (who, incidentally, is not a Roman Catholic) to the Revd. Fr. R. Bresciani, of the Verona Fathers, London. Mr. Bangot later paid me a visit in Oxford and there amply confirmed the written reply that I have quoted.

[14] Professor Evans-Pritchard has been asked his opinion about *liagh* as the lexical equivalent of 'believe'. He maintains, as I understand him, certain reservations on the point.

The more closely we consider this situation, even in the favoured circumstances that attend it, the more perplexing and obscure it seems; and not only because, as Evans-Pritchard remarks, 'it is in the nature of the subject [sc. religion] that there should be ambiguity and paradox' (1956: 318). Nor is the real difficulty that of assessing the relative reliability of contradictory reports, for the evidence, both linguistic and descriptive, is unusually abundant, explicit, and checkable. The problem is indeed of a far more profound and consequential kind.

Let us accept that the Nuer possess in their language a means for the subtle discrimination of psychic states, that the language is well understood and recorded by foreign students, and that there are at least two words (as well as circumlocutions) which can be translated as 'believe'. Even then, we remain completely ignorant of what is the interior state of the Nuer toward their god. We have no idea, so far as phenomenal evidence goes, whether or not they experience a distinct state of belief or of 'spiritual' awareness when they speak of themselves by either of the words in question. All we know is what their language permits them to say about their relationship to a mystical personage. But the terms of this language do not in themselves constitute evidence of any specific state or experience; they can in fact be quite variously translated, and the divergent interpretations cannot be reconciled on simply linguistic grounds. Just as the observers' contradictions do not reflect contradictory empirical data concerning the interior states of the Nuer, so by contrast a complete accord on the equivalent of 'believe' in the Nuer language would still not supply evidence of an experience of belief.

Nevertheless, it is through language in the main that we must seek to identify such an interior state, and it may be that a linguistic comparison will help to locate the problem in a more revealing perspective. In any event, the normal recourse of a social anthropologist, when faced with a refractory issue, is to look for similar situations in otherwise disparate cultural settings; for these may at least show whether the problem is contingent, and peculiar to a particular form of civilization, or whether it is of a more constant (not to say inevitable) and general kind. In such a comparative focus the clearer definition of the problem may thus make it more amenable to analysis. To that end, therefore, it may prove useful to make a brief comparative survey of comparable issues in the translation of other languages.

3

Comparison

I

The difficulty in the translation of the concept of belief is not by any means confined to the Nuer case, but has been reported from numerous other societies.

Nida, in his article on problems of translating the Scriptures into Shilluk, Anuak, and Nuer, makes a typically useful introduction to our survey with his statement of the situation in Anuak (1955: 60):

In many Biblical contexts the Anuak words *yiey* and *ngadho* are neither one adequate in themselves to translate 'believe' or 'faith', for *yiey* implies only intellectual assent and *ngadho* is closer to hope or trust than to faith. However, the combination of these two words is an equivalent of 'believe' in such phrases as 'believe in the Lord Jesus Christ'. In such a context the combination of words implies not only agreement with but personal trust and confidence, coloured with hope.

It is most disappointing that Nida happens not to have directed his supremely practised attention to the same issue in Nuer, but in this related language (cf. Anuak *ngadho*, Nuer *ngath*, trust) we are nevertheless presented with familiar factors. In particular, Nida's comments on the effect of the combination of the two separate Anuak words brings out the importance of the psychological vocabulary available to the Anuak as compared with that to which the translator is accustomed in his own language.

The rest of the examples may simply be catalogued briefly in order to build up a cumulative impression of characteristic facets of the question.

In Navaho there is no word by which the English word 'believe', as employed in the Scriptures, can be exactly translated. There is a word, '*oodlá*', meaning 'to-believe-something-(unidentified object)', but in biblical translation it is necessary to complement this with other words meaning 'to trust in or depend on'. This expedient can make up a phrase such as *boodlágo ba'olí*, 'him-believing him-he-trusts', in order to convey an exclusive trust and commitment (Edgerton 1962: 33).

In Hindi, 'faith' and 'believe' are variously rendered. *Visvas* is reported to have established itself in missionary translations, but *nischay* is also used in the sense of belief as evidence or assurance, and *sachchai* as well, in the sense of 'faithfulness'. 'The Faith' is rendered as either *mat* or *dharm*, i.e., by additional and unrelated words. 'Belief' has also been conveyed with *pratiti*, though apparently exception can be taken to this (Hindley 1962: 112–3).

The Kikchi, of Guatemala, express both 'believe' and 'obey' by the same word (Nida 1947: 4; cited in Koper 1956: 139 n. 15; cf. Nida 1964: 51), and the same usage is reported of the Cuicatec of Mexico (Nida 1964: 51). 'In the Cuicatec and Tzeltal languages of Mexico there is no way of distinguishing between "to believe" and "to obey"....These Indians reason...that these words should be one. "But if you believe, do you not obey?" they say. "And if you obey, does not this show that you believe?"' (Nida 1952: 21–2).

In the Philippines, four dialects, namely Cebuano, Ilocano, Pampango, and Tagalog, all use separate words to express distinctly 'belief' and 'trust', in the following senses: (a) 'to believe that a person is telling the truth', 'to believe a fact or statement'; (b) 'to trust or put faith in the person himself' (Waterman 1960: 28).

The Uduk, on the border of Ethiopia, say that 'to believe in God' is 'to join God's word to the body'. The Shipibo Indians of Peru render 'to believe in God' as 'to be strong on God'; and their neighbours to the south, the Piro, say that to believe is literally 'to obey-believe'. In the language of the Huichol Indians, on the western slopes of central Mexico, 'to believe' is 'to conform to the truth' (Nida 1952: 119, 121, 122).

In a wider and very instructive comparison, Bratcher and Nida supply a passage of comment on the translation of 'believe' in Mark 1: 15, 'believe in the gospel', an account which valuably brings together a wide sampling of evidences from a number of different languages. They report that finding suitable equivalents for the key word 'believe' is very complicated, 'for such expressions as *believe a report*, *believe a person*, and *believe in a person* are frequently treated in other languages as quite different types of expressions'. Since belief or faith is 'so essentially an intimate psychological experience', they write, it is not strange that so many terms denoting faith should be highly figurative and should represent 'an almost unlimited range of emotional "centres" and descriptions of relationships', e.g.: 'steadfast his heart' (Chol), 'to arrive on the inside' (Trique), 'to conform with the heart' (Timorese), 'to have in the insides' (Kabba-Laka), 'to make the mind big for something' (Putu), 'to make the heart straight about' (Mitla Zapotec), 'to cause a word to enter the insides' (Lacandon), 'to leave one's heart with' (Kuripako), 'to catch in the mind' (Valiente), 'that which one leans on' (Vai), 'to have no doubts' (San Blas), 'to hear and take into the insides' (Karré), 'to accept' (Bare'e). Moreover, although these phrases are used to express faith, it must not be concluded that they can be used automatically in all types of context, so that difficulties in the translation of 'believe' still remain (Bratcher & Nida 1961: 38–9).

The western Penan, in the interior of Borneo, use the word *ayu* for 'believe' in such a context as *ayu pia' nah*, believe what he says. The word also means, however, 'to use', as of a tool or a weapon; and in addition it means 'to wear', as of a loincloth or a necklace. Its instrumental connotation can be glimpsed, furthermore, in such a phrase as *ayu nah maneu' kelepu'*, in order that he may make a blowpipe.[1]

The combination in one word of the notions of belief and use is found similarly in the Wewewa dialect of Sumba, in eastern Indonesia.[2] It takes a specially interesting form in the Bare'e dialect of Celebes, in which it is found in company with a very wide scope of meanings, namely: to take or use something, accept, believe, trust, hold dear, take into account; and, in compound forms, to suppose, opine, hope, etc. (Adriani 1928: 6–7, s.v. *aja*).

From Roti, also in eastern Indonesia, there is a reported set of homonyms under the term *hèle*. This can mean (1) to pick up, (2) to select, (3) bird-song, (4) to hinder, obstruct, weary, (5) tight, strong, firm, to make fast, fix, appoint, determine, agree upon (Du. *vaststellen, bepalen*). As a derivative from this last sense, *hèle* also means 'to trust, believe' (*vertrouwen, gelooven*).[3] Its uses are illustrated by the glosses: 'however pleasing his words may be, do not trust him'; 'he acted as though he was firmly convinced, as though

---

[1] Field inquiries, 1951–2, 1958.

[2] Professor Dr. L. Onvlee, personal communication (11 January 1968).

[3] I owe this reference to the advice of Dr. James J. Fox, who has himself conducted research on the island of Roti. I am obliged to him, also, for the information that the entry in the dictionary is not entirely correct: sense (3), in particular, should read 'to sing (in a ritual context)'.

he believed it'. As a further derivative, grammatically, *namahèlek* is translated as 'belief', *geloof*, and as 'trust', *vertrouwen*, a word which in Dutch focuses on the idea of confidence.

II

The Indonesian examples lead to a wider topic of investigation.

Probably the most common and widespread word for 'believe' in Indonesian cultures is *perchaya* or some variant of it. A standard Indonesian dictionary defines it thus: (1) the state of considering that something is true; (2) to think that something is true, to acknowledge the truth of something (Poerwadarminta 1954: 532, s.v. *pertjaja*). In Wilkinson's dictionary of peninsular Malay the word is rendered as: 'to trust; to believe; to have confidence in'. We can recognize these senses of the concept in a phrase such as *jangan kita perchaya yang demikian*, let us not believe such things. The word may also connote, however, an element of understanding as well, as in *perchaya angin* (the latter word meaning 'wind' or 'air') for 'belief that is not real; acceptance without comprehension'. Finally, as far as the entry in this dictionary goes, it conveys the idea of trust: *orang yang keperchayaan*, 'a man in a position of trust, a servant in whom implicit reliance is placed' (Wilkinson 1901: 456, s. v. *pěrchaya*). It would not be a simple or brief task to establish all the connotations of the word, in one or another form, throughout Indonesia, and a few representative examples will have to serve. In Javanese it appears as *pracaya*; in Toba Batak as *porcaya*; and in Busang as *pěrsaya* (Gonda 1952: 252, 77, 51). It is found also well into the interior of Borneo, where it is reported to be employed by the Kayan, Kenyah, Punan Bah, and Bukitan (Urquhart 1955: 203, s.v. 'believe').[4]

Now the word *perchaya* is not Malayo-Polynesian, as are nearly all of the indigenous languages of Indonesia, but is derived from the Sanskrit *pratyaya* (see, e.g., Gonda 1952: 443). It is instructive, both here and for later reference, to look at its original meanings in that language. The main renderings in the dictionary are as follows: belief, firm conviction, trust, faith, assurance, certainty of; proof, ascer-

---

[4] There seems to be no way of investigating decisively the possibility that Penan *ayu* is related to *perchaya*. In any case, the latter word has nothing to do with to use or wear (which in Malay, for instance, is *pakai*). Compare also the Bare'e *aja* (pronounced *aya*).

tainment; to acquire confidence, repose confidence in; conviction; conception, assumption, notion, idea; fundamental notion or idea; consciousness, understanding, intelligence, intellect; analysis, solution, explanation, definition; ground, basis, motive or cause of anything; the concurrent occasion of an event as distinguished from its proximate cause; an ordeal; want, need; fame, notoriety; an oath, usage, custom; religious meditation; a dependent or subject; a householder who keeps a sacred fire. In addition to this very wide range of meanings there are also a number of words which are formed from *pratyaya*, giving such meanings as: one who awakens confidence; seal, signet; a certain or distinct answer; etc. (Monier-Williams 1899: 673, col. 3).

III

A comparative survey of this kind could be very lengthily extended, but my present purpose will be accomplished if I give just one more example. I have not the competence to deal with it properly, but a few lines will indicate some of its potential interest.

The word in question is the Chinese *hsin* 信. This offers an especially intriguing case for investigation, though one in which the difficulties would be even more compounded. The ancient senses of the character were: truthful, true, sincere; indeed; to believe; to trust; good faith (Karlgren 1964: 109, no. 384a; cf. 1942: 114, gloss 85; 1946: 123, gloss 1014). The standard renderings in modern dictionaries are: faithfulness, reliable, sincere, true; believe, trust, follow; pledge, credentials; seal, letter; news (Karlgren 1923: 94); to believe in, to trust; truth, sincerity, confidence; pledge or token, etc. (Mathews 1931: 408–9). Richards cautions particularly that it is not to be equated with any of the western senses of truth, trust, loyalty, or fidelity, and suggests that 'faith', in the sense of good faith, perhaps comes nearer to the meaning (1932: 42).

Inferences from the formation of Chinese characters are hazardous, but it may be remarked nevertheless that *hsin* is composed of the radical for 'man' combined with that for 'speech'. Richards interprets this as 'a man standing by his word' (1932: 42), though this is possibly to take the character too pictographically and also to read an English idiom into it. Karlgren has simply 'a man's word' (1923: 94); and McKenzie (1970: 254–5) renders it as 'sincerity (a man of his word)'. The fundamental reference, anyway, would thus appear to be to social communication rather than to a relationship with, or dependence upon, spiritual power; to public status rather than to an inner state. This inference is strengthened by a comparison with terms constructed with *shih* 示, the radical for religious terms (Karlgren 1923: 260): e.g., *li*, rite, ceremony; *shen*, spirit, god; *tsu*, ancestor; *chi*, *ssŭ jang*, to sacrifice; *tao*, *ch'i*, to pray; *ch'an*, to pray, meditation; *hsi*, blessing; *hsiang*, good omen, happiness; *chih*, to respect.

This notion is likely to repay special attention, not only because it is prominent in the language of an ancient and very great civilization, and one that contrasts so far with either Europe or India, but because it belongs to an autonomous psychology that in some regards appears to frame a radically distinct view of human capacities and their relationship to the nature of things (see Richards 1932).

IV

A number of consequential points have already emerged, I think, from this survey.

The first consists in a clearer and more evidential recognition of the bewildering variety of senses attaching to words in foreign languages which are indifferently translated by the English 'believe'. The second is that, whereas it may often seem possible, in comparing other languages, to isolate one prominent sense from each set of connotations and then to treat this as the equivalent in each of the English word 'believe', there are languages in which senses that to an English interpretation are quite disparate are nevertheless so conjoined, and so equally expressed, as to make it unjustifiable to abstract any one of them as definitive. Thirdly, there are apparently languages in which, as Evans-Pritchard thinks is the case in Nuer, there is no verbal concept at all which can convey exactly what may be understood by the English word 'believe'.[5]

[5] Mr. Malcolm Crick has kindly directed me to the following observation on this point by Max Müller: 'If we take such a word as faith, or "to believe", it may seem to us very simple and natural; but that the idea of believing, as different from seeing, knowing, denying, or doubting, was not so easily elaborated, is best shown by the fact that we look for it in vain in the dictionaries of many uncivilized races' (1897, 2: 448).

In his earlier work, *The Science of Thought* (1887), Müller presents a list of 'the fundamental concepts expressed by Sanskritic roots' (619–32). There are 121 of these, but there is no entry for 'believe'. It is worth

All of this contrasts extremely with the plain statements made by ethnographers to the literal effect that the peoples whom they study 'believe' this or that, or 'believe in' certain matters. Such statements are commonly made, as we have seen, as confidently as if they were phenomenal descriptions of public acts; but the complexity and dubiety that is constantly present in the translation of the concept should now make us wonder more deeply whether reports of the kind can be so confidently accepted.

The context of the query is the mutual adjustment of psychological vocabularies and the variant classifications of human capacities that these express. In any individual case there is then the more particular question whether there exists a verbal concept that is equivalent to belief; and in the majority of the instances surveyed it appears that there may not be.

For the purposes of biblical translation, which are especially revealing, minute qualifications may have to be made in the employment of vernacular terms, and sometimes new phrases may actually have to be concocted in order to express the particular religious sense that is intended. Nevertheless, even missionary translators (by far the most aware), while discriminating in their apprehension of indigenous concepts, either do not pay comparably explicit attention to what it is that they have to convey when they translate belief-statements (see Koper 1956), or else, it seems, they rely on the dogmatic conceptions of their faiths and on their own personal conviction of the reality and the central inspiration of belief. It is as though the faculty of belief, and perhaps even the necessity to believe, were thought to be given in human experience and to be adequately recognized in Greek, Latin, and modern European languages. The task, in these circumstances, is hence to discover the linguistic means by which other peoples recognize this faculty; or, if their languages do not exactly enough provide for the expression of religious belief, then the resources of the alien languages can still be satisfactorily manipulated, it seems to be supposed, in order to fabricate an appropriate idiom of belief.

Yet the range and extreme disparity of the meanings attaching to the very many alien terms which are identically rendered as 'belief' must lead one to doubt whether this word can possibly accommo-

remarking, also, that a chief contention of Müller's in writing about the science of thought is to show that 'there is no such thing as intellect, understanding, mind, and reason, but . . . all these are only different aspects of language' (x; cf. 69).

date such variegated conceptions as it is called upon to convey. Alternatively, if we can somehow be persuaded that it does furnish a set of valid equivalents, then we must surely ask whether it can possess such clarity and precision of denotation as to make it useful in ethnographical description or conceptual analysis.

An essential difficulty does indeed reside, as Evans-Pritchard suggests (1956: vi; cf. 1965: 12–14), and as the comparative evidence marshalled above has demonstrated, in our own words. Let us therefore look next at the notion of belief in English.

4

Tradition

I

The relevant definitions of the English word 'belief', in the Oxford dictionary, are:

Belief. . . . 1. The mental action, condition, or habit, of trusting to or confiding in a person or thing; trust, confidence, faith. . . . Trust in God; the virtue of faith. 2. Mental assent to or acceptance of a proposition, statement, or fact, as true, on the grounds of authority or evidence; the mental condition involved in this assent 1533. 3. The thing believed; in early use, *esp.* a religion. Now often = opinion, persuasion. . . . Intuition, natural judgement 1838. 4. A creed.

Believe. . . . I. *intr.* 1. To have confidence or faith *in*, and consequently to rely upon. . . . 2. To give credence *to*. . . . 3. To believe *in* (a person or thing), i.e., in its existence or occurrence 1716. II. *trans.* 1. To give credence to (a person in making statements, etc.). . . . 2. To give credence to (a statement). 3. . . . To hold it as true *that* . . . , to think ME. 4. To hold as true the existence of—1732.

This familiar set of conventional and established connotations could be augmented by a consideration of current idiom, in which 'to believe' may also connote 'to suspect', 'to expect', and so on. In American English, moreover, the idiom is yet further extended, and a much greater use is commonly made of 'believe': e.g., 'I do believe' may express a simple statement of opinion; 'I believe I won't', in response to an offer of a drink, just means 'No, thank you'; and such phrases as 'I do believe I don't care to', as a polite form of refusal, emphasize even more the everyday reliance on belief-statements. In the English language, therefore, the concept of belief is not simple but covers a very wide range of meanings. The definitions indicate no central or essential meaning, and it is obvious why the English word must be hard to translate into other languages.

A full demonstration of this source of confusion calls for a grammar of belief, in the form of a socio-linguistic inquiry into the types

40

and functions of belief-statements in the current use of the English language. This in turn would form the ground for a conceptual analysis of belief-statements as expressions of ideology, rather like Newman's *Grammar of Assent* (1881), perhaps. Investigations into these aspects of the question are certainly most desirable, and ideally they should have preceded a comparative study such as this; but they are not essential to the present purpose of setting out the initial hindrances to the translation of the notion of belief between English and exotic tongues.

The first of the hindrances is the sheer proliferation of senses attaching to the English words 'belief' and 'believe'. This proliferation is not a reflection of some arbitrary development or conceptual confusion, but results from a long linguistic tradition. The several meanings of 'believe' are the products of a continual elaboration upon a more elementary base in Indo-European culture. The concept of belief is an historical product, and in order to understand its present scope we have to begin with the history of the word, i.e., with its etymology (see page 42, Fig. 1).

II

In Middle English (ca. 1100–1475) the verb *bilēven* already had the following main senses: to believe (in a doctrine, in God, etc.), 1150; to profess a faith or religion, 1330; to accept (a statement, a doctrine, etc.) as valid or true, to accept as authoritative, 1325–; to give credence to, have confidence in, 1225; to have (a certain) opinion or conviction, think, believe, expect, 1390 (Kurath & Kuhn 1956: 856–7). Thus from the Norman Conquest to the beginning of printing there existed an established variety of meanings which have endured into present usage.

In late Old English, to go further back, the word was *bileafe*, which from the twelfth century replaced the OE *ġelēafa*. The verbal form was *belȳfan* or *belēfan*, which replaced, by prefix-substitution, the earlier *ġelēfan* (West Saxon *gelīefan*) = Old Friesian *gelēva*, Old Saxon *gilōbian* (Dutch *gelooven*), Old High German *gilouben* (German *glauben*), Gothic *galaubjan*, a normal development from the Common Germanic (except Old Norse) **ʒalauƀjan*, to hold dear, cherish, trust in, from **ʒa-* + **lauƀ*, dear, lief (Onions 1966: 87). The Germanic **ʒa-*, which is possibly identical with the Latin *com-*, had originally the physical connotation of 'with' or 'together'. This yielded the notion of association and hence of appropriateness, suit-

ability, and collectivity, the final stage being the notion of completeness and perfectivity, a special application finding expression in the
use of the prefix in past participles (1016, s.v. *y-*; see also Grebe 1963,
s.v. *glauben*; cf. *lieb*).

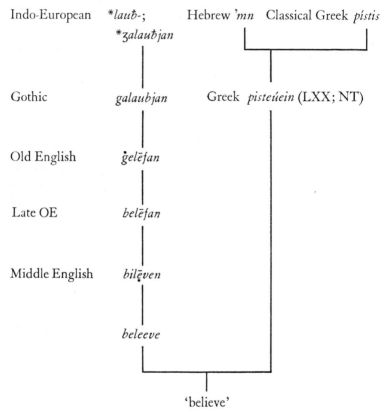

Indo-European   *lauƀ-;   Hebrew *'mn*   Classical Greek *pístis*
                 ʒalauƀjan

Gothic   galaubjan   Greek *pisteúein* (LXX; NT)

Old English   ġelēfan

Late OE   belēfan

Middle English   bilę̄ven

                 beleeve

                        'believe'

Pokorny makes a more profound investigation than do the sources
from which these earlier forms are taken, and he covers a larger
number of cognate forms. According to this authority, the Common
Germanic *laub* is itself to be related to the Indo-European *leubh-*,
meaning 'to love, want, desire'. From this root there have derived a
numerous family of words in Sanskrit, Greek, Latin, Albanian, the
Germanic languages, and Lithuanian (Pokorny 1948–: 683–4; cf.
Buck 1949: 1206, art. 17.15).

A convenient survey of many of these derivative forms is to be
found in Grandsaignes d'Hauterive, who renders *leubh-* as 'prendre

plaisir, aimer' and brings together this telling collection: Skt. *lúbh-yati*, he desires strongly; Lat. *lubet*>*libet*, he is pleased by; *libido*, desire. The Latin gives Fr. *libidineux*>English libidinous; Italian *libito*, will, desire; Spanish *libídine*, lust. The Germanic languages have Gothic *liufs*, dear, and *galaubjan*, to believe; English love, lover, believe, belief; German *lieb*, dear, *Liebe*, love, *lieben*, to love, cherish, *glauben*, to believe, *Glaube*, faith, *erlauben*, to permit, *Urlaub*, leave, *Lob*, praise, *loben*, to praise (Grandsaignes d'Hauterive 1949: 108).

Even so compressed an account as this has been demonstrates strikingly the crucial value of an etymological examination of the notion of belief in English. It is indeed, as embodied in the words 'belief' and 'believe', an historical product; and, in spite of the similarities to Germanic concepts in particular, it has assumed a distinct and complicated character of its own.

From a root denoting 'love' or 'desire', it has come to mean not only 'trust', which can readily enough be connected to the idea of love (as we now conceive it, at any rate), but also the assessment of something as true, not to mention the variety of connotations such as 'expect' which are more distant from the original concept. The singularity of this development is well illustrated by, for example, the contrast between the English 'believe' and Spanish *libídine*, lust, lewdness. This divergence, moreover, is only one instance of the wide variegation of the large family of words which have a common origin in the IE **leubh-*. Consider no more than a brief list of some of the more prominent senses that are to be found among the derivatives in the languages cited above: love, cherish, trust, desire, want, permit, leave, praise, commend, approve, believe, opine, think. This semantic differentiation is the result of migrations, political divisions, deliberation, fashion, intellectual circumstances, and other contingencies in the use of language. The process continues, and just as no one could have predicted the present variety of meanings, so the future uses and transferential developments of the word 'believe' and its congeners cannot possibly be forecast. All we can be certain of is that the words in question will acquire yet more connotations, and that the associated notions of belief will become even more intricate.

It is plain, therefore, that the general notion represented by the English verbal concept of belief is complex, highly ambiguous, and unstable. No wonder there is such constant difficulty in putting it into other languages, and that conversely the English words 'belief' and 'believe' require such glosses and qualifications if they are to convey the concepts or attitudes of alien cultures.

III

But even these obstacles to translation are only one side of the question. It is not just a word that is at issue, but a concept; for a word can acquire, serially or by accretion, a number of meanings in its history, and an idea can retain an essential constancy in spite of its passage into a number of languages.

The notion of belief has not only a lexical history in the Indo-European tongues, traceable phonetically through the form of the English word, but it has also an ideational history, and this leads back to unrelated languages and to a world of meaning with which communication is even more hazardously inferential. The English concept of belief has been formed by a Christian tradition, and the religious acceptation of the word relates in the first place to the Christian faith. But this religion itself has a history, and if we are to grasp something of the origin and development of the concept of belief we need to trace it back ideologically to the Old Testament.

In describing man's relationship to God, two contrasting groups of ideas are employed in the Old Testament.[1] These are fear and trust, and although they are fundamentally different they are so connected that the fear of God is often simply the term for faith. The word groups denoting these attitudes are evenly balanced. None of the verbal stems is of specifically religious origin, and their use in religion seems to have arisen out of profane roots. A root of central importance is '*mn* (אמן). This can mean,[2] in a secular context,

---

[1] As any student of theology will at once recognize, I have based this section directly and for the most part verbatim on the edited translation of Bultmann and Weiser's fascinating article on Πίστις in Kittel's great encylopedia (Bultmann & Weiser 1961; Kittel 1932). This, incidentally, is one reason that in what follows I write without distinction of either 'belief' or 'faith'.

I have also profited very much, if less patently, from van Dorssen's learned and invaluable dissertation on the root '*mn* in the Hebrew of the Old Testament (1951).

[2] That is, it can have certain meanings in one particular form, namely the *qal*, of the Hebrew verb. Three other forms (*niph'al, hiph'il, pi'el*) make important distinctions in other relevant contexts, but it has not seemed necessary to register such complications in setting out the usages that are examined here.

a child's mother, nurse, attendant, guardian, foster-father; it is used of a child wrapped in something, or as being carried; and it can further connote education or nurture. It is reported to be difficult to determine which of these ideas is the original, and also to ascertain whether there is a connection between such employments of the word and its religious usage. There is, however, another and much wider range of use which has a special significance. The usual translation of *'mn* in this usage is 'firm, certain, reliable', but this is no more than an approximation which does not represent its ultimate and fundamental meaning.[3] This can be seen in those passages where the profane use of the verb is connected with a thing: it then expresses suitability for a particular purpose, as of a tent-peg fastened in a sure place; it is used of a dynasty, in order to say that it will not die out; it is applied to lasting afflictions and grievous diseases, with reference not only to their persistent continuance but also to their effects; it can mean that a source of drinking water will not fail; and, finally, it is further used of a statement which is proved to be true because it corresponds with the facts of the case. These examples clearly show that an unvarying translation with only one word is not possible. The root *'mn* is 'a general concept the content of which is determined differently in each case by the particular thing it describes'; 'it declares that in any given instance the qualities to be attributed to the subject in question are actually present' (Bultmann & Weiser 1961: 5).[4] When it is used of persons, the word can describe qualities which in themselves are quite different, and it is this capacity which makes it possible for the great number of the different manifestations of God's activity to be summed up

[3] This assertion has a bearing on the position adopted by Professor Dr. H. G. Schulte Nordholt in his inaugural lecture (1967). Relying on this interpretation of the Hebrew, he proposes that the most demanding activity of man is the struggle to believe (*geloven*), in the sense of 'to acquire certainty' (6). His main argument does not suffer thereby, but the translation of *'mn* does not quite provide the support that he suggests (34 n. 4).

On the question of the 'ultimate' meaning of *'mn*, incidentally, a full investigation would have also to take into account the Egyptian *mn*, which meant 'to remain, to be fixed in one place, etc.'. When used of persons, this word meant 'to stay, to survive, to persist'; when applied to things, such as buildings, memorials, or statues, it meant that they stood permanently (Erman and Grapow 1925–31, 2 [1927]: 60, 61).

[4] An interesting comparison is formed by the Sumbanese word *ndewa*, usually translated as 'soul' or 'spirit', which may also be rendered as 'that which gives things their existence, their nature, etc.' (Onvlee, in Swellengrebel 1941: 120).

45

in one term. As Weiser well phrases the matter, it is 'a formal concept' (Weiser 1935: 89).[5]

These facts enable us to grasp something of the import of the root '*mn* in the verbal form *he'emīn*, to believe. In profane usage, to believe a report, etc., is to be aware of and to accept as true the thing reported, and at the same time it includes an attitude appropriate to the thing reported. When used toward persons the word emphasizes, according to our authorities, the attitude that is associated with the English word 'trust', and this in a mutual sense: thus 'it is the reciprocal relationship which makes trust what it really is and not merely a one-sided connexion'.[6] The term is employed similarly toward God, and signifies to recognize and to acknowledge the relationship into which God enters with man, so that 'the reciprocal relationship between God and man is part of the essence of faith' (Bultmann & Weiser 1961: 11). The special character of his relationship, as described by *he'emīn*, has to do with the fact that 'the setting and origin of the religious usage of the stem '*mn* is to be sought in the OT tradition of the sacred covenant of Yahweh' (13), and this covenant is, of course, the sign of an exclusive relationship between God and his chosen people. Isaiah played a decisive part in giving the ultimate depth of meaning to

[5] In this respect it resembles the notion of *mana* as interpreted by Lévi-Strauss, namely as being simply a form, or a symbol in a pure state, which is capable of incorporating any symbolic content whatever: it is 'une valeur symbolique zéro... un signe marquant la nécessité d'un contenu symbolique supplémentaire à celui qui charge déjà le signifié, mais pouvant être une valeur quelconque...' (1950: xlix–l).

I should acknowledge, however, that Barr objects to Weiser's interpretation as bearing the marks of a philosophical–theological origin, and contends that this formal gloss goes 'far beyond what can be documented as a linguistic fact from the uses of forms from this root' (1961: 180).

[6] On the connection with the idea of firmness, Barr maintains that 'any semantic development from the sense of 'firmness, sureness' was made with reference not to the 'firmness', 'steadfastness', and 'sureness' of God, but to the sureness and certainty of the one who trusts or believes' (1961: 184–5). With particular reference to the Hebrew '*omenot*, doorposts, and also perhaps to 'the "guardian" series', he thinks it may be possible 'to explain some of these usages as derivatives from the sense of "trust"' (186).

How hard these matters are for a comparativist is shown, on the other hand, by Pfeiffer's contrary emphasis on the reciprocity of activity and passivity which, according to him, is characteristic of the Old Testament. In this view, the burden of belief rests on man's consciousness of insignificance and powerlessness in relation to the firmness and reliability of God (Pfeiffer 1959: 164).

'*mn*, with a crucial emphasis that has never dropped out of the later history of its usage. For him, faith is an altogether special form of existence for those dependent on God alone; faith and existence are identical (15–17). Hence, although the term '*mn* sums up all the ways by which men express in their lives their relationship to God, *he'°min* is nowhere in the Old Testament used for the relationship with other gods. The root bth, meaning to be in a state of security, is used with relation to God and it is also used to denote confidence in idols; but '*mn* is used only of God and can never express a relationship to other gods.

There are other roots that are used to express faith in God, namely *hsh*, to seek refuge, to make oneself safe, and *qwh*, *yhl*, and *hkh*, which are verbs of hope; but for our purpose the root '*mn* is the most important, for it is this verbal concept, with its 'very wide range and flexibility' (32), which prevailed in Judaism and which contributed definitively to the formation of the Christian conception of faith.

In the third century B.C. the Old Testament was translated from the Hebrew into Greek, in the version later known as the Septuagint, and in this rendering the Hebrew *he'°min* is almost invariably conveyed by the Greek πιστεύειν (*pisteúein*). This verb is one among a number of grammatical forms centering upon the notion of *pístis* and connoting, in classical usage, trust, confidence, loyalty, certainty, firm conviction, etc. Treaties and oaths are objects of *pisteúein*, as are persons who are trustworthy and can be relied upon; but the formations with *pist-* did not become technical terms of religious language in classical Greek. Nor did *pístis* become a technical term in religion, though it prepared for such a possibility by its usage as 'reliance upon' a divine oracle, and also by the fact that in the sense of 'conviction' it can have the existence of a deity as its object (38–9). In the early Greek world it was customary, rather, to express the belief that there are gods by the word *nomízein*, to recognize, acknowledge. In later times *pisteúein* could be said instead, and this was in accordance with the acquisition by this word of the meaning 'to believe'. That gods existed was a fact that had its own proper certainty, but it was not at all self-evident and it presupposed an obstacle to be overcome. A man had to be educated by knowledge to believe in the incorporeal, and this theoretical conviction, allied with piety, became a recognized premise of belief in the writings of Plutarch, Plotinus, and Porphyry. The use of *pístis* as a technical term in religious language was further encouraged by the fact that

47

E

it became a key word in the propaganda of proselytizing religions, not only in Christianity. When the Septuagint was compiled, therefore, the term readily proposed itself as the translation of the Old Testament *he'ᵉmin*, especially since the latter word not only means in part 'to trust' but also, like *pístis*, 'to acknowledge'.

The concept of faith in Judaism, in its special senses and developments (particularly in its relation to the Law) in rabbinical writings, did not so decisively contribute to the history of our own notion, and from the Septuagint we may pass therefore directly to the New Testament. In this, *pisteúo* was used formally, with only slight departures from Greek linguistic usage. Together with related forms, it conveyed the ideas of reliance, trust, credence, etc., but the frequent expression *pisteúein eis*, to 'believe on' (a phrase now indissolubly part of English usage), is found neither in classical Greek nor in the Septuagint, but is peculiar to the New Testament. The noun *pístis* has in Greek the twofold meaning of 'loyalty' and 'trust', yet in the New Testament it is scarcely used in the former sense. There are other special usages which might be noted, but in the main there is a clear and direct derivation to be traced from classical Greek usage into our notion of belief.

In primitive Christianity, *pístis* became the predominant designation of the relationship of man to God, but it acquired particular applications in the New Testament. *Pisteúo* often means to put faith in the words of God, and it therefore applies to the scriptures, to what is written in the law and the prophets, to what the prophets said or simply to the prophets themselves, to Moses, and similarly to what God is saying at present, e.g., through an angel. It is brought out particularly that to believe is to obey; it was chiefly Paul who emphasized that the nature of faith is that of obedience. The element of trust is not so prominent, but it is especially marked where Old Testament and Jewish influence is strong. Trust in God is indeed mentioned relatively seldom, though 'trust' is in fact a prime meaning of *pístis*. The Old Testament meaning of 'loyalty' is still discernible in *pístis*, and in other respects also there is a clear persistence of Old Testament and Jewish tradition into the New Testament; but there also developed a specifically Christian usage which must be distinguished from all such inherited meanings.

The primary meaning is the acceptance of the kerygma (message) of Christ (69); the early Christian kerygma brings the message that there is one God and together with it the message concerning Jesus Christ. The element of trustful hope becomes less prominent, and 'the *pistis eis* . . . looks first and foremost at what God had done, not at what he is going to do' (70). Paul makes it plain that the Christian faith consists in recognizing Jesus as Lord, and at the same time in accepting ('believing to be true') the miracle of the resurrection. Different forms of *pisteúein* are in fact used in order to describe the relationship to God and that to Christ. There is a personal relationship with Christ which is analogous to that with God and yet differing from it. Faith in Jesus Christ, in what is judged to be its original and proper sense, is not obedience to the Lord who has always been known: on the contrary, it is by faith that the existence of this Lord is first perceived and acknowledged (75). 'In the OT the godly man believes (in loyalty and obedience) in God by reason of what He does; . . . In the NT it is precisely that which God does which is to be "believed"' (83). Hence the meaning of *pisteúein* has developed, and has become differentiated, so that in most cases it means 'to accept the message'. The 'faith' is simply the designation of the religion, and the 'believers' are the Christians. In John, believing procures salvation, and to believe is to renounce the world. This doctrine is associated with a conviction so firm that knowledge also is implied; 'as all knowledge must be imbued with faith, so faith comes to be its true self by knowledge' (108) and, by a significant qualification, is accomplished through love (109–10).

This summary exposition of the long historical formation of the notion of belief, as inherited and shaped by the Christian tradition, has made, I fear, a grievous compression of the far longer and scrupulously coherent account by Bultmann and Weiser; and I can only hope that I have not too much mangled the exquisite conceptual carefulness of the original. Naturally, too, I have had to omit a great deal, so that the true impact of the past has been unduly lessened, but the main ideological influences and their several effects should nevertheless have become plain enough.

Our conception of belief, so far as it has been religiously moulded, is demonstrably an historical amalgam, composed of elements traceable to Judaic mystical doctrine and Greek styles of discourse. Those two distant and contrasted cultures merged in the Septuagint and continued to make their distinctive kinds of impress on the New Testament. The Gospels differed among themselves in the conceptions of belief that they called upon or proclaimed, and a further differentiation was brought about by Paul and by later commentators. These literary elaborations of the central theme of belief were not resorbed into a homogeneous conception, though reformers and

49

sectarian movements continually tried to impose their own forms of unity, but were only perpetuated and multiplied through centuries of dogmatic strife, theological explication, and the arduous ingenuities of translators. From the conflation of '*mn* and *pístis* an increasingly extensive and complex conglomeration of meanings has come lengthily down to us; and after all the accretions and giddy twists of sense we now find ourselves, even within a specifically Christian context, with a notion of belief so dispersed, intricate, and ambiguous as to create yet more perplexity and uncertainty.

IV

We can thus distinguish, if only schematically in this place, two convergent lines in the development of our notion of belief: one manifesting itself in a series of related lexical forms in the Indo-European family of languages, and the other in a religious history that combines Jewish, Greek, and Christian concepts.

In the pre-Christian merging of cultural premises, it was in fact an Indo-European language, namely Greek, which was semantically commingled with Hebrew in the translation of the scriptures. But the Greek word that was adopted in order to express the Hebraic ideas of belief is unconnected with the set of words in other Indo-European languages which derive in common from *leubh-*. Already, therefore, in this first decisive conjunction of traditions, a division from Indo-European forms of thought was introduced at the same time as these were made the vehicles of Semitic conceptions.

A feature of the utmost importance is the continual reformulation of the criteria and patterns of belief in Hebrew and Greek texts, and in the establishment of the Christian faith. I have concentrated on this latter development, since it has had such a profound and explicit influence on European civilization; but it should not be overlooked that conceptual changes also accompanied the lexical variations which preceded the Authorized Version, i.e., before the English language and Christian traditions were crucially conjoined into the literary formulations of belief that we have inherited.

When these two separate traditions are conceived together, against so extended a time-scale and so complex a background of styles of thought and forms of social life, the grounds for difficulty in understanding and translating the English verbal concept of belief can readily be seen to be very numerous and bewildering.

5

Theories

I

The disparate senses that make up the notion of belief are so patent and yet problematical, and they touch so directly on traditional concerns in epistemology, that we might expect philosophers to have reordered the varieties of the concept, or at least to have reduced these to a more explicit economy of meaning. There is the encouragement, also, that philosophy is not confined (ideally, at any rate) by linguistic or religious traditions. 'The philosopher is not a citizen of any community of ideas: that is what makes him into a philosopher' (Wittgenstein 1967a, sec. 455). Yet, in spite of this presumed advantage, the philosophers' attentions to the problem have in fact multiplied distinctions and have fabricated new grounds for uncertainty.

A full review of philosophical disquisitions on belief is out of the question here,[1] and a summary of commonly agreed opinions on the topic would be even less feasible; but it will be helpful to call to mind, in the first place, the views of four prominent philosophers (two in the eighteenth century, two in the twentieth) whose views have a close and special interest in the present inquiry, and whose writings will help to guide our more empirical investigation. These excerpts will be followed by reports of two more concentrated analyses of belief which have recently been published by modern linguistic philosophers.

The purpose of this chapter is not to provide a full or critical account of the ideas of each of the philosophers cited, but only to introduce the variety of theories that philosophers have advanced in their repeated attempts, over the past two centuries and more, to arrive at a satisfactory account of belief.

[1] A very useful survey is to be found in Price (1968), but since he does not mention the views of Kant or Wittgenstein, or the modern philosophers to whom I later refer, there is little overlap in our accounts. His examination of Hume's theory, however, is extensive and deserves particular recommendation.

II

Hume, in 1739, found belief to be 'an act of the mind [that] has never yet been explain'd by any philosopher', and he quickly made clear where the real difficulty lies.

The idea of an object is, he writes, an essential part of a belief in it, but not the whole. 'We conceive many things, which we do not believe.' Reasoning concerns the existence of objects or of their qualities; but to conceive the existence of any object adds nothing to the simple conception of it. In the same way, 'the belief of the existence joins no new ideas to those, which compose the idea of the object. When I think of God, when I think of him as existent, and when I believe him to be existent, my idea of him neither encreases nor diminishes' (1888: 94).[2] But since it is certain that there is a great difference between simply conceiving the existence of something and holding a belief about it, and since this difference does not lie in the constituents of the idea that is conceived, it follows that it must lie in the manner in which we conceive it. Hume asks, then, 'Wherein consists the difference betwixt believing and disbelieving any proposition?' (95).

To answer this question he goes back to what he regards as the sources of all our ideas, namely 'impressions' or perceptions. Our ideas are copied from our impressions, and the only way to vary the idea of a particular object is to increase or diminish its 'force and vivacity', i.e., the degree to which it resembles its original. 'So that as belief does nothing but vary the manner, in which we conceive any object, it can only bestow on our ideas an additional force and vivacity.' An opinion or belief, therefore, may be most accurately defined as 'a lively idea related to or associated with a present impression' (96).

The effect of belief is to make an idea approach an impression in force and vivacity; it is indeed 'nothing but *a more vivid and intense conception of any idea*' (119–20), 'so that there can be no suspicion of mistake' (101). Belief, therefore, 'consists merely in a certain feeling or sentiment; in something that depends not on the will, but must arise from certain determinate causes and principles, of which we are not masters. When we are convinced of any

[2] Page references, still, are to the Selby–Bigge edition in the Oxford printing of 1888.

matter of fact, we do nothing but conceive it, along with a certain feeling . . .' (624).

But what is the nature of this feeling, Hume inquires, and does it resemble any other 'sentiment of the human mind'? This is an important question, as he stresses, for if the feeling is unique we must despair of explaining its causes, and must consider it as 'an original principle of the human mind'; whereas if there are other feelings like it, we can hope to explain its causes by analogy, and trace it to more general principles.

Yet when Hume tries to define the feeling of belief, he encounters very considerable difficulty. 'Even when I think I understand the subject perfectly, I am at a loss for terms to express my meaning. . . . When I would explain this *manner*, I scarce find any word that fully answers the case' (629). Part of the problem is that it is 'very difficult to talk of the operations of the mind with perfect propriety and exactness', because common language does not make precise enough discriminations (105). So Hume writes that he can only endeavour to explain the feeling by calling it a superior 'force', or 'vivacity', or 'solidity', or 'firmness', or 'steadiness'; but he confesses that it is 'impossible to explain perfectly this feeling or manner of conception'. All he can do, accordingly, is to invoke the feeling that everyone has, and to resort simply to the word 'belief', which is 'a term that every one sufficiently understands in common life'. In the end, he concludes (629), we can go no further than to assert that belief is:

something *felt* by the mind, which distinguishes the ideas of the judgement from the fictions of the imagination. It gives them more force and influence; makes them appear of greater importance; infixes them in the mind; and renders them the governing principles of all our actions.

As this final quotation indicates, I have passed over a number of stages in Hume's examination, as well as certain of his more incidental observations on belief. We shall take these up later, at places where they will acquire their full relevance.

III

Kant, in the *Critique of Pure Reason* (1787),[3] agrees with Hume in

[3] Page references are to Kemp Smith's translation (London: Macmillan, 1929; second impression, with corrections, 1933). The original text has been referred to also at certain points of special importance. I have kept very close

focusing on the sense of conviction, but instead of defining belief by reference to the vivacity of an impression, he classes it with a number of mental occurrences having to do with 'holding a thing to be true' and the grounds for this kind of judgement.

If a judgement that something is true is valid for everyone, its ground is objectively sufficient and the holding of it to be true is entitled conviction; whereas a judgement residing only in the special character of the individual is mere persuasion. Now 'truth depends upon agreement with the object', and the true judgements of all individuals must be in agreement with each other. The touch-stone by which we decide whether a judgement that something is true is conviction or only persuasion is therefore external, namely 'the possibility of communicating it and finding it to be valid for all human reason' (645). This test has only a subjective value in detecting a merely private judgement or persuasion; it does not in itself procure conviction or establish an objective validation.

There are three degrees in holding a thing to be true, in its relation to conviction, namely opining, believing, and knowing. Opining is both subjectively and objectively insufficient; whereas knowledge, by polar contrast, is sufficient on both counts. Believing lies midway between these two: 'If our holding of the judgement be only subjectively sufficient, and is at the same time taken as being objectively insufficient, we have what is termed *believing* [*glauben*]' (646; cf. 1787: 850). A subjective sufficiency is termed conviction; an objective sufficiency is termed certainty. When we believe, we are convinced; but we lack the grounds for regarding even so firm a judgement as certain knowledge.

Beliefs can be classed as contingent or as necessary. A contingent belief, which nevertheless forms the ground for the actual employment of means to particular actions, is called 'pragmatic belief'. The usual test, Kant avers, of whether what someone asserts is merely his persuasion or 'subjective conviction, i.e., his firm belief', is betting. This reveals, by the scale of risks found acceptable regarding the assertion in question, that pragmatic belief always exists in some specific degree (648). A man may propound his views with such a positive and uncompromising assurance that he seems to have ruled out any possibility of error; but a bet disconcerts him.

to the wording of the places cited, even where no quotation marks are provided; this is not only safer, when writing about Kant, but instructively brings out the contrast with Hume.

If, in a given case, we represent ourselves as staking the happiness of our whole life [upon a conviction], the triumphant tone of our judgement is greatly abated; we become extremely diffident, and discover for the first time that our belief does not reach so far.

There is also a 'doctrinal' kind of belief, which is conceived in cases where judgement is purely theoretical, such that nothing can actually be done about the object of the belief. An example is Kant's own conviction—'on which I should be ready to stake my all'—that at least one of the planets that we see is inhabited.[4] Another is the doctrine of the existence of God. Such cases bring out the ambivalent character of belief: from the objective point of view, the expression of belief is an expression of modesty; yet at the same time, from the subjective point of view, it is an expression of the firmness of our confidence.

The term 'belief' refers only to the guidance that an idea gives me, and to its subjective influence in that furthering of the activities of my reason which confirms me in the idea, and which yet does so without my being in a position to give a speculative account of it.

Finally, there is the type of 'moral' belief. This is marked by the absolute necessity that one must in all things conform to the moral law.

I am particularly conscious that so compressed an account is most inadequate to Kant's rigorously coherent thought, and to the ramified implications of his technical vocabulary, but these brief abstracts should indicate well enough for the present some of his main ideas about belief.[5] In particular, it is already clear how divergent are Kant's views from those of Hume.

IV

The next great philosopher on whom I wish to call is Wittgenstein. Since he is the central figure in the argument of this book, and its chief inspiration, we can defer a detailed examination of his ideas until later chapters. For the present, we need only register his appearance on the intellectual scene, as far as the problem of belief is concerned, and establish as shortly as possible the main tenor of his thought.

[4] See also Kant 1797: 112–29: 'Eine Vergleichung zwischen den Einwohnern der Gestirne.' (Cf. Lovejoy [1936] on the 'plurality of worlds'.)

[5] See further Eisler 1961, s.v. 'Glaube'.

Wittgenstein's interest in the notion of belief declared itself very early in his work, in 1916, with the question that opens the present inquiry: 'Is belief an experience?'[6] He returned to the problem repeatedly, and towards the very end of his life the topic still exercised him (1969: 72). Throughout his work, he ingeniously put a series of questions about belief which in some respects strike far more deeply than do the ordered arguments of his predecessors. It is a question whether his own conclusions are ultimately of much more decisive help in dealing with the difficulties that we have encountered; but he certainly succeeded in giving a quite new cast to the whole issue.

'This is how I think of it,' he says (1953: 191-2):

Believing is a state of mind. It has duration; and that independently of the duration of its expression in a sentence, for example. So it is a kind of disposition of the believing person. This is shown me in the case of someone else by his behaviour; and by his words. And under this head, by the expression 'I believe...' as well as by the simple assertion.

This dispositional view of belief, set out in an uncharacteristically consecutive form in the passage cited, is supported and elaborated by many more scattered and allusive remarks in a number of different places. It would be possible to combine these into an integrated disquisition on believing, but to do so would be foreign to Wittgenstein's own style of investigation, and moreover it would not be the best way to take advantage of his thought.[7]

Let us therefore merely note, for the present, that Wittgenstein's summation makes no place specifically either for feeling or for truth. He has in fact excellent views on the former aspect, and on much else besides in connection with believing, but it will prove more effective to adduce these ideas below as occasion offers.

V

The fourth major philosophical example that I wish to introduce is Stuart Hampshire's *Thought and Action*, not simply on account

---

[6] 'Ist der Glaube eine Erfahrung?' (1961: 89). The published translation rather impairs the clarity and effect of the question by rendering it as: 'Is belief a kind of experience?'

[7] A compact and sympathetic account of Wittgenstein's views on belief is to be found in Hudson (1968).

of the author's observations on belief, but also because these form part of an admirably integrated disquisition on philosophical argument and styles of discourse in their general connection with forms of social life. Where he touches especially on the empirical interests of social anthropology is in his constant emphasis on actions and judgements, i.e., on the consequences, within any given social setting, of the intentions and beliefs which by his definition constitute thought.[8]

In Hampshire's view, beliefs must to some degree be stable if they are to count as beliefs at all, but they need not be present to the consciousness. Any man carries about with him an enormous load of settled beliefs about the world, which he has never had occasion to question and many of which he has never had occasion to state (1959: 150):

They constitute the generally unchanging background to his active thought and observation. ... The culture of which he is part is formed partly by the beliefs in which he grew up, almost without noticing them, and partly by the habits of action of social behaviour that are unthinking, unquestioned, but not unintentional.

Nevertheless, conventional though beliefs may be, 'the whole point and purpose of a belief is that it should be true' (150).

Belief has a content which, fixed by the conventions of language, determines by itself the reasons that are required to support it. To express a belief in words a man must 'find within a language the right words to represent his thought *correctly*' (152). Yet one does not decide to believe (158):

When a statement is brought to my attention, and the question is whether I believe it or not, the decision that I announce in the words 'Yes, I believe it' is not a decision to do anything; nor can these words constitute an announcement that I have attempted or achieved anything. I have not decided *to* believe; I have decided *that* the statement in question is true.

Still, one can decide to act, and this is another defining feature of belief. Just as thought cannot be thought unless it is directed to

[8] In general, this splendid work of intellectual art demands the serious attention of any social anthropologist whose conception of his subject, and of what it might be transformed into, approaches that which inspires the present essay. At all events, it deals with topics that are inevitably of common interest to both speculative and empirical disciplines, and the inquiries of the most pragmatical of anthropologists are likely to be improved by some acquaintance with it.

a conclusion, so, Hampshire asserts, beliefs which never guided action would not count as beliefs. 'If a man is to attach any meaning to the alternative of belief or disbelief, he must in each case envisage some possible consequence' (159).

VI

The views which have been cited are for the most part relatively minor and dispersed observations about belief which have been abstracted from works on far larger matters. Recently, however, philosophical notice has been directed more precisely to the topic, and we can next glance at two modern analyses which are exclusively devoted to the notion of belief and are thus more concentrated and more technical in their arguments.[9] The advantage in considering these is not merely to add to a catalogue of opinions, but is that the papers in question usefully supply us with further points for investigation.

The first analysis to be taken up is the paper entitled 'On Belief', by Griffiths (1963). One does an injury to its very detailed argument by failing to rehearse it as a whole, and with due recognition of its original power of persuasion, but all I want to do here is to pick out certain assertions which may lead us somewhere in a comparative context.

'I am an authority on what I believe,' writes Griffiths (129), and also, 'certainly, the concept of belief is not only applicable with authority to ourselves, but with confidence to others' (138). This is a point of quite special importance for ethnographers, for it implies that 'we are able to tell, if not incorrigibly, what others believe', and this presumably without any differential consideration of language or culture. Such an ability is not just a matter of learning the relevant canons of truth, for although there can be no distinction between believing something and believing it to be true (134), yet belief must involve more than merely entertaining a proposition—and that additional component cannot be understood in terms of truth (135). More fundamentally, 'the search for [any] internal marks to distinguish all cases of belief is fruitless: there is nothing in common between beliefs that is not shared by non-beliefs.' But Griffiths maintains, nevertheless, that 'Belief is a discriminable mode

[9] The papers in question have been reprinted in a collection of essays on knowledge and belief (Griffiths 1967); page references are to this collection.

of consciousness' (137), i.e., discriminable in the way that doubting, willing, and wondering are all discriminable modes of consciousness. The central problem is then posed as follows: 'Belief is not explicable in terms of other concepts, such as assertions, action or evidence: so how can there be any necessary connexions between these and belief?' (139).

Griffiths responds that belief is nonetheless 'somehow' connected with truth,[10] and that 'the connexion between belief and truth is that belief is *appropriate* to truth' (140). This conclusion is immediately qualified, though, by the declaration that it does not say what belief is, nor does it establish any necessary connection between belief and any actual condition: it establishes a connection which does not necessarily hold but which ought to hold. Yet to say simply that belief is appropriate to truth has a crucial place in the argument, for it answers the question how belief is identified as a public concept. 'It is only this tenuous connexion which reaches out from the unanalysable private state of mind to the public world' (140). The concept of belief is thus only possible at all, Griffiths maintains, if we presuppose standards of appropriateness which link belief with what is believed.

It follows that any qualitative characteristics that one may associate with belief cannot be essential for its identification; it is for this reason that we cannot say that belief is necessarily a feeling. On the other hand it is a mode of consciousness. Though not essentially marked by a difference of quality, it is not merely nothing for us.

The concept of belief, by this view (142), thus involves canons of truth, standards of evidence, and conventions of appropriateness, which must of course be couched in the idiom of a particular language. In other words, we are inevitably in the sphere of social institutions, i.e., we are again confronted with the confusing variety and contingency which we have already glimpsed in our ethnographical survey.

VII

As a last example of a strictly philosophical application to the problem of belief, let us more rapidly cite some of the salient points

[10] Cf. 'There is obviously some connexion between the concepts of knowledge and belief. ... What the connexion is it is very difficult to say' (Griffiths 1967: 10).

in the second paper referred to, Mayo's 'Belief and Constraint' (1964).

Mayo's initial premise is that the question of the relation between belief and truth is central to any discussion of belief. Truth is independent of belief, since anything that is believed can be false. But belief is not independent of truth, for what is believed must be either true or false, and even if it happens to be false it is still believed to be true. We need not follow him in the entire progress of his argument, which in the main attempts a development of that advanced by Griffiths, and may come directly to one of his later passages where he attempts to resolve a very prominent difficulty.

There are three aspects of belief, Mayo writes, which are often dismissed as inadequate criteria for saying of other persons that they believe. These aspects are: (a) what a person says; (b) his behaviour being such as would in fact be conducive to his presumed goals if the proposition in question were true; and (c) his feelings of conviction, warm glows of assent, etc. Griffiths, he objects, seems to have concluded that, since no one of these is a sufficient condition for the presence of belief, no set of them is either, so that we can only say that belief is 'not nothing' and resign ourselves to a schematic categorization in terms of what is appropriate. But, Mayo goes on (158):

I see no reason why we should not regard (a) to (c), either singly or in conjunction, as criteria—though never logically sufficient criteria—for the assignment of the belief concept; since there is a high correlation, not merely inductive, both among them, and between them and the dispositional core of belief. In other words, belief is what usually goes with assertion, or with acting in a certain manner easily interpretable in the light of usual goals, or even with certain feelings, etc.

From this point the argument passes through several positions (which one can only commend to the reader) and thus to the concluding section, in which Mayo elaborates a gloss to Wittgenstein: 'Having a belief is not having something which favourably disposes me towards something else—the fact believed—but rather, to have a belief *is* to be favourably disposed towards something else: to asserting (or accepting) the proposition believed' (161).

VIII

In recounting some of the main arguments advanced by philosophers, and in isolating certain of the criteria of belief that they employ or propose, we have not been drawing up a representative conspectus of theories but have been trying to find reliable bearings for a further reconnaissance into the notion of belief.

These we certainly now have, for in spite of the premises and propositions that the philosophers hold more or less in common, they display a clearly divergent set of opinions on the matter. Indeed, the first lesson they teach is that even a philosophical stance, unconstrained in principle by particular languages or cultural traditions, is no guarantee of analytical agreement, let alone unanimity, on the essentials of belief. Feeling, truth, disposition, action, and so on are not so much demonstrated constituents or circumstances of the supposed phenomenon of belief (though they could be taken for such), as they are definitional devices for grasping an extremely elusive concept. It is an interesting feature of the major arguments, moreover, that they are not much directed against other interpretations or (where this is chronologically possible) against one another, but that each is an independent sally against the ground thought to be occupied by the subject of the problem. The span of time that they cover, also, stresses the equivocal character of the topic, for there is no decisive supersession of ideas from one theory to the next: Hume and Kant address us just as directly as do Wittgenstein and Hampshire. Even the languages in which the arguments are written have apparently no effect on our understanding of their views or on our judgement of these: both Kant and Wittgenstein wrote in German but are usually read in English translations, and it is a little curious (or, at any rate, not a fact to be taken for granted) that this should make no difference.

In any event, the overriding conclusion is that more than two hundred years of masterly philosophical application have provided no clear and substantial understanding of the notion of belief. As a matter of fact, it rather looks as though we were getting further and further away from any satisfaction of this kind. The papers by Griffiths and by Mayo, for instance, make (it seems to me) a markedly ambiguous impression which serves well to show the dilemma we are in. There is a great contrast, that is, between on the one hand the learned and very careful attention which these modern philosophers devote to the question of belief and, on the other hand, the vague and inconclusive positions at which they eventually arrive. Now I do not want these latter epithets to be taken as indicating the slightest disrespect for their thought or for the philosophical movement to which they belong (the contrary is indeed the case), but I cannot see that the state of actual affairs calls for a different description.

My sense of dissatisfaction can be partly explained by returning for a moment to an anthropological situation. Suppose that an ethnographer is being newly despatched to the field, and that we desire him to make special inquiry into the matter of belief among the people whose world of meaning he is to attempt to understand. If we are to accept the recommendations of these latter-day philosophers, what are we going to advise the ethnographer to look for or to ask about?

He cannot start with the word 'belief' (assuming a local equivalent for this to be already in a dictionary, or to be otherwise ascertainable), for to do so would be only prejudicial to the entire inquiry. What he has to do, rather, is to discriminate a mode of consciousness, let us say, in terms other than 'belief', and in doing so to find out whether and in what senses there are corresponding linguistic usages which he can critically translate as expressing or describing belief. Well, he can certainly investigate canons of truth, to begin with, but how can he look for something (namely belief) which is only 'somehow' connected with truth? Or could his field manual any more usefully include the instruction that the connection to be discovered is that any hypothetical belief will be 'appropriate' to truth, and that he must therefore seek standards of appropriateness? Alternatively, could he look for what 'goes with' an assertion or with the other phenomena (not forgetting the 'etc.') listed by Mayo, and thence conclude that he had identified belief among the people under study? More narrowly, if he found that these people were 'favourably disposed' toward asserting or accepting a certain proposition,[11] could he thence infer that they were also in an inner (mental, psychic) state of a distinct kind for which the correct description would be 'believing'? Furthermore, if the ethnographer wanted to find out whether they had a certain feeling of belief, how would he do this? He would have to find a word first, and

[11] I have left out from the original phrasing the adjective 'believed' (qualifying 'proposition'), which admits a tautological interpretation.

then ask whether the utterance or conception of that word had a characteristic emotional concomitant. But how could he know that the word was the right equivalent of 'belief' if the distinctive sign of this latter notion were taken to be the feeling itself?

There are many other such questions raised by the papers under discussion, but it is enough simply to consider these initial and obvious queries in order to see that the ethnographer has not been furnished with a clear and decisive set of operational criteria for the discernment of belief.

The main reason, it seems to me, is that the modern philosophers just referred to have intended to analyse the logic of the notion of belief in a general acceptation of the English word. That is, they have to a certain extent, this being delimited by the common connotations of the word, taken for granted what is in fact radically problematical. Their procedure thus makes implicitly so many cultural presuppositions that it is unlikely to cope with the full range of our comparative concerns.

The philosophers could well make the rejoinder, of course, that they have done what is properly their job, especially when this is conceived as the philosophy of common linguistic usage, and that they have not tried to make an advance in empirical psychology or in ethnographical technique. But our present intention is to investigate a supposed human capacity, and to do so without regard to cultural differentiation or academic specialization; and it is not ungrateful to report that even the most genial philosophers have not given us a sure guidance in that venture.[12] Nor, therefore, is it unduly temerarious to propose that we now need to make a renewed search for criteria of belief.

[12] There has latterly appeared a collection of papers, *Language, Belief and Metaphysics* (Kiefer & Munitz, eds., 1970), which contains a separate section devoted to aspects of belief. This is welcome evidence of a concerted redirection of philosophical attention to this problematical subject, and references to some of the papers (those by Danto, Hartnack, and Williams) have been interpolated at a few places below; but these recent investigations, professional and exact though they are, similarly do not supply the kind of guidance that is called for.

F

6

Criteria

I

Belief does not necessarily depend upon possibility; something can be believed even when it is recognized to be impossible.

'I believe because it is impossible.' Tertullian's famous paradox has lost none of its force, yet it has been much misquoted, so before we say anything about the grounds for 'that odde resolution' (Browne 1643, pt. I, sec. 9) let us get the declaration straight. He is commonly represented as having said, 'Credo quia absurdum', I believe because it is absurd. Hocart has a variant, 'Credo quia non intelligo', I believe because I do not understand (Hocart 1927: 28). What Tertullian actually wrote was: 'Prorsus credibile est, quia ineptum est; . . . certum est, quia impossibile', it is to be believed, just because it is out of the question; . . . it is certain, because it is impossible.[1] Mnemonically contracted, the assertion is: 'Credo quia impossibile', I believe because it is impossible. In any form, though, the proposition offers shock enough to the conventional foundations of our critical judgement.

Sir Thomas Browne contended in the same vein, but more plainly, that 'to beleeve onely possibilities, is not faith, but mere Philosophy' (1643, pt. I, sec. 48; 1955: 62); and the theologians, expectably, have made much of Tertullian's contradictory paradigm. It has a sense, after all, or at least it makes an impact; yet it is still no more than a paradox. It offers an affront to common usage and to common sense; it does not substantiate an alternative connotation of belief, but instead relies for its effect on the meaning that it conventionally

---

[1] *De Carne Christi* (written 208 A.D.), cap. V. I am indebted to the Revd. Fr. Michael Singleton for supplying me with the source.

A modern philosopher, incidentally, further glosses the passage by referring to 'the ridiculous things' that Tertullian believed (Griffiths 1967: 141), a phrase which scarcely accords with the solemnity of the beliefs in question or with Tertullian's reverent submission of his reason.

has. All the same, we need to remark that the notion of belief can meaningfully be given this curious twist, whereas other psychological verbs cannot so readily, if at all, be manipulated in a like sense. We should not say, for instance, 'I think so, because it is impossible' or 'That is what I wish, because it is impossible,' and we could not understand someone who said 'It is to be feared, because it is impossible,' or 'It is to be hoped, because it is impossible.' Yet this is just the form of proposition in which the notion of belief can be used. It is no fundamental objection that this usage belongs to a particular universe of discourse, namely theological propositions. Maybe it is true that it has a sense only in propositions about God: certainly it could not be said of an ordinary mortal that those things which Tertullian believed of the Son of God (his birth, death, and resurrection) should likewise be believed against all common possibility; and still less could it be said in such a case that they were certain (and thus to be believed) because they were impossible. But if the notion of belief can have this theological application, whether or not in other contexts, then the point is made that belief does not depend necessarily even on possibility. We cannot determine the criteria of belief by arbitrarily excluding a certain usage, and one so prominent and long-lived, because it is self-contradictory. This is the sort of thing that people say, or to which they attach a perfectly serious meaning, and it is our business to understand what they are doing.

Actually, it may not be only in theological discourse that belief and impossibility are conjoined. A man could well say, I think, that he believed his dead son was present even though he knew this was impossible; or another might say that he believed his mistress would return to him despite all the circumstances that he knew made it impossible. If we tried to analyse such statements, it would be significant that they are expressions of the deepest emotional attachment, comparable perhaps to devotion to God. We should have to notice that the usage would not make any sense in trivial contexts; e.g., a man could not convey anything that was intelligible if he said he believed his motor car would run without fuel even though he knew this was impossible. Indeed, we might be led to think that it was precisely a sign of an ultimate personal significance when the verb 'believe' was used in situations where what was asserted was conceded to be ordinarily impossible. For the present, though, I merely suggest that such formulations of belief in the impossible do make sense.

65

Not only this, but the criterion of possibility can even be made a factor in the classification of objects of belief:

There are two ways to define believing. It is simplest to put this in the negative. You can say that you do not believe in something when that thing exists; for example, that you do not believe in religion, and religion certainly exists. Or you can say that you do not believe in something which certainly does not exist and is impossible; for example, that you do not believe in Santa Claus.[2]

In other words, the grammar of belief takes no account of the possibility that the object does or does not exist; in either case, perfectly intelligible belief-statements are equally valid.

Indifference to the constraint of possibility is a curious property in a psychological verb, but it is certainly a distinctive mark of the notion of belief. We can say that we believe because something is impossible, or that we believe in spite of the admitted fact that something is impossible, and we can sort out formally equivalent beliefs according to whether their objects are regarded as possible or impossible.

II

Belief is not a guarantee of reality, and it does not necessarily depend on the reality of what is believed.

Hume argued that belief is 'an act of the mind, which renders realities more present to us than fictions' (1888: 629). His example is that of two people who sit down to read a book, one taking it as a 'true history' and the other as a 'romance'. They receive the same ideas, and in the same order; and the belief of the former reader, and the incredulity of the latter, does not hinder them in putting the very same sense upon what they read. But the influence of the book is not the same on each. The one who believes it as a true narration has 'a more lively conception' of the incidents, and enters deeper into the concerns of the characters; whereas the other, who takes it all for a fiction, has 'a more faint and languid conception' of these particulars.

[2] I owe this idea to my elder son, Tristan. The statement was written down verbatim at the time he made it (shortly after his eleventh birthday, in fact, when he was a pupil at the Dragon School, Oxford). He put it in the negative because he could not bring himself to conceive believing something that was impossible, and I regret that he had not yet heard of Tertullian or the learned doctor.

By this account, belief has a connection with reality, in that we believe what we take to be real. If I look out of my window, as I write this, I see a chestnut tree, which by all the usual tests I judge to be real; and I can express this judgement by asserting that I believe there is a chestnut tree there.[3] If, in some other place, someone later gives me a report of that identifiable tree, for instance that it has been struck by lightning, my reception of the report will have a 'vivacity', Hume would claim, stemming from my past impressions and constituting my belief in the reality of the tree.

But we cannot infer, conversely, that we believe, or ought to believe, when we have merely a firm and lively conception such as ordinarily convinces us of the reality of something. Hume forgets, in the first place, the example of dreams.[4] In these, the vivacity of the impressions can be complete.[5] but it does not follow that we therefore believe them. By this I mean that we do not necessarily believe them when we judge them as dreams. While we are actually experiencing dreams, we apprehend them as real and we usually do believe them. It is only occasionally that we observe to ourselves, in a moment of detachment, that we are dreaming; or we try desperately to escape an intolerable situation by urging upon ourselves that it is, or must be, only a dream. Typically, indeed, the passions are so vivid that dreams acquire a reality of their own which is peculiarly intense.[6] Dreams are real when we are in them—only then they are not 'dreams'. They do not become dreams until we wake, and it is then that we are faced with the question whether we believe them. One reason that this is a question is that the sentiments associated with dream-images persist into waking consciousness, even when we have rationally discounted the content of the dream; they can colour our experience throughout the succeeding day, sometimes with such evocative and inescapable presence that only fresh dreams can expunge them. This is a particularly vivacious

---

[3] Though Kant denied this. 'No objects of *empirical* knowledge are matters of belief' (1800: 103).

[4] That is, in connection with belief and judgements of reality. He does allude to dreams in the *Treatise* (bk. I, sec. III), but only to mention, as the introduction to an analogy, the moral instruction that some suppose them to afford.

[5] 'Wir leben und empfinden so gut im Traum als im Wachen' (Lichtenberg 1958: 293).

[6] 'Es ist ... im Traum die Vorstellung lebhafter und das Bewusstsein und Denken geringer' (Lichtenberg 1958: 318).

impression of reality, yet even so there is a question as to whether dreams are matters for belief. Mankind has generally responded to their apparent reality by elaborating various means of interpretation: dreams are genuine encounters of the migratory soul during sleep, for example, or they are veridical premonitions of events to come. By such interpretations, dreams are indeed to be believed, and the only uncertainty is how reliably they can be interpreted. The question then shifts to the credibility of the analysis, so that even when the maximum confidence may be reposed in dreams as reports of reality, whether past or to come, this conviction that they are refractions of the real does not in itself entail that they shall be believed. Alternatively, of course, it may not be admitted that they are at all fit subjects for belief, in spite of the recognized vivacity and continuance of their effects; the sceptical may deny that they have any real meaning or that they can consistently be interpreted in real terms. If, thus, it is true, as Hume maintains, that 'the belief, which attends our memory, is of the same nature with that, which is deriv'd from our judgements' (154), then we have to make a distinction between memories of dreaming experience and memories of waking experience. This distinction will depend upon criteria of reality other than the lively impression of reality which occasions the concurrent beliefs. As far as dreams are concerned, therefore, belief is not a guarantee of reality, and it does not depend on the judgement that what has been so vividly experienced is in itself real.

The topic of dreams leads to that of art, in which there is an external play upon the imagination by means of factors which are publicly observable. Hume takes it for granted that to read a book as a 'romance', or work of fiction, is to conceive its characters and events in no more than a faint and languid manner; but the truth of the matter appears to be quite contrary. It is historical narratives, on the whole, which produce this effect in us, however firmly we may accept them as true; whereas it is precisely the power of art that it procures, for a time at least, a belief in what we already know from the beginning is not even intended to be factually true. This is so, not only in the case of narrative fiction, but also in ballet, opera, and any form of drama. We respond to the pathos of 'Petrushka' as we scarce can do when reading of the worst miseries that man has suffered; 'Checkmate' is stylized in the extreme, yet it works poignantly on the beholders by its imaginary depiction of the real force of brutal death and the doomed contention of precarious life; 'Tristan und Isolde' is conventional and stagey in its presentation, to the point that in some eyes it can appear heavily absurd, but to the Wagnerian it is so overwhelmingly real as the emotions of common human affairs may almost never be. Thus, too, Sir Thomas Browne confessed that he could 'weepe most seriously at a Play, and receive with a true passion, the counterfeit griefes of those knowne and professed Imposters' (1643, pt. II, sec. 5). While we are in the thrall of works of art, then, we tacitly assent to their reality, and find ourselves responding to this impression, in a manner for which the appropriate linguistic description is none other than belief.

This response is made possible, in the first place, by the absence of the element of intention in the circumstances. In aesthetic experience, as Hampshire has well brought out, the thought of the possibility of action is for a time partly suspended: 'The recognized value of aesthetic experience is partly a sense of rest from intention, of not needing to look through this particular object to its possible uses' (1959: 119). In our contemplation of art we participate in the object but are uncommited; we do not have to think about what to do next, to compare possible courses of action in their relation to present experience, and this freedom from active responsibility permits the attitude of belief. We may say afterwards that we did not really believe Petrushka was demented with unrequited adoration, or that Isolde was desolate at the death of Tristan; but this denial does not (ex hypothesi) report what we felt and were convinced of at the time. It makes no difference, either, that works of great art are few, and ideal performances seldom met with; what counts is what was the case at the time of the experience. One does not say that one was not in love once with a certain person, merely because one no longer is; the love was real at the time, and 'love' is the right word for that experience. In just the same way, we should not deny the state of belief in the representations of art, even though that degree of rapture may be as rare as true love, merely because in retrospect (when criticizing the performance, for example, or comparing it with others) we are no longer in the same state. Naturally, there are differences, too, between the two conditions. If you distract someone from his lively contemplation of a work of art, in which he is wholly engrossed, and ask whether he really believes what is going on before his eyes, he will not affirm (unless he is being pretentious) that he does. Jerked out of his involvement, and faced with a coldly rational question that puts another aspect of his personality to the test, he may even brusquely deny that he was in any such state or could describe his state by that word. On the other hand, if you ask whether he really loves his mistress, he will respond (unless he is forced to be uncandid) only with asseverations of unfailing devotion. But these circumstances of duration and continuity are nothing to the point; there is no grammatical or psychological compulsion which should make us say that belief is not belief unless it is as enduring, and as unlimited by occasion, as (ideally) love is. What counts is what actually goes on, and by this criterion I suggest that it makes perfectly acceptable sense to say that works of art can be, and are, believed; but it would be only a very contrived and stultifying gloss to assert that art is reality.

We are much influenced in all this, I think, by our conventional classification of forms of experience. Life is divided by our language into reality, dreams, and art; so we tend to assume that these forms are empirically distinct, and hence that they demand description in different terms. But if we consider experience phenomenally, i.e., simply (so far as this is feasible) in terms of what really happens, the delineations blur and lose their power of distinction.[7] A discriminable mode of experience may be equally characteristic of real life, dreams, and responses to art. But of course it may not have the same value or function, either privately or in a social context, in each kind of setting: inferences from dreams can be hazardous if followed up in public action, and the conventions of art are not normally applicable in society. Social restraint and a prudent concern for survival conjoin, thus, to maintain an accepted classification of experience. 'Belief', I suggest, is one of the linguistic means by which we recognize and maintain this useful set of categories. So people implicitly believe, it might commonly be said, in what is real; they do not actually believe their dreams (because they disavow them later, or because not all dreams count, or because they have to be minutely interpreted first, and so on); and they do not believe at all in the representations of art. These, at any rate, are the kinds of assertions and distinctions that the verbal conventions of English incline us to make; but experience, straitly scrutinized, teaches otherwise. If anything can be said to be believed, these partitioned

[7] As a matter of introspective observation, in any case, it is hard to concede the reality of these compartments: 'Die Träume verlieren sich in unser Wachen allmählich herein; man kann nicht sagen, wo das Wachen eines Menschen anfängt' (Lichtenberg 1958: 293).

forms of experience can all similarly be believed; and it makes no difference that they are accounted real or unreal.

At a more ordinary level, we judge reality according to evidences other than the vivacity of impressions, but whatever bases of judgement are resorted to belief does not necessarily depend on real and decisive evidence. 'At the foundation of well-founded belief lies belief that is not founded' (Wittgenstein 1969, sec. 253). Also, 'For most people, disbelief in one matter is based on blind belief in another' (Lichtenberg 1958: 455), not on evidence. As Griffiths (1967: 133) has put it:

Any attempt to reduce belief to entertaining *p* while having evidence for *p* must fail on two counts: first, because 'having evidence' must itself involve beliefs about the evidence, and secondly, because people undoubtedly believe things on many occasions without evidence at all.

Notoriously, indeed, people do believe without evidence, or upon insufficient evidence, or even without considering whether evidence is called for. It is even an accepted usage that people are said to believe precisely when they admit that they have not adequate empirical evidence to justify the assertions they make. Conversely, the presentation of such empirical evidence does not in itself constrain belief. This is pathetically well known from the cases of those who refuse to believe that their sons really are dead in distant wars. There is a gap, as it were, between entertaining the evidence (such as might quite persuade another, or even the subject in other circumstances) and believing the conclusion to which it clearly leads.

In discourse about religious topics, e.g., whether illness is a punishment for sin, or whether there will be a Day of Judgement, those who agree upon the evidential phenomena may not only disagree about whether the propositions are to be believed, but they will disagree in a context to which evidence is not even relevant. The reasons advanced are not ultimately evidential, and discussion cannot be concluded on empirical grounds. More than this, 'the point is that if there were evidence, this would in fact destroy the whole business' (Wittgenstein 1966: 56). Here, too, belief is independent of canons of reality.

III

Belief is not a logical character of propositions; their validity does not depend on whether or not they are believed.

Assertions of belief need not be the termini of chains of correct inference; nor, conversely, is it essential that valid logical grounds shall be discoverable for their defence or explication. Men commonly believe without reasons, and without being able to supply reasons if they are pressed for a logical justification of what they say they believe. In one rather vague but still acceptable connotation, 'belief is an act of the mind arising from custom' (Hume 1888: 114), custom being understood as everything which 'proceeds from a past repetition, without any new reasoning or conclusion' (102). This will ultimately include tradition and the historical pronouncements of authority. Beliefs derived from these sources can be challenged, but commonly they are accepted and passed on without any logical exploration on the part of those who hold them. When a belief is explicitly proposed, moreover, a logical exposition may induce someone to entertain the proposition with an increased readiness to accept it, or even to give his assent to its validity as the conclusion to a correct argument, but such logical grounds will not in themselves constrain him to believe.

Religious discourse brings out in a particularly marked degree something of the logical peculiarity of the notion of belief. In the Christian tradition, for example, there has for centuries been a continued emphasis on the ontological, cosmological, and teleological arguments for the existence of God; but it is a plain fact that many men of normal understanding, who concur in the recognition of the laws of logic and the phenomena in question, do not accept the arguments as sufficient grounds for belief. The alleged proofs have been pressed and elaborated by masterly logicians into the most minute and subtle forms, yet 'it is highly improbable that anyone who had no belief in God was ever led to believe in God by any of the standard "proofs" of God's existence' (Bevan 1962: 344). From another point of view, MacIntyre maintains to the same effect (1957: 209):

There is no logical transition which will take one from unbelief to belief. The transition is not in objective considerations at all, but in the person who comes to believe. There are no logical principles which will make the transition for one.

Between believer and non-believer, consequently, there may not exist the possibility of a logical transition of thought, nor even the grounds for contradiction.

Wittgenstein's lectures on religious belief, as latterly reported, make this impediment to a logical confrontation enigmatically plain (1966: 53):

Suppose I say that the body will rot [after death], and another says 'No. Particles will rejoin in a thousand years, and there will be a Resurrection of you.'

If someone said: 'Wittgenstein, do you believe this?' I'd say: 'No.' 'Do you contradict the man?' I'd say: 'No.'

Would you say: 'I believe the opposite', or 'There is no reason to suppose such a thing'? I'd say neither.

Suppose someone were a believer and said: 'I believe in a Last Judgement', and I said: 'Well, I'm not so sure. Possibly.' You would say that there is an enormous gulf between us. If he said 'There is a German aeroplane overhead', and I said 'Possibly. I'm not so sure', you'd say we were fairly near.

It isn't a question of my being anywhere near him, but on an entirely different plane.

In this particular case, the likelihood of a communication of conviction between the parties to the dialogue is much affected by the formulation of the proposition in question; for whereas logic is powerless to constrain belief, the forms of art have a non-logical power which can very well persuade, and this subtle resource is quite lacking from the blunt and unlikely assertion that personal particles will join up in an individual resurrection. Yet even the sublime form in which belief in resurrection was cast by Sir Thomas Browne[8] cannot conceal the absence of logical connection, and the consequent hindrance to a transition of thought, between statements of religious belief and non-belief.

It is apparently a distinctive feature of belief-statements in general that they are, as Wittgenstein's illustration shows, on a special plane. The co-ordinates of this plane are of course the problem behind our entire investigation, and we are not yet in any position to determine what they may be. But the point to be

---

[8] 'I beleeve that our estranged and divided ashes shall unite againe; that our separated dust after so many pilgrimages and transformations into the parts of mineralls, Plants, Animals, Elements, shall at the voyce of God returne into their primitive shapes, and joyne againe to make up their primary and predestinated formes.... At the last day, when those corrupted reliques shall be scattered in the wildernesse of formes, and seeme to have forgot their proper habits, God by a powerfull voyce shall command them backe into their proper shapes, and call them out by their single individuals' (1643, pt. I, sec. 48; 1955: 62). If the reader does not like my argument, yet is unacquainted with this glorious master of the English language, at least he will get this thrilling return from his application.

made for the moment is clear enough: there is a logical peculiarity about assertions of belief such that they cannot be contradicted.

The first reason for this, clearly, is that an assertion of belief is a report about the person who makes it, and not intrinsically or primarily about objective matters of truth or fact which others may equally apprehend. Even though the proposition may be a dogmatic one, and be uttered in company with others as a common declaration of faith, a man's assertion that he believes is ultimately a reference to an inner state. Others may doubt his asseveration, and can say that they do not think he really believes (or can believe, given the circumstances) what he says. In this case there is a contradiction, but it attaches to the veracity of the person making the declaration and not to the truth of the belief in question. If, however, he says 'I believe *p*' and someone else responds 'I do not believe *p*,' there is no contradiction, for the latter is saying nothing about the inner state of the believer.

A second reason that belief-statements cannot be contradicted is that the very premises of apparently rival assertions may be so disparate that the opposed propositions cannot be brought into any logical correspondence. To revert to Wittgenstein and his example, if someone says that he believes in a Day of Judgement, it is utterly inappropriate to offer the appearance of contradiction by returning, 'No, I don't believe there will be such a thing,' and it is pointless to try to give an explanation by going on, 'I don't believe in . . .'— for, as Wittgenstein brings out in a revelatory remark, 'the religious person never believes what I describe' (1966: 55). This realization leads to the consideration of premises and contexts which go far beyond the elementary logic of belief, and into the appreciation of 'ways of thinking and acting' (56) which constitute the grounds for assertions of belief. In this region also the special character of belief-statements is not logical, and their validity does not depend on whether or not they are actually believed.

Lichtenberg characteristically combines aphoristic paradox and level observation (1958: 455) when he phrases the logical peculiarity and the indeterminate resolution of questions of belief in these words:

There is a great difference between believing something and not being able to believe the opposite. I can very often believe something without being able to prove it, just as I can disbelieve something without being able to refute it. The side that I take is not determined by strict proof but by preponderance.

74

Not only this, but in the matter of belief it is notoriously possible to take both sides; i.e., to hold together opinions so contrary that if one is true the other cannot be. This acute form of contradiction, within one and the same individual, is even a characteristic aspect of belief; mutually incompatible propositions can be concurrently believed, whereas such a flagrant challenge to the validity of each and the coherence of the whole would never be admitted if they were considered as items of knowledge or empirical judgement. Pascal in fact went so far as to laud this unlimited facility of logical accommodation as a distinctive merit of belief: 'Le croire est si important! Cent contradictions seraient vraies' (*Pensées*, no. 260; 1964: 144).

It is, then, a peculiar feature of belief-statements that although they have a logical form their assertion or acceptance does not depend on logical validity but rather upon what we might call a circumstantial cogency. Logic and belief are independent.

IV

Although belief is not determined or characterized by logical necessity, there are grounds to consider whether necessity of another kind can on occasion or in specific cases be employed as one criterion of belief.

Kant writes that, from a practical point of view, once an end is accepted the conditions of its attainment are hypothetically necessary. This necessity is subjectively sufficient if I know of no other conditions under which the end can be attained; in this case my assumption and the holding of certain conditions to be true constitute a merely contingent belief. But if I know with certainty that no one can have knowledge of any other conditions which lead to the proposed end, then I subscribe to a necessary belief (1787; Kemp Smith trans., 1933: 647).

This is of course a comprehensible distinction between modes of belief, according to whether they are contingent or necessary, but it can be taken as no more than the exploitation of a certain usage of the word 'belief' (*Glaube*). Clearly, if anything practical can ever be known with such certainty, then it is grammatically admissible to term such knowledge a belief; and if (what is even more unlikely) anything can be so certainly known to be the exclusive conditions of the attainment of a given end, then it has to be conceded that this belief is necessary. But it is a rather uninstructive procedure to posit this doubly suppositional circumstance as the grounds for ascribing necessity to a belief. Logically, it is a tautology, for what is absolutely and exclusively certain is thereby necessary; and grammatically it is merely a recommendation to adopt a usage which the connotations of 'belief' already permit.

Nevertheless, Kant particularly adverts to a necessary mode of belief in the context of morality. 'Here,' he writes, 'it is absolutely necessary that something must happen, namely that I must in all points conform to the moral law' (650). But this specific example serves still less in the end to provide us with a criterion of belief, for it depends on the 'one possible condition' under which this end can connect with all other ends, and thereby have practical validity, 'namely, that there be a God and a future world'. And this, as Kant at once concedes, cannot be known: 'my conviction is not *logical* but *moral* certainty; and... it rests on subjective grounds (of moral sentiment)'. He himself straightway considers the 'questionable' character of basing this 'rational belief' on the assumption of moral sentiments; and he only extricates himself by advancing an argument, which is unconvincing enough, about negative beliefs (651), i.e., the inability to prove with certainty that there is no God and no future life. Obviously, however, this inability by no means proves the necessity of the beliefs in question.

Naturally, there is a burden to Kant's argument, and a point to his usage, which an extended exegesis could bring out; but that is an enterprise which can have no place in our rapid survey of possible criteria. Yet the question about necessity remains. Let us approach it from another direction. Rather than ask whether there are beliefs which are necessary (or propositions which are necessarily to be believed), let us ask whether necessary propositions can be believed.

Kant, at any rate, thought not: 'No objects of rational knowledge (knowledge *a priori*) are matters of belief, whether their knowledge be theoretical, e.g., in mathematics and metaphysics, or practical in morals' (1800: 105; 1885: 59). Recently, likewise, Braithwaite has explicitly omitted from his analysis of religious belief (1967: 38) the type of beliefs in logically necessary propositions:

Direct knowledge of these I am pretty clear is something into which belief does not enter: my seeing that $2+2=4$ is not a believing. My attitude towards such a proposition is more like that towards a proposition about a sense-datum: I have only to understand the words to know whether the proposition is true or false.

But one looks in vain for any argument, or instructive confrontation with differing opinions, in these declarations. They exhibit an intention to retain a common connotation (in German and in English) of the word in question, and one can understand perfectly clearly that certain propositions are not to be regarded as objects of belief; but what is not at all explored is the question why one should fall in with this intention. Nor is it clear what objects of rational knowledge are to be discounted. Kant instances what he regards as our practical knowledge of morality, on the ground that 'one must be *absolutely certain* whether something is right or wrong' (1800: 59); but neither Braithwaite nor any other modern philosopher would be likely to put moral certainties on a par with the necessary propositions of mathematics. There is not much point in excluding necessary propositions from the scope of belief if it is not made clear what is the scope of necessity.

For Wittgenstein the matter is not at all so evident, or one that can so readily be settled by the stipulation of a certain grammatical usage. His paradigm is the question whether mathematical propositions can be believed, e.g., 'Can someone *believe* that $25 \times 25 = 625$?' (1967a, sec. 407). He takes up issues of this kind in various places, and in different contexts, but one of his most probing investigations is to be found in his remarks on the foundations of mathematics (1965, secs. 106–12). Here he takes the case of someone who is assured of an incorrect arithmetical calculation, namely $13 \times 13 = 196$, and who believes this. The person will be surprised then to discover that he cannot arrange 196 nuts in 13 rows of 13 each. 'But I feel a temptation to say: one can't *believe* that $13 \times 13 = 196$, one can only *accept* this number mechanically from someone else.' This observation contains an incidental difficulty, in that by a common and well established acceptation (Hume, Hampshire) beliefs are in fact largely accepted, from tradition or from some other source of authority, so that there is not that disjunction between believing and accepting. However, Wittgenstein at once asks: 'But why should I not say that I believe it? For is believing a mysterious act with as it were an underground connexion with the correct calculation? At any rate I can *say*: "I believe it", and act accordingly.' Hence, in considering what one is doing when one believes that $13 \times 13 = 196$, he answers that 'it depends on what you can do with the equation. . . .' The test of the belief is thus practical, and does not focus on any operation that led up to the belief. The calculation may be mistaken, but the readiness to employ the result will show that it is nevertheless believed; and it would be arbitrary to reserve the word 'believe' only for cases of correct calculation.

Alternatively, Wittgenstein asks what someone is believing if he believes an incorrect calculation. 'How deep does he penetrate, as one might say, with his belief into the relation of these numbers? For—one wants to say—he cannot be penetrating right to the end, or he could not believe it.' But when, Wittgenstein asks, has he penetrated into the relations of the numbers? Just while he says that he believes? Surely not, for this appears to be so only because of the superficial form of our grammar. 'For I want to say: "One can only *see* that $13 \times 13 = 169$, and even that one cannot *believe*".' In saying this one is drawing a line between a calculation with its result and an experiment with its outcome.

When I believe that $a \times b = c$ . . . I am not believing the mathematical proposition, for that comes at the end of the proof, it is the end of a proof; I am believing that this is the formula that comes in such-and-such a place, which I shall obtain in such-and-such a way, and so on. And this does sound as if I were penetrating the process of believing such a proposition. Whereas I am merely . . . pointing to the *fundamental* difference, together with an apparent similarity, between the roles of an arithmetical proposition and of an empirical proposition.

None the less, it is a fact of language that we do say we believe in either type of proposition. What is interesting, then, is the kind of circumstances in which we say that we believe $a \times b = c$, and what is characteristic of them, in contrast with the circumstances of such a statement as 'I believe it is going to rain.' For there is a contrast, such that it can well be objected that surely one does not believe a mathematical proposition; and although this objection may be no more than an implicit appeal to the authority of a grammatical usage, the usage does have an authority. Again, it may be said that one cannot believe that the multiplication 13×13 yields 169, 'because the result is part of the calculation'; and one does not believe separately the process of multiplication. And it is even a question, furthermore, what it is that one calls a multiplication: whether it is only the correct pattern which one recognizes, or whether a wrong multiplication (e.g., $13 \times 13 = 196$) counts too.

The deeper Wittgenstein goes, therefore, the plainer it becomes how hard it is to *decide* whether or not necessary propositions can be believed, and in what circumstances, and by what contrasts and similarities with empirical propositions, they may be said to be believed or not.

Yet a further source of difficulty is the judgement that 'it is impossible to know and to believe the same thing at the same time' (Price 1935 [1967: 42]; cf. Hartnack 1970: 115). Logically necessary propositions are objects of rational (*a priori*) knowledge, and therefore, by this account, they cannot also be believed. But this assertion of impossibility is not grounded in any logical necessity: it is a report on what is tacitly assumed to be a grammatical convention governing the use of the verb 'to know'. This is shown by two means. First, if someone wished to maintain to the contrary that it was indeed possible both to know and to believe the same thing at the same time, he would encounter no inherent impossibility, no contradiction, in the assertion: it would be grammatically permissible for him to make it, and he would be committing no logical error. Second, there are in fact propositions of the kind which are common, comprehensible, and acceptable in certain types of discourse. A Christian will find no difficulty in asserting that he knows God exists, and also that he believes God exists; indeed, his very profession of belief signifies in part his complete assent to what he claims to know. There must be others, too, who would find nothing 'impossible' in saying that they knew it was unforgivably wicked to murder little children in gas chambers, and also that they believed it was wicked to do so. It is true enough that the enunciation of such pairs of propositions, asserting both knowledge and belief with respect to the same thing at the same time, might advance different grounds for each of the verbs. A religious, for example, may give certain reasons for claiming to know that God exists, and other reasons to explain why he says he believes God exists. But the adduction of different grounds for the constituent parts of a compound proposition, in the report of a complex judgement or inner state, does not in itself make it impossible to conjoin knowledge and belief.

There are many other factors and distinctions to be taken into account, when assessing the role of necessity in belief, but the general conclusion seems to be clear enough already. Although assertions of belief are often analysed, or defined, by reference to necessity, there is apparently no real argument to the effect that necessity is a criterion of belief or, alternatively, that belief is to be distinguished by contrast with necessary propositions.

G

V

'The whole point and purpose of a belief, and of the kind of thought that leads up to it, is that it should be true' (Hampshire 1959: 150). Beliefs are 'those thoughts that I endorse as true' (Hampshire 1965: 98).

There can be no distinction between believing something and believing it to be true; but people can believe what is untrue and disbelieve what is true. As Mayo writes (1967: 47):

Truth is independent of belief, since anything that is believed can be false.... But belief is not independent of truth, and this in two ways: (1) what is believed must be either true or false...; and (2) what is believed, even if it happens to be false, is believed *to be true*.

Hampshire maintains that conversely 'a belief is something that *can* only be abandoned by the subject as being false' (1965: 85). This is correct if it is taken to mean that the subject finds that a thought to which he has subscribed is untrue, withdraws his endorsement, and then appreciates that he has abandoned that belief. It would not be correct, however, to say that beliefs are abandoned only in this explicit and conscious way; for just as we are said to acquire beliefs unconsciously and uncritically, and may assert them to be true only when attention is directed to them, so we can abandon such beliefs without express purpose or decision, and only later realize that we no longer hold them to be true.

Nevertheless, there are certainly a number of aspects under which it can be said that belief is implicated with truth. This is so not only for the subject, enclosed in his private world of inner judgements, but for others also. Every assertion of belief is a claim on credence; a man who says that he believes something asserts that it is true, and thereby that others also ought to believe it.

These connections with truth form some of the necessary conditions for the employment of the verbal concept of belief, but they do not provide us with a distinctive criterion of belief. Assertions of belief, after all, are not primarily or directly statements about the truth-value of propositions: they are statements about whomsoever utters the propositions. 'The language-game of reporting can be given such a turn that a report is not meant to inform the hearer about its subject matter but about the person making the report'

(Wittgenstein 1953: 190). None of the considerations attaching to truth is sufficient to explain what state of that person is reported by the assertion that he believes.

VI

Whether belief is an act of the will is a question that has long occupied philosophers and theologians, but without any decided outcome.

Descartes maintained a clear distinction between the capacity to understand and the capacity to chose among propositions by free will: 'For by the understanding alone I neither assert nor deny anything, but I merely conceive ideas about things which I may assert or deny'; 'In asserting or denying, pursuing or fleeing those things that are proposed by the understanding, we act in such a way that we do not at all feel ourselves constrained to do so by any external force' (Descartes 1647, méditation IV). By this account, then, belief (although the word itself does not figure in this context) is voluntary.

This is a view that has survived, and is particularly clearly expressed, in current Roman Catholic philosophy. Thus Lonergan outlines 'the typical process of true belief' as consisting of the following five stages: (1) preliminary judgements on the value of belief itself, on the reliability of the source, and the accuracy of the communication; (2) a reflective act of understanding that grasps 'the value of deciding to believe some particular proposition'; (3) the consequent judgement of value; (4) the consequent 'decision of the will'; and (5) 'the assent that is the act of believing' (Lonergan 1958: 708). Thence he concludes (709):

It is a free and responsible decision of the will to believe a given proposition as probably or certainly true or false.... Moreover, in its antecedents, the decision to believe may be said to resemble any other decision;... the decision to believe is a decision to produce in the intellect the act of assenting to a proposition or dissenting from it.

To the same effect, Pieper, in his monograph on belief, asserts repeatedly and without hesitation that one can only believe when one wishes to do so (1962: 39): 'belief depends on the will' (40). He does not make an argument to demonstrate as much, nor does he analyse the influence of the will in accepting something as 'real and true' on the testimony of others (31), but he is entirely definite in maintaining that a deliberate act of the will is what constitutes believing (42). 'No one who believes *must* believe; belief is by its nature a free act' (59).

Yet Hume, on the other hand, was equally definite in his view that 'belief consists . . . in something, that depends not on the will, but must arise from certain determinate causes and principles, of which we are not masters' (1888: 624). One indication of this fact is that 'experience may produce a belief . . . by a secret operation, and without being once thought of' (104); and, as we cannot perform an act of the will without conscious thought, so it follows that a belief produced by that secret operation was not the result of a decision. Or, as Lichtenberg characterized the phenomenon, 'First we *must* believe, and then we believe' (1958: 506); i.e., we find ourselves believing, without any intention to do so, and under some hidden compulsion the product of which we then regard as true.

Kant's position is that 'Those objects alone are matters of belief in which assent is necessarily free, that is, not determined by objective reasons independent on the nature and interest of the subject' (1800: 106; cf. 1885: 60). But this formulation does not in itself make plain what is supposed to be the influence of the will in arriving at such an assent. If the objects of empirical knowledge and the certainties of logic and (presumptively) morality are, by stipulation, not to be counted as matters of belief, in that they are objectively determined, then by a contrastive definition the variety and fluctuation of beliefs about other matters must be ascribed to a mode of assent that is not imposed externally upon the subject; that is, beliefs are conditional upon free assent. Yet from the premise that beliefs are not necessary and are not objectively determined, it does not follow that they are the consequences of decisions. In a later formulation, in fact, Kant writes unambiguously that 'the will has no direct influence on assent [*Fürwahrhaltung*]; that would be quite absurd' (1800: 113). Moreover, as Hume brought out, we hold many beliefs under the persuasion of sheer custom, and although we may freely assent to them we did not acquire them by any acts of deliberate assent. It is one thing to say that we regard our beliefs as 'formed in response to free inquiry' (Hampshire 1965: 87): it is quite another to say that they are formed by acts of free will. According to Hampshire, as we have seen in chap. 5 above, an announcement of belief is not a decision to do anything: 'I have not decided *to* believe; I have decided *that* the statement in question is true.'

There are thus very marked and long-continued disparities of philosophical opinion about whether belief is voluntary. There has been no resolution, but the question remains of fundamental importance. Hampshire even regards this point of difference in the philosophy of mind as being 'of the greatest importance in the assessment of human powers and virtues: indeed it is one of the dividing lines in philosophy' (1959: 155). But the difficulty, as he continues, is to see by what method of argument the difference could possibly be settled. In this case the testimony of ordinary language, at any rate, is most unreliable.

There is in English a whole range of idioms which assimilate belief to acts of the will, yet none can withstand critical scrutiny. We say, for instance, that we 'cannot' believe something, as though it were in our power to believe or not as we decided (e.g., Marty 1970: 20); but when we introspect in search of the exercise of that power we find that none of the philosophical dubiety is at all relieved—and, of course, if it were that easy a matter the dubiety could scarcely have survived. If, after saying that I cannot believe, I suddenly assert 'Yes, I can', I do not thereby switch from disbelief to belief, and I cannot by any firm intention alone bring myself to do so. This is a matter of common experience, testable on the spur of the moment, yet our language tends to persuade us to the opposite. We say, also, of a man who discovers some unpalatable fact, e.g., that his mistress is unfaithful, that he 'will' not believe the evidence, as though it were precisely a matter of will whether he believed it or not; yet it may be quite plain from his distress or consternation or anger that he does indeed accept that she has done him wrong, and that his assertion of disbelief, or of refusal to believe, is itself no more than a sign of how disagreeable he finds the realization. Again, we say that a man cannot be 'forced' to believe the evidence of his own eyes, as though under sufficient duress he would abandon his resistance to belief and give in; but in such a situation the real difficulty may rather be to induce him to interpret the evidence in a certain sense, to adopt one chain of inference instead of another, and so on, or perhaps it may simply be the difficulty of getting him to admit that he does believe it. As a final example, we can speak of a 'willing suspension of disbelief', as though in the plainest way possible a man might deliberately manipulate his power to believe or not, whereas this at any rate is not what goes on in that complicated state of mind. Perhaps the best way to put it is to say, as does Kant in his discussion of the influence of the will on assent, that to defer or reserve judgement consists in the resolution not to allow a merely provisional judgement to become a definite one (1800: 113). We do indeed reserve judgement, or we entertain a proposition without judging it, or we provisionally adopt a position to which we decline to commit ourselves; but we cannot suspend disbelief any more than we can procure belief within ourselves. To revert to the topic of the power of art, we might better say that in some cases the alleged suspension of disbelief is actually a state of belief, only on grounds that we should not normally admit.

Mayo suggests that the only way of escaping this dilemma, between the conventions of language and the forms of experience, is to re-interpret the mechanical metaphors of constraint, force, and so on (1967: 152), and certainly this is one recourse. But there is still 'no way of showing that the idioms in common speech which point to one decision are to be preferred to the idioms which point to an opposite decision' (Hampshire 1959: 156). More positively, Mayo suggests in effect that the analogy between belief and action is inappropriate and misleading, and that comparison with other states of mind is more helpful (Mayo 1967: 153).

The question, whether we can choose to believe, is paralleled, not by the question, whether we can choose to act, but by the question, whether we can choose to feel, intend, etc. Which is indeed the same question, the answer to which appears to be no.

We can exhort someone to act, he continues, and we can also perhaps exhort him to act in a certain frame of mind (as we adjure people to cheer up or to pull themselves together, which works sometimes), but we cannot mean to imply that it is really up to him to decide what frame of mind he chooses to do it in, or which of a range of feelings he chooses to select.

Now these alternative analogies (with feeling or intending) may well be found more persuasive than the metaphor of action, but we still have the choice whether to adopt this figure of speech or that; and this option is not decided by logical or experiential considerations alone. The way in which we talk about human powers, and specifically about the voluntary character of belief, is in part a matter of ideological tradition of or moral commitment. The linguistic usage reflects a theory, and we have to decide among theories

84

that are connected with different forms of social life. For instance, as Hampshire observes (1959: 156):

It may be that in a society in which a man's theoretical opinions and religious beliefs were held to be supremely important, a man's beliefs would be considered as much part of his responsibility as his behaviour to other men.

An example of this outlook is the Catholic tradition, latterly expressed by Lonergan, that belief is a free and responsible decision of the will; and European history is notoriously replete with the consequent reprobation, oppression, and burning of men because of their wilful failure, or refusal, to believe. 'A particular moral outlook, connected with particular forms of social life, will show itself in the distinctions that are stressed in the forms of common speech' (Hampshire 1959: 156). Such linguistic usages survive, however, long past their practical relevance, and despite their unsuitability for the description of experience; but so long as they are current they exert an insidious influence toward the conception of belief as a voluntary faculty. It must be admitted, all the same, that this is a philosophical conclusion and not a matter of pragmatic psychology. When Borges was advised by a doctor that his insomnia was unimportant, on the ground that the body benefited just the same from the long rest in the dark, he was not at all sure of the argument; but, he reports, 'I did my best to believe it' (in Burgin 1970: 63), and this effort did in the end get him to sleep easily. Psycho-somatic therapies of this kind do work, but merely to phrase the means to a cure by reference to belief does not in itself demonstrate anything about the reality of an intentional capacity to believe.

Hampshire's useful emphasis on forms of social life, also, can certainly lead to a clearer recognition of the effects of linguistic and ideological tradition, but it cannot of course make supererogatory a critique of those informal premises about human capacities which are part of a cultural tradition. My own view is that Hampshire is correct in his argument that it is wrong to represent a belief as an action (1959: 155),[9] but this conclusion depends on a conception of action which itself is open to dispute.

This is typical of the issue. The best of minds are at odds, the most persuasive of arguments brings no resolution (see also Williams

---

[9] Cf. Wittgenstein (1967a, sec. 51): 'believe' belongs to a group of verbs, including also intend, mean, suspect, etc., which 'do not stand for actions'.

1970), and linguistic usage provides conflicting and indecisive evidences. But at least it is sure that no readily discriminable act of the will can be assumed as a criterion of belief.

VII

The idea that belief is an act of the will nevertheless takes a distinct and prominent form in religious discourse, and this usage calls for separate comment. The view in question is that which describes religious belief as a spiritual commitment.

This topic presents a special difficulty, for the Christian literature alone is vast and interminable; doctrinal differences proliferate and flourish; and in the end most theologians acknowledge, in any case, that they are trying to utter the unutterable. I have therefore selected just one recent account, and from that I shall need to take only a few statements. It happens to be written by a Jesuit, and I ought to declare that I prefer such a source (for the present purpose) to an account written by, for instance, a fundamentalist. From my point of view here, the great advantage possessed by the former is that of a long and intensely analytical tradition of scholarship. The religious premises are quite another matter, of course, but for a careful illustration of one traditional conception of religious belief we cannot in my opinion do better than to turn to that church which before all others supports its claims to credence by philosophical argument. There may be differing views on this, but I think that the acceptation of belief which we are about to examine is a paradigm case which has much in common with the kind of commitment that is recognized by other sects and faiths.

In a contribution to a symposium on religious belief, Clarke plainly concedes that the core of Christian belief is not at all, 'as any competent Christian theologian will explicitly admit', the intellectual acceptance of a set of propositions held as true on exclusively intellectual grounds. 'It is rather first and foremost an existential, global and unconditional commitment of loving trust to a person, that of Jesus of Nazareth . . .' (1964: 145). Furthermore, no amount of conceptual analysis and refined formulation will ever be able, we are told, to grasp and express exhaustively the living core of communion with Christ. 'This is a *mode of existence*, of personal existence, and not *primarily* a set of propositions held to be true, though the latter point to and safeguard the former' (146).

It is plain that these statements define a position which is radically different from that of the modern philosophers who have been cited above, for their concern, by contrast, is precisely with conceptual analysis, i.e., with 'the intellectual acceptance of a set of propositions held as true'. The philosophical impact of Clarke's declaration is obviously important in itself, but he makes also a further claim (147) which has to do with the main direction of our inquiry, namely that:

It is this personal core which makes possible ... the capacity to transcend all particular cultural contexts and culture-bound modes of explication.

It is true, of course, that the tenets of a universal and proselytizing religion, and one which so stresses the act of faith, must include some such provision; but Clarke's formulation has the special interest, in relation to comparative ethnography, that it so explicitly refers to cultural contexts and to the influence of traditional notions on the exercise of analytical thought.

There are nevertheless considerable difficulties of vocabulary in Clarke's statement about belief as a personal commitment. Evidently a commitment of this nature is (as by its very description it must be) an act of the will, and it is central to the belief. But this decisive act is not the same as belief in a proposition that has only limited implications. Many would doubtless assent to (say they believe) the proposition that Jesus of Nazareth was an historical personage, but this in itself plainly would not at all commit them to the belief that he was the Son of God and so on; whereas the spiritual commitment in question, which is superadded to the assent, has total consequences, to the extent that the purported act of belief entails a special mode of personal existence. This is far more even than the complete acceptance of a body of doctrine: it is a style of life, and this enduring personal engagement is held to be the expression of belief.

Yet it is not at once obvious in what way, apart from the extreme character of the quasi-description that is offered, this kind of self-commitment differs from certain other personal undertakings of a determined kind. For instance, a man who marries commits himself in a pretty absolute manner, and so does someone who offers himself as a hostage, or one who even stands bail in some great amount. In such cases, too, what is evinced may well be a 'loving trust' in individuals, of the same general kind perhaps as that which Clarke writes of. More generally, a teacher may commit himself to his profession as a style of life, and show by doing so and by continuing in it the strength and fervency of certain ideals that he holds; and nurses or social workers may similarly act out in their lives a commitment that entails a particular mode of existence, one inspired throughout by ideals such as might commonly be termed beliefs. But in all these cases the believing can be said to obtain, in the end, only with regard to propositions that embody the ideals or values that are at work. The commitment to these propositional values is not simply, to adopt Clarke's wording, the merely intellectual acceptance of a set of propositions held as true on exclusively intellectual grounds: there is a firm and continued attitude on the part of the subject, and it is this, over and above mere assent, which makes his engagement describable as a commitment. Under this aspect there are very many circumstances in which an affective commitment is made, and there is no patent distinction of nature or setting which divides religious faith from these. Given this extensive class of types of self-commitment, therefore, we are confronted with various occasions, resolutions, and constancies of behaviour which are not typified by religious belief but have a far more general incidence. If they are all, whatever their several objects, describable by reference to belief, then the allegedly special features of religious commitment lose their putative singularity and the concept of belief is not elucidated by a religious paradigm. As far as any act of the will is concerned, religious belief then remains open to the objections that have already been rehearsed in sec. VI above. Alternatively, if there is indeed a psychic state or act of the mind that is peculiar to religious belief, it would appear to be not an act of the will but something else, and what that is even the religious cannot well say.

In any case, declarations of the kind that we have been examining are often not represented as being true descriptions such as will convey information of a public sort to others; and in this sense they cannot even be apprehended by the uninitiated, let alone be assessed or acted upon. They seem, rather, to serve two main functions. On the one hand they are a form of code among the faithful, signalling mutually a common adherence, against the world, to a way and purpose of life. On the other, their very impenetrability conveys to outsiders that what they speak of is significant in that it is ultimately ineffable, and in this way they hint at a supremely desirable mode of experience. Only believe, they enjoin, and your eyes will be opened, the scales will fall, and you shall perceive the divine truth in all its unutterable glory.[10] In neither case, though, do such assertions of belief provide a literal description of what this state is or of how, by an act of self-commitment, it is to be entered. Presumably such adjectives as 'existential' and 'global' record for the believer, and call to mind in others of his faith, a blissful apprehension of which he and they are personally quite persuaded; but these epithets cannot readily be construed as specifications of any definite state of mind that can be voluntarily assumed.

Admittedly, this has been a very bare and truncated consideration of a matter of living faith, but even the most extended explication could not obviate the fundamental difficulty that 'there is not much hope for an independent analysis of religious language' (Williams 1955: 207). The first and most intractable obstacle is the very notion of belief as a wilful act of complete commitment, and there are many attendant difficulties as well, but this combination of psychological obscurity with unanalysable propositions rules out a distinctive commitment as a criterion of belief.

VIII

'The influence of belief is at once to enliven and infix any idea in the imagination, and prevent all kind of hesitation and uncertainty about it' (Hume 1888: 453), 'so that there can be no suspicion of mistake' (101).

This is perhaps the most commonly agreed criterion of belief, that it is marked by a 'firmness and strength of conception' (Hume 1888: 627), i.e., by a degree of conviction. But there is no agreement at all on the extent and kind of connection between belief and certainty or conviction. Kant, indeed, made a distinction between these two attributes: conviction is subjective sufficiency, whereas certainty is objective sufficiency (1787: 850). I may be convinced of what I believe, but this does not make it certain, for what is certain must be so for everyone. Belief, because it is founded on merely subjective reasons, does not give a conviction that can be communicated to others, or command universal assent, like the conviction that comes from knowledge: 'Only I myself can be certain of the validity and immutability of my practical beliefs' (1800: 106).

[10] This, at any rate, is one formulation. There is a quite different view, namely that 'what actually causes anyone to believe in God is direct perception of the Divine' (Bevan 1962: 345).

Belief is thus an inferior mode of holding something to be true; it is not a special source of knowledge, and it is held with varying degrees of conviction. The touchstone of firmness of belief is betting, and the degree of 'subjective conviction' can be gauged by what the subject is prepared to stake. Far, therefore, from preventing hesitation and uncertainty, belief by this account always contains a recognized element of uncertainty. Even when the subject is firmly convinced of his belief, he will yet be required to concede that it does not automatically procure an equal conviction in others: 'the expression of belief is, from the *objective* point of view, an expression of modesty, and yet at the same time, from the *subjective* point of view, an expression of the firmness of our confidence' (1787: 855). The lack of full objective certainty (namely that which would qualify the proposition as knowledge) is always, in some variable degree, an impairment of the conviction with which something can be held to be true. In fact, Kant most explicitly describes belief as 'a kind of consciously imperfect assent' (1800: 102 n.).[11] In this case, there can well be suspicion of mistake.

Prichard puts this point of view in the plainest possible way when he asserts bluntly that 'when we believe something we are uncertain of it' (1967: 63), and this is of course a perfectly normal acceptation of the word. But then it is also perfectly normal, particularly in religious discourse, to consider belief as admitting no uncertainty at all: 'Faith is incompatible with doubt' (Newman 1849: 228).

It is surely an accepted connotation of the concept of belief that a proposition in question must be held with some conviction, but there is a curiosity about English usage (and German, too, for that matter) in this regard. If we imagine a scale of positive certainty, ranging from utter conviction down to the very slightest assent, the English language marks off various points along its length with separate designations: e.g., one can be absolutely certain, sure, persuaded, and so on through stages of increasing dubiety. Not only does English have this apparatus of graded acceptance of a proposition, but any language must make some such provision in its epistemological vocabulary. The language need not be at all subtle in its lexical discriminations, and the degree of conviction can easily be expressed merely by the use of, for instance, the word for 'certain' plus one of a number of qualifiers such as any language can be expected to contain. (The Penan do so by means of the word *atek*,

11 '. . . Eine Art des mit Bewusstseyn unvollständigen Fürwahrhaltens.'

certain, modified by others signifying truly, nearly, slightly, and so on.) Such a scale of conviction, however it may be marked off, is a general feature of language and a common preoccupation in discourse; yet in English, despite the array of distinct terms for several degrees of certainty, the verb 'believe' is used nevertheless to indicate any point whatever on the scale. A belief, particularly of a religious kind, can be a matter of absolute and irrefragable conviction; but it can also be, in extreme contrast, the slightest supposition, conjecture, or expectation.

By this ready linguistic test, therefore, Hume is justified in his view of the importance of conviction, and Kant is also right in his; but of course neither is wholly or exclusively right about the class of all assertions of belief. In this event, we may well say that an assertion of belief connotes some degree of conviction; but this feature is not sufficiently precise or characteristic to serve as a criterion. It is rather as though one were to say, with equal generality, that every material body has a temperature: the assertion is true enough, but it makes a difference whether any particular body is red-hot or just this side of absolute zero. Moreover, conviction (like temperature) is a state that fluctuates according to circumstances, and this typical variability makes it yet less feasible to resort to conviction in the determination of belief. For example, it may be said of a man that he holds a constant belief in that he makes the assertion in question, on appropriate occasions, over a long period. But if the degree of conviction with which he utters the proposition can vary from occasion to occasion, wherein lies the constancy? In the form of words with which he makes the assertion of belief? In that case the utterance is sufficient in itself to establish the report that he believes, and the degree of his conviction is irrelevant to the issue whether or not he actually holds the belief or holds it constantly. It is not a quibble, either, to observe that it is open to debate what shall count as a long period; this judgement, also, apart from its arbitrary element, may vary with the type of belief in question, and so correlatively will the estimation of constant conviction. On the other hand, since the semantic range of the verb 'believe' is so extremely extended, it is not feasible to gauge the significance of an assertion of belief without taking into account the apparent or inferable degree of conviction with which it is uttered. In this case, and in this respect, it is difficult to say that the belief is constant, since the conviction with which it is held or expressed is liable to fluctuate. This variability has nothing to do necessarily with the grounds for the belief: the evidence, the logical validity of the formulation, and ultimately the truth (if ascertainable) of what is believed may all retain their objective justification, while the subject's conviction—even in association with an identical proposition repeated regularly over a period—may oscillate between extremes of confidence.

The unreliability of conviction as a criterion of belief becomes still more patent when we consider what could be meant, in this regard, by a report that two persons held the same belief. We should then have to take into account (assuming this to be practicable) the degree of conviction with which at a certain time each of them held that belief, and it is not likely that this could be at the same pitch. It might even be concluded that, by a given standard somehow determined, only one of them actually believed, while the other was insufficiently convinced and merely presented the externals of belief. Moreover, since conviction fluctuates, the assessment of their individual commitments would be continually unhinged, as now one and then the other underwent an accession of proper conviction. These difficulties, finally, are multiplied as the number of individuals concerned increases, to the point that evidentially it could not possibly be said that the members of a society believed anything in common.

It is logically necessary that a belief be held with a degree of conviction, so we can say nevertheless that conviction must be a component of belief; but it is not a distinctive feature of belief, and it is not a practical criterion. And even if the centrality of conviction, a feeling of certainty, were granted there would still remain yet another difficulty in resorting to it as a criterion. This is brought out by Wittgenstein in considering the question 'What does it mean to *believe* Goldbach's theorem?' (1953, sec. 578). He asks, namely, what this belief consists in:

In a feeling of certainty as we state, hear, or think the theorem? (That would not interest us.) And what are the characteristics of this feeling? Why, I don't even know how far the feeling may be caused by the proposition itself.

Conviction is thus a most uncertain feature to rely upon in any objective investigation of belief. This however does not mean that there is no other mode of feeling that might serve as a criterion.

IX

'Belief is more properly an act of the sensitive, than of the cogitative part of our natures' (Hume 1888: 183).[12]

It is a natural concomitant of the subjective character of belief that it is commonly thought of in connection with some feeling. This is especially the case with religious discourse, in which declarations of faith and doctrinal adherence are customarily phrased in emotive (and even erotic) terms. This is a familiar fact in the European tradition, and comprehensible, but it is none the less rather remarkable. The curiosity of the situation emerges well in Freud. He defines 'belief' as conviction of the accuracy (alternatively, the truth) of a statement, and later says, quite acceptably, that 'a believer has certain ties of affection binding him to the substance of religion' (1928: 44, 81). We are indeed accustomed to this connection, yet all the same it is neither necessary nor, on common premises, expectable that a judgement of accuracy shall be accompanied by affection. Admitted, it is possible to make a disjunction between assent to a proposition (e.g., 'There is a God') and the feeling which is prescribed as appropriate to the subject of that proposition; but in this context the assent known as 'belief' entails the feeling and is in part an emotional commitment. Not, however, that the feeling is necessarily or solely one of affection. As Malcolm says (1964: 107),

Belief in God encompasses not only trust but also awe, dread, dismay, resentment, and perhaps even hatred. Belief in God will involve some affective state or attitude, having God as its object, and those attitudes could vary from reverential love to rebellious rejection.

Religious beliefs are an extreme case, but they draw attention dramatically to the feeling-tone generally ascribed to propositions of belief. When we say that someone knows something, or thinks something, or calculates, and so on, we do not imply that he is also in some emotional state; but the report that someone believes is, in common usage, inseparable from the implication that he experiences some feeling, if only the alleged feeling of certainty, about what he believes.

Belief, however, is not singular in this respect. There are other psychological verbs which carry the same implication. The connotation of feeling is, for example, one possible ground of distinction

[12] Cf. Wittgenstein (1953, sec. 574): 'Believing is not thinking.'

underlying Wittgenstein's assertion that 'the concepts of believing, expecting, hoping are less distantly related to one another than they are to the concept of thinking' (1953, sec. 574). Believing, then, is one of a class of emotive psychological verbs. Moreover, just as with expecting, the emotion (or at least a definitive emotion) is determined by the circumstances: in one situation love is appropriate, in another, hatred, and so on. This does not mean, though, that any one such emotion excludes the possibility of another. Simple emotions are, I take it, hypothetical constructs; experientially, any emotional situation is complex, and it is a matter for investigation to determine what emotions are or are not mutually compatible. To say therefore that an assertion of belief may be accompanied by a variety of emotions does not exclude the possibility that a particular one of them, or some set of them, may still be an emotional state that is peculiar to belief.

Is there, then, any such discriminable feeling? I do not mean Hume's very general 'vivacity', or intensity of impression, but a more specific and isolable sentiment. Is there a feeling, that is, not of certainty or of any other supposed attribute or component of belief, but of belief itself? The issue can be publicly resolved only by resort to the facts of language. In English we can feel happy or dull or resentful, or in any one of hundreds of identified emotional states, but can we feel 'believing' or 'belief-ful'? The obvious answer, as a matter of established linguistic usage, is that we cannot. The English language makes a very prominent place for the concept of belief, but it does not provide for the expression or recognition of a concomitant feeling. (The adjective 'credent', archaic and rare as it is, moreover, does not serve this purpose.) The linguistic test is not final, of course, for not every significant psychic phenomenon is designated by a distinct word. In any case, a presumed inner state must be capable of innerly investigation; so we have to ask ourselves, individually, whether we can discern any feeling of belief in association with (not necessarily together with) any type of proposition in which we are prepared to say that we believe. My own answer is that there is nothing of the kind; inquiries of others elicit no more positive report; and I cannot discover that previous authors have ever demonstrated as much. We have had every historical, cultural, and linguistic inducement—save the ultimate epithet that is in question—to conceive a feeling of belief, or even to form one, yet it appears almost certainly not to exist.[13]

13 There is an incidental interest, too, in the fact that Descartes, who is so

Why, then, should we ever contemplate the existence of a feeling in connection with belief? Let us approach the question by reverting for a moment to the topic of conviction. Wittgenstein says that we speak of a feeling of conviction because there is a 'tone', such as is characteristic of feelings, of conviction (1967, sec. 513). Similarly, he asserts that 'there is a tone of belief, as of doubt' (1953, sec. 578). So we might be inclined to think that there will be a corresponding feeling of belief as well. But this is not the argument. Instead, Wittgenstein writes (1953: 225):

We should sometimes like to call certainty and belief tones, colourings, of thought; and it is true that they receive expression in the *tone* of the voice. But do not think of them as 'feelings' which we have in speaking or thinking.

This is in part a cogent injunction, as far as conviction is concerned: there is indeed a tone of conviction in the voice, and this is recognizable in the utterances of any language and in the expressive conventions of any culture. But is there really a tone of belief?

I suggest, as I am in fact convinced, that there is not. What we can hear in the asseveration of a belief, in the sense of a firmly held view, is firmness or conviction. In a confession of faith the tone may indicate, and be intended to indicate, reverence or humility or many another posture of the inner self; but what we cannot detect, or try to affect, is a tone characteristic of belief. When, for instance, a Kodi priest proceeds through the standard invocation to spirits and the deities, he can be said presumptively to believe in the existence and powers of these mystical beings (if questioned on the point he will assuredly reply in terms which could be conventionally translated to this effect), but I am pretty sure that even to Sumbanese ears there is no tonal indication which signifies or expresses his belief. A man, also, who protests to his mistress that he believes implicitly in her fidelity can put a passionate and earnest emphasis on his declaration, but nothing in his tone of voice will convey, apart from the significance of his words, his avowal that he believes in her. The same conclusion follows, more generally, from any attempt to distinguish by tone of voice alone between statements that are

insistent on the voluntary character of assent, makes no place in his extensive catalogue of sentiments (1649, pt. 3) for a feeling of belief.

In this Cartesian context, we may consider in addition the implications of Danto's acute observation: 'In large measure, we are going to have a different analysis of belief as we move to a different view of the mind–body problem' (Danto 1970: 126).

H

believed and those that are not believed. The tones that can go with assertions of belief are certainly discriminable and they are very numerous, including grievous doubt as well as buoyant confidence, anguished realization as well as glad assent, but none of them is a tone of belief and none is a distinctive accompaniment of utterances that are believed.

This is not to say, though, that there is no connection of any sort between belief and tone of voice. The interesting thing, indeed, is that the tone of voice can be used to signify, and may even naturally express (when not modulated by the etiquette of the situation), the fact of *dis*belief. But this curious phenomenon does not entail the converse facility; and the contrast caps the demonstration that there is no 'tone of belief'. We are thus in a position to go back to Wittgenstein's premise. Belief, he says, is a 'tone of thought' (*Tönung des Gedankens*), and it is this which receives expression in the tone of voice. Now it would be more than unreasonable to reproach him with employing a metaphor of the kind in this realm of investigation, but it is after all a metaphor and one is at rather a loss to know what to make of it. Wittgenstein resorts elsewhere to a similar figure, when he speaks of belief as 'a particular colouring of our thoughts' (1953, sec. 578), in the more explicit terms 'ein Farbton der Gedanken', but this phrase does not provide a better aid to the sense. There is no common English usage corresponding to Wittgenstein's expressions, and they convey in themselves no exact description or, I find, useful indication of whatever phenomenon is in question. Testing again, therefore, by the inevitable introspection, I can only report that the metaphorical 'colouring of thought' corresponds to no distinct inner experience or state. But this conclusion is by no means entirely negative in effect. Wittgenstein's postulated colouring may not serve as a causal explanation, but the internal inspection in search of it places us in a more secure position to consider the next issue.

We have briefly examined a line of derivation: a tone of voice expresses a feeling which is a response to a colouring of thought. At all three points this chain of inference has been thought defective, but the problem of a feeling in connection with belief can still be further explored. There is in fact a very good reason why such a connection might be postulated. There may be no feeling of belief, but there *is* a feeling associated with (actually, provoked by) a challenge to a belief.[14] The feeling is physical, and it is characterized

[14] This point has latterly received pleasing confirmation by Price, who

by two symptoms: a sharp intake of the breath, and a sudden tension in the solar plexus. Doubtless there are other manifestations, and physiological changes as well, but these features appear to be the most marked and the most readily sensed. The causal proposition that such a reaction is provoked by challenge to a belief does not depend on the definition of what is to count as a belief; or at least not until we reach the lower end of our hypothetical scale of commitment (sec. VIII above), where it may not matter especially whether a minimal 'belief' (supposition, expectation) is justified or not, in which case a challenge may call into question nothing of particular importance. We might refer to the stronger commitments as 'significant beliefs', i.e., judgements and evaluations that really mean something to the subject, and of these at any rate it can be confidently asserted that a challenge to any one of them, without consideration of what kind of belief it may be, will bring about the feeling in question. It makes no difference whether the challenge is to a belief in a religious proposition, in a moral value, in a social form, or in a person: an affront, even if it can be seen to have no substance, produces the emotional effect. There are exterior bodily changes, too, such that we can observe in others certain responses which, being involuntary and little under the power of deliberate suppression, are far better indicators of an inner state than the tone of voice is likely to be. These physical signs include a momentary pallor, a start or a brief rigidity of posture, a set facial expression (or, alternatively, an agitated expression, depending in part on convention), and sometimes other more minor indications. Is this complex bodily alteration then the evidence for a specific feeling associated with belief? It would make a slightly roundabout demonstration, but it might serve. We may not have a distinct feeling as we believe (while we are the locus of whatever phenomena are supposed to constitute that state), yet as soon as we are confronted with disbelief the intensity of our reaction signals the fact and the degree of our commitment to the proposition believed. There is a parallel here with the asymmetric feature of tone of voice (which does not express belief but can signify disbelief), and once more the conclusion is negative.

The feeling provoked by the challenge of disbelief is not

makes a brief allusion to the phenomenon: '... belief sometimes shows itself by the distress or dismay one feels when others deny the proposition believed' (1968: 295). Bertrand Russell, incidentally, conjectures that there may exist in addition a 'disbelief-feeling' (1921: 250).

symptomatic of belief. We have only to ask ourselves if the feeling is associated with other situations as well in order to see this. The identical effect can be produced by situations of fear, surprise, intellectual realization, aesthetic impact, and by innumerable other circumstances and factors. To be shot at, for instance, to conceive an idea or formulate the solution to a problem, to hear the opening chord of a Balinese *pelegongan* or 'Liebestod', to come face to face with a stunning picture or a desperately desirable woman—all these, and countless other 'breathtaking' situations (as we significantly call them), can provoke the feeling which at first seemed to offer a distinctive sign and gauge of belief. That feeling is simply a species of shock, not a singular evidence of belief.

A last resort, in this event, might be to respond that it does not matter in the end what particular feeling accompanies an assertion of belief, just so long as there is some feeling in some sort of connection with it. This contention might indeed be admitted, in the sense that an emotional character could be regarded as a component in the notion of belief; but so vague and perhaps sporadic a feeling could not serve as a criterion by which to discriminate belief from other inner states.

For all the persuasive verve of Hume's declaration, therefore, we still cannot find that belief is 'something *felt* by the mind' (1888: 629). And if we could do so, we should still have to grapple with the fundamental difficulty pointed out by Wittgenstein (1953: 181):

Even if someone had a particular capacity [*Fähigkeit*] only when, and only as long as, he had a particular feeling, the feeling would not be the capacity.

X

'Neither man nor any other being ought ever to be thought possest of any ability, unless it be exerted and put in action' (Hume 1888: 311).

One active sign of belief is, as Kant pointed out, betting; or, more generally, a readiness (expressed in action) to take risks. 'What you say won't be taken as the measure for the firmness of a belief. But, for instance, what risks you would take' (Wittgenstein 1966: 54).[15]

[15] The punctuation in the printed source places a question mark, inappropriately, at the end of each of these sentences.

This is a decisive enough test of the degree of confidence with which anyone actually subscribes to a proposition, but of course it is not only that. In gambling, for example, people bet on issues where they are anything but certain, and sometimes when in fact they know that their cards are not strong enough. For that matter, they may bet with some other intention than merely to win a wager; they may make a bet precisely in order to cloak a different motive, such as inducing others to bet on a doubtful or even hopeless outcome. It is true that stratagems of the kind can have a chance of working only because betting, or being prepared to take a risk, is generally taken as evidence of true conviction; but the practice of conventional deceits, meant to convey merely an impression of confidence, has the consequence that we cannot rely on risk-taking as a guarantee of belief. Everything depends on context, and on the determination of motives which may never be securely discoverable. There are admittedly many types of situation which approach the hypothetical ideal, and where the firmness of a man's 'belief' could not much be called into question; e.g., an officer who believes it is his duty to safeguard his men and hence risks his life to save one who is lying wounded in the open, or a mediaeval Spanish Jew who goes to the stake rather than commit the spiritual offence of apostasy. Yet even these extreme examples are open to other interpretations, and ultimately it is only by putting an ideal construction on them that they can be made into behavioural evidence of belief. For the rest, there are altogether too many other possibilities, of motive and circumstance, to allow any safe inference to this effect. But, in any case, why should betting or risk-taking be regarded as evidence of belief rather than of something else? It may, in the best of cases, be taken as qualified evidence of certainty or conviction in something that is proposed; or it may be seen instead as evidence of a bold resolution, or recklessness, or incapacity to appreciate the risks, and so on. What reason have we, though, to accept it as a token of belief? It is not enough that the person in question should assert that for which he takes great risks or even suffers a pious death, for this precisely is the paradigm case which leads us to ask whether taking risks is indeed independent evidence of belief.

Perhaps a less demanding test than risk-taking would serve better as a behavioural indication of belief; for example, that belief is that which provides guidance to action. Kant proposed, in fact, that a belief could be defined as 'an assent that is sufficient for action'

(1800: 103);[16] and Hampshire asserts that 'beliefs which . . . never guided action, would not count as beliefs' (1965: 159). These statements are grammatically correct enough, i.e., they are consistent with the acknowledged usage of 'glauben' and 'believe', but they are not co-extensive with the range of connotations of the verbal concept of belief. For instance, the word can denote a condition of such doubt and uncertainty that no one would be likely to embark on any action on the basis of it. Conversely, not all actions can usefully be regarded as based on belief; e.g., if an infantryman is forced into an advance by the menace of his superior's pistol, he may well be said to believe that if he refuses he will be shot, but it would not be an acceptable description to say that his action was guided by belief (rather than by fear, shame, hopelessness, etc.) or that his state of mind was one of belief. Moreover, there are beliefs which need have no expression in action; e.g., beliefs about the inscrutable purposes of God, or about conjectured beings on other planets. It might be contended of course that the mere utterance of a belief is an action, which indeed in a sense it is: 'Words are also deeds' (Wittgenstein 1953, sec. 546). But since we can know nothing of the beliefs of others unless they declare them, the utterance is no more than a necessary condition of describing them as beliefs. Since, therefore, there is no necessary or general connection between belief and action, it is to some extent arbitrary to select action as a criterion of belief.[17]

Are there then other behavioural signs of the presumed state of mind? It is difficult to know what signs could constitute acceptable evidence. It is a notorious matter of common experience, after all, that the conventional externals of religious belief do not entail a real adherence to the doctrines that they are supposed to acknowledge. Genuflections at the altar, prostration on a prayer met, and bloody sacrifice tell us equally little about the internal states of those who perform these public actions. No rite shows by its performance that the participants do or do not hold a certain attitude towards— 'believe'—the ideological premises of what they do. Much of social conduct, also, is cloaked in a comfortable obscurity about real motives, and there are no sure signs that the protestation or enactment of a belief is accompanied by any special and characteristic

[16] 'Ein Fürwahrhalten, welches genug ist zum Handeln, d.i. ein Glaube.'
[17] See further Kenny (1963: 63): 'There seems to be a difference... between emotions and other states of mind, such as beliefs.... Beliefs, by themselves, do not lead to action; whereas desires and emotions do.'

state of mind. Even when we are convinced that a person genuinely believes what he says he believes, our conviction is not based on objective evidence of a distinct inner state. If it were possible for us ever to have this knowledge, then all the social dissimulation would not matter, for in that case there would be a true archetype which the dissemblers artfully affected; but this is not so, and all we actually have are assertions of belief and the acts and postures which may conventionally accompany them. If these culturally formulated tokens of belief are taken away, or discounted, does anything remain?

We have already rejected the suggestion that there is a tone of belief to be detected in the voice, but Wittgenstein also maintains that there is another behavioural sign, namely the facial expression: 'It cannot be doubted that we regard certain facial expressions, gestures, etc. as characteristic for the expression of belief' (1958: 144).[18] A man's face does not have a constant appearance, but it is nevertheless possible to draw a picture of his physiognomy: a picture in which the face smiles does not show how it looks when weeping, but it does permit inferences. 'And in this way it would be possible to describe a kind of approximate physiognomy of belief' (1967a, sec. 514).[19]

But is this really so? We certainly do give such signs, as Wittgenstein goes on to mention (sec. 515), of delight and comprehension, but is there really any facial sign that is distinctive of belief? Since the alleged expression is not described, we do not know what exactly to look for; but my own conclusion, at any rate, is that there is no more a physiognomy of belief than there is a tone of belief. We can see fear or expectation or calculation in a man's face, but we cannot tell from his visage that he believes. His physiognomy does not portray an enduring disposition to believe, and it does not express at any particular time the momentary fact that he is entertaining or contemplating a belief. This, indeed, is what our linguistic forms might lead us to expect. A man's habitual expression can be described as signalling a benevolent or a spiteful disposition, but how could it be said to express a believing

---

[18] Also: 'It is advantageous in treating our problem to consider parallel with the feeling or feelings characteristic for . . . meaning what one says, etc., etc., the facial expression (gestures or tone of voice) characteristic for the same states or events' (1958: 144).

[19] '. . . Eine Art ungefähre Physiognomie.' The published translation has '. . . average physiognomy'.

disposition? Someone could look credulous, perhaps, but this would mean only that he was 'disposed to believe' (*S.O.E.D.*), not that he was the locus of a specific disposition describable as belief in a certain proposition or whatever was at issue. In common usage, also, this adjective has more usually the derogatory connotation that a person is apt to believe on weak or insufficient grounds, so that it carries the implication of naïvety, ignorance, or unintelligence, and none of these attributes is what we are looking for.

On the other hand, if it is not an habitual inclination that is in question, what would a passing facial expression reflect of the person's belief? Not the proposition, of course, or a set of related propositions, or any type of proposition. If, moreover, the expression does not specifically correspond to the utterance of a belief, or to the bodily acknowledgement of a belief, to what then could it possibly correspond? For believing is not an action (Wittgenstein 1967a, sec. 51). As Hampshire has put it, I do not decide to believe, I decide that a statement in question is true; or, as it might otherwise be phrased, I decide that I believe it. But this realization has no revelatory physiognomy. A man may be of a decisive disposition, and by the habitual set of his features he may also give a decisive impression (as politicians, military men, and magnates evidently try to do); but neither the inner formation nor the public face will be able to declare or reveal that his decisiveness, or his particular decision, has anything to do with belief. This is confirmed by Wittgenstein's own parallel (1953: 188) with the case of fear:

> What is fear? What does 'being afraid' mean? If I wanted to explain it at a *single* showing—I should *play-act* fear. Could I also represent hope in this way? Hardly. And what about belief?[20]

The answer is, I think, that one cannot possibly play-act belief: there is no facial expression, either natural or (so far as I know) conventional, which can be put on for this purpose, and there is no bodily act which can be taken as a sure and distinctive sign of believing.

'An "inner process" stands in need of outward criteria' (Wittgenstein 1953, sec. 580), but in the case of belief these are just what we cannot discover in any form of action.

[20] See also: 'If a person has not yet got the *concepts*, I shall teach him to use the words by means of *examples* and by *practice*' (1953, sec. 208).

XI

Belief, according to Hume, gives the ideas of the judgement a firmness, solidity, or steadiness, and renders them 'the governing principles of all our actions' (1888: 629). It is not therefore simply an isolated act of assent, decision, or commitment, nor is it only (if at all) a distinct feeling: it is something persistent. To employ the language of modern philosophy, it is a disposition.

Unfortunately, however, 'the word "disposition" has been used in too many different senses' (Hampshire 1959: 164), and to call belief a disposition scarcely makes the issue clearer. The dictionary tells us that a disposition is a turn of mind, the state or quality of being disposed, or an inclination, etc. (*S.O.E.D.*); but these formulations are either themselves unclear or they rest on presumptions which have been shown by our preceding examination to be insufficient or unreliable. Wittgenstein, who is most prominently associated with a dispositional view of belief, frames at one point (1953, sec. 149) the following definition:

If one says that knowing the ABC is a state of mind, one is thinking of a state of a mental apparatus (perhaps the brain) by means of which we explain the *manifestations* of that knowledge. Such a state is called a disposition.

But of course we know nothing directly, without the mediation of language, about any mental apparatus in connection with knowledge, and we know nothing at all about any state of the brain such as could be relevant to the investigation of belief.[21] Nevertheless, there are phenomena which are interpreted as manifestations of the disposition. Wittgenstein says of belief that it is shown in the case of someone else by his behaviour, and by his words; but both common experience and the course of our preceding search for criteria make it plain that nothing can be certainly inferred from the observation of behaviour or from the assertion of belief. There

[21] W. Grey Walter states that there is objective evidence, in the form of neuro-electrical events, of the genesis of a person's intentions, that a subject's decisions can be predicted through an electrical machine, and that 'we can identify objective accompaniments of spontaneous volition and creative reflexion' (1969: 36–7). But he does not claim, and so far as I know it has not been proposed elsewhere, that a distinct inner state of the kind that belief is taken to be can be distinguished by this means in the functioning of the brain.

are conventional acts and utterances which are recognized as appropriate to belief, and there may be some advantage in referring these to a unitary source in a disposition; but unless that disposition can be specified in some further respect (as a discriminable mode of consciousness, for example) we may not be any clearer about the nature of belief than we are when we refer the acts and utterances to some hypothetically distinct mental faculty or process.

If we inquire further into the manifestations of the belief disposition, we find that it has certain rather interesting characteristics. It has duration, says Wittgenstein, and this independently of the duration of its expression in a sentence, for example. How do we know this? Well, there are recurrent acts and utterances which we regularly designate as signs or expressions of belief. These are the evidences that we start from when we identify a persistent state of mind. But what comes in between these recurrent signs? Nothing that we know of. And if we lack such evidences during the intermissions, in what consists the duration? These questions are not merely Zenonic objections, or sophistical criticisms of the notion of continuity: they are direct and inevitable responses to the suggestion that belief is a state of mind that has duration. We have no need to resort to classical paradoxes, or to limiting cases in logic, in order to see that in this respect the suggestion leads to a dead end.

Of course, it could be said that the very recurrence of certain evidences is just what we mean by duration, just as when (Berkeley notwithstanding) I am pragmatically satisfied of the continued existence of the chestnut tree outside my window because whenever I choose to look out it happens still to be there. According to this view of the matter, a man's belief in the Trinity can be said to have duration in that he repeatedly, for example every Sunday morning, recites the Creed; or that a Purum's belief in an agricultural god has duration because every year, after the harvest, he makes a sacrifice; or that an ancient Greek's belief in the goddess of child-bearing had duration because whenever his wife gave birth he made an offering at the temple. But as we increase the time-span between the observances, or make it more adventitious, the idea of an enduring state of mind becomes progressively more difficult to accept. And, in the third example, suppose the woman had only one child, so that there was no repetition of the act of offering; or none at all, so that there was no conventional occasion to give public evidence of a disposition to act in such a manner. Where then resides the belief? In a readiness to offer to the goddess if only she would give a child, or to declare the belief in response to a query on the part of an ignorant outsider? But then the existence and the duration of the belief would be, so far as manifestations in the individual are concerned, no more than hypothetical.

When Hampshire states that beliefs generally must be to some degree stable if they are to count as beliefs at all, he is writing in conformity with a grammatical convention. The stability is a property that we must ascribe to beliefs if we are to respect the meaning of words as given in common use; and we are thus led to interpret this linguistic presumption of stability as the manifestation of a persistent disposition. And when he continues with the assertion that beliefs 'are not in their nature episodic, as are actions with their accompanying intentions' (1959: 150), he makes a statement about something the nature of which cannot be known except episodically.

'Really one hardly ever says that one has believed, understood or intended something "uninterruptedly" since yesterday. An interruption of belief would be a period of unbelief, not e.g. the withdrawal of attention from what one believes' (Wittgenstein 1967a, sec. 85). Does one ever at all say that one has believed something uninterruptedly? Surely one does not; nor could one reasonably say so as an act of communication with others, for although the statement would be syntactically correct it would not be a recognizable vehicle of information. It is not even plausible, for that matter, since one is not uninterruptedly (as a matter of reportable fact, not figuratively) in any state of mind, even love or fear, for very long at a time. Always, and very rapidly indeed, there are fluctuations in whatever conception or mood may be thought of as a state of mind; and it would be extremely odd if belief, of all such states, were exceptionally constant. And how would we know if it were so? Could we know by constantly attending to what we believe, e.g., to the import of a certain proposition? Such an unremitting attention is itself a psychic impossibility; and even for so long as it might be feasible, one's interpretation of the proposition would continually vary. 'I said to myself, "I cannot possibly believe that"—and while I was saying it I observed that I had already believed it a second time' (Lichtenberg 1958: 488). Nor, even more certainly, could one attend to the state of belief in itself, as something separate from that which is believed: 'I can attend to the course of my pains, but not in the same way to that of my belief...'

(Wittgenstein 1967a, sec. 75). So far, indeed, we have been able to discover nothing of the kind to attend to.

XII

A constant hindrance in an inquiry of this sort is, as Hume found, that it is 'very difficult to talk of the operations of the mind with perfect propriety and exactness; because common language has seldom made any very nice distinctions among them', and this, he continues, is a source of obscurity and confusion, doubt and objection (1888: 105). In the appendix to his *Treatise* (629) he confesses:

Even when I think I understand the subject perfectly, I am at a loss to express my meaning. . . . I scarce can find any word that fully answers the case, but am obliged to have recourse to every one's feeling, in order to give him a perfect notion of this operation of the mind.

He resorts on occasion to a variety of evocative descriptions such as force, vivacity, solidity, firmness, and steadiness, in order to distinguish that feeling which (as he thinks) is peculiar to belief, but in the end he has to admit that he finds it 'impossible to explain perfectly this feeling or manner of conception' (629).

Kant, in his turn, encounters a comparable difficulty (1787: 855):

The term belief refers only to the guidance which an idea gives me, and to its subjective influence in that furthering of the activities of my reason which confirms me in the idea, and which yet does so without my being in a position to give a speculative account of it.

Perhaps, then, there really is some kind of inner state or process corresponding to the word 'belief,' only one that we apprehend intuitively and which (like many sensations, emotions, and impulsions) is recalcitrant to definition. The quandary may be similar, that is, to the one we are in when we try to define or analyse physical sensations and aesthetic impressions. We do not say that these experiences are illusory or factitious simply because we cannot render an objective account of them, or specify the criteria by which they can be recognized and discriminated. Perhaps, therefore, belief too is just such a state: real enough, but practically impossible to describe. At least, this possibility allows us to guess how it is that Richards can resort to the enigmatic figure: 'We should beware of supposing that believing or not is like turning a light on or off. It is much more like focusing or not focusing the eyes' (1942: 170). This sounds as though it means something, and even something quite penetratingly apposite to an enigmatic state of mind; but it is intriguing rather than revealing, and apparently one still has to know what belief is before one can see that the metaphoric description makes sense.

Yet even this obscure indication looks positive when compared with the wording of the conclusions arrived at by modern philosophers. Griffiths' inquiry into the concept of belief is very scrupulous and reasonable, as we have seen, but by the end of it he has retreated into a position that is scarcely locatable, let alone defensible. Belief, he thinks, is a discriminable mode of consciousness, in the way that modes of consciousness such as doubting, willing, and wondering are all discriminable, and this, he affirms, 'is something of its own sort'. He concedes that this account may be thought to say nothing and to provide no answer, but to this objection he responds that it is still preferable to certain other theories which he argues to be false, 'and if I say nothing, I at least say nothing false'. He maintains, indeed, and on grounds that we can well appreciate, that the upshot of his investigation, to the point cited, is that 'belief is the kind of concept which makes the question "What is belief?" unanswerable' (Griffiths 1967: 138). It is, then, an 'unanalysable private state of mind' (140), such that any qualitative characteristics (e.g., feeling) that one may associate with it cannot be essential for its identification. 'On the other hand, it is a mode of consciousness. Though not essentially marked by a difference of quality, it is not merely nothing for us' (142). We can certainly take it as a gauge of the problematical state of the notion of belief that a professional philosopher can have to content himself, and try to placate his readers, with such a description of his predicament.

Mayo says of Griffiths' remarks that they reveal 'the ghost of psychological empiricism' which his colleague has not quite exorcised (1967: 154); but he in his turn gets no nearer to a helpful description than to propose that belief is what usually 'goes with' assertion, or with acting in a certain manner easily interpretable in the light of usual goals, or even with certain feelings, etc. (158). It is not at all clear, either, how this proposal is to be construed, and still less how it could be practically applied. How is one to tell, by these indefinite and contingent features, what belief is? After all, 'belief consists not in the nature and order of our ideas, but in the manner of their conception' (Hume 1888: 629), and this much at least seems to be agreed; but Mayo's conclusion certainly would not reduce any of Hume's puzzlement about the description or the determination of that manner of conception. If belief 'usually' goes with assertion, for instance, how are we to distinguish those hypothetically unusual situations in which it does not? How indeed are we to know whether or not it is a usual accompaniment unless we first know what it is? Parallel difficulties also beset the acceptance of the other 'aspects of belief' delineated by Mayo, quite apart from the invalidating fact, which he declares, that in any case those aspects are never 'logically sufficient criteria' (158).

The philosophers, then, are evidently in an extreme difficulty, and one that is typical of investigations into the notion of belief. It is a fair judgement, I think, that they are simply and totally baffled by the descriptive task of stating the criteria of belief. It is unquestioningly treated as a discriminable mode of consciousness, but when they try to describe belief it proves to be indeterminate and unanalysable. In these respects, and without pronouncing on the ultimate reality of the interior state or whatever it may be, we should thus have to conclude that there are no criteria of belief.[22]

Where, then, do we get the notion of belief from? From the verb 'believe', and its inflected forms, in everyday English usage. Statements of belief are the only evidence for the phenomenon; but the phenomenon itself appears to be no more than the custom of making such statements.

[22] I should perhaps make it quite plain that I do not pretend to have examined all conceivable criteria, but only that those which I have adduced have special claims to attention. While not denying, moreover, the hypothetical aptness of further criteria, I tend to think that the detection of so prominent a natural capacity as belief is taken to be should not really need such hyperacuity of analysis as they would seem to entail.

7

Classification

I

'Concepts lead us to make investigations. They are the expression of our interest, and direct our interest' (Wittgenstein 1953, sec. 570).

A concept, in a standard acceptation, is the idea of a class of objects.[1] The name of the class that we are examining is 'belief'. What are the defining features of this class? We have not been able to discover any distinctive criteria, and it has proved hard to conceive that the word really denotes any homogeneous class of phenomenal objects, whether these be propositions, inner states, or external signs. Our linguistic predispositions constantly persuade us to assume some unitary principle or object of classification underlying the usages of belief; yet however much we turn about the concept, and scrutinize it under new aspects, this unitary feature is just what we cannot find.

Take the conclusion arrived at recently by an able philosopher (Price 1969: 487) who has carried out the most extended critical analysis of belief since the eighteenth century:

If our long and devious investigation of the epistemology of belief has shown anything, surely it has shown that belief is a complex attitude which may manifest itself in many different ways.

Our own survey has brought us to a position from which we can easily see the grounds for this statement of the issue, but it has also precluded an entire agreement with such a conclusion. Even if belief is taken to be complex, as must certainly be admitted, can so extreme a variety of 'manifestations' plausibly be ascribed to a single attitude? Is it a reliable description, or at all informative, to say that belief is an attitude? (For that matter, what is an

---

[1] *Shorter Oxford English Dictionary*, s.v.

attitude?) Is belief really any such thing, in fact, as might exhibit manifestations? Nothing so far, at any rate, has given us reason to agree with even the implicit premises to Price's careful inquiry, let alone to accept its highly qualified outcome.

By what means then are we to apprehend this concept, the class of varied phenomena that are termed beliefs? What do these have in common? There is not anything evidently in common among the phenomena surveyed in chap. 6, to look no further, and it has seemed impossible to determine any aspect of the usages of belief under which they might thus constitute a class. Well, perhaps they have nothing in common and do not form a class in that conventional regard. Perhaps it is the uncritical acceptance of a word, rather than the peculiarities of belief as a phenomenon, that we need to concentrate on. The question then becomes: Need the various connotations of a verbal concept have anything in common?

This is a problem to which Wittgenstein devoted a great deal of his work, and I wish to argue that it is his revelations about thought and language that will show us a way out of our present difficulty. In order to appreciate this analytical advance, let us further construe the definition of a concept as the idea of a class of objects. We have taken it for granted that a class is, as the dictionary defines it, a number of individuals known by a common name in virtue of some respect in which they are alike. When we describe a class we specify what is common to all members of it; and when we say that an individual belongs to that class we ascribe to it whatever property or properties that it has in common with the other members of the class. This traditional conception of a class is basic to formal logic, forms part of our implicit psychology, and is confirmed by the practical employment of substantives in language. An excellent illustration of this conventional acceptation of the notion of a class is to be found in a nineteenth-century pictorial technique which not only displays the view that Wittgenstein argued against, but which also demonstrates an interesting convergence in the history of ideas.

In 1879, Francis Galton, after conversation with Herbert Spencer, turned his restlessly curious mind to the task of discovering what were the 'typical characteristics' in the faces of intellectual families and of criminals, the former constituting a class formed by heredity, the latter a class formed by psychological tendencies. The method consisted in superimposing tracings of their features, or alternatively in making a brief exposure of each face on to one photographic plate.[2] The results, he wrote (Galton 1879: 133), were peculiarly convincing:

These ideal [composite] faces have a surprising air of reality. Nobody who glanced at one of them for the first time, would doubt its being the likeness of a living person, yet ... it is no such thing; it is the portrait of a type and not of an individual.

Now it is precisely in such a way, it has generally been thought, that concepts are formed in the mind. Common features are noticed among a number of individuals and are abstracted; these features then compose a definition of the class that is made up by the individuals. It was this analogy that struck Vygotsky (1962: 80) in 1934:

According to the classical school, concept formation is achieved by the same process as the 'family portrait' in Galton's composite photographs. These are made by taking pictures of different members of a family, so that the 'family' traits common to several people stand out with extra-ordinary vividness, while the differing personal traits of individuals are blurred by the superimposition. A similar intensification of traits shared by a number of objects is supposed to occur in concept formation; according to traditional theory, the sum of these traits *is* the concept.

Vygotsky's investigations showed, however, that in reality the path by which adolescents arrive at concept formation 'never conforms to this logical schema'. Instead, he argued, concept formation is a complex movement of thought, 'constantly alternating ... from the particular to the general, and from the general to the particular'. The various means by which children progress from the apprehension of unorganized congeries of things to true concepts are described in his chap. 5, 'An Experimental Study of Concept Formation.' For the moment, though, we need only stress the relevance of his results to the definition of a class by reference to a common feature. The concept of belief has been treated as though it reflected a class of states of mind or experiences which shared a common definitive characteristic; but Vygotsky's psychological experiments prove that a concept is not necessarily formed in this way.

In 1933-4, in the period when Vygotsky's work was to appear in its first Russian edition, Wittgenstein was dictating to his class at Cambridge the investigations which were later to become known

[2] Galton decently acknowledges, as well as Spencer's parallel idea, the prior invention of the method by A. L. Austin, of New Zealand, who had written about it to Charles Darwin on 6 November 1877.

I

as *The Blue Book*. A dominant concern in that work was to expose the far-reaching consequences of 'our craving for generality'. This craving is the resultant, he writes, of a number of tendencies connected with particular philosophical confusions. The first is the tendency 'to look for something in common to all the entities which we commonly subsume under a single term' (1958: 17). For example, we are inclined to think that there must be something in common to all games, and that this common property is the justification for applying the general term 'game' to the various games,

whereas games form a *family* the members of which have family likenesses. Some of them have the same nose, others the same eyebrows and others again the same way of walking; and these likenesses overlap. The idea of a general concept being a common property of its particular instances connects up with other primitive, too simple, ideas of the structure of language. It is comparable to the idea that *properties* are *ingredients* of the things which have the properties. . . .

Another tendency, he continues (18), is to think that someone who has learned to understand a general term, e.g., 'leaf', has thereby come to possess a kind of general picture of a leaf, as opposed to pictures of particular leaves.

We say that he sees what is common to all these leaves; and this is true if we mean that he can on being asked tell us certain features or properties which they have in common. But we are inclined to think that the general idea of a leaf is something like a visual image, but one which only contains what is common to all leaves. (Galtonian composite photograph.)

It is an intriguing coincidence that both Vygotsky and Wittgenstein should in the same period have taken Galton's composite portraits in order to illustrate the traditional definition, which they similarly desired to controvert, of what a concept is. It is odd, too, that whereas both of them seized on the metaphor of a 'family', Vygotsky stayed close to Galton and called family traits those features common to several people, whereas Wittgenstein designated as family likenesses a number of traits which occurred sporadically, none of which might be common to all of the individuals. The contrast between these acceptations is itself a telling demonstration of the danger which may lie hidden under the surface of a familiar and non-technical word: for Vygotsky, the word 'family' was most apt to express the common-features view of a concept,[3] yet for

[3] See also, however, the place at which Vygotsky adduces the example of

Wittgenstein it was just the word with which to escape from that view.[4]

Whatever the idiom resorted to, the craving for generality has, according to Wittgenstein, another main source, namely our preoccupation with the method of science. By this is meant, for instance, the method of reducing the explanation of natural phenomena to the smallest possible number of primitive natural laws, whereas it can never be the philosopher's task, Wittgenstein maintains, to reduce anything to anything: 'Philosophy really *is* "purely descriptive"' (1958: 18). In this connection, he explains, instead of speaking of a craving for generality he could well have said 'the contemptuous attitude towards the particular case' (18) or 'contempt for what seems the less general case' (19). But however the tendency responsible may be described, the consequences of adhering to the conventional definition of a class or a general concept have been serious (1958: 19–20):

'family names', e.g., Petrov, as an instance of complex thinking, in which the bonds between components are concrete and factual rather than abstract and logical (1962: 61).
  [4] Another dimension is given to the metaphor, incidentally, by Dugald Stewart's previous observation: 'I am inclined to think that what we call *family-likeness*, consists rather in a similarity of expression than of features...' (1792–1827, 3 [1827]: 5; original emphasis). Bergson, too, writes that memories present themselves grouped into 'families' according to their relations of 'kinship' and resemblance (1901: 710). Cf. Durkheim and Mauss on the significance, in the study of classification, of the etymological connection between 'family' and 'genus' (1963: 8).
  In a more explicitly philosophical parallel, and so long ago as 1765, Lichtenberg (1968, 1: 13) wrote:

Nature does not create *genera* and *species*, she creates *individua*, and it is our shortsightedness which makes us look for resemblances, so that we shall be able to retain in our minds many things at once. These concepts become more and more inaccurate the larger the families that we make up.

Wittgenstein does not mention Lichtenberg's name in the *Tractatus* or in the *Philosophical Investigations*, but G. H. von Wright tells us that Wittgenstein 'esteemed him highly' (in Malcolm 1966: 21), and we have it from Stern that he spoke of him with 'great admiration' (1959: 161 n.). Von Wright, in making the point that Lichtenberg's conception of philosophy as linguistic analysis (*Sprachkritik*) is represented in modern times by Wittgenstein, nevertheless thinks it 'out of the question' that Wittgenstein was influenced by Lichtenberg (von Wright 1942: 215, 217). But the metaphor of the 'family' (*Geschlecht, Familie*), in connection with the constitution of classes, does make an interesting association between them, all the same.

The idea that in order to get clear about the meaning of a general term one had to find the common element in all its applications has shackled philosophical investigation; for it has not only led to no results, but also made the philosopher dismiss as irrelevant the concrete cases which alone could have helped him to understand the usage of the general term.

Now all of this will have struck any philosopher as an exceedingly bare and elementary exposition of a well-known development in modern philosophy. I could not very well claim that it was anything else, but to that professional objection I must make the defence that this revolutionary reappraisal by Wittgenstein of the notions of class and concept has so far had no marked effect on the thinking of social anthropologists, at any rate, and they are precisely the people in whose work such a reappraisal could have the widest consequences (Needham 1971c). Philosophers may think it strange, also, to cite the preliminary and fairly diffuse *Blue Book* rather than the more rigorous recapitulations in the *Philosophical Investigations*, written ten or more years later, but I begin with the earlier work mainly because of the date: to mark the convergence of Wittgenstein's philosophical criticism with Vygotsky's psychological experiments, and also to stress how many decades it may take for even the most genial idea to have its effect on work outside the discipline in which it was first propounded. In any case, if there are readers who are interested in the concept of belief but have not well appreciated the momentous significance of this turning-point in conceptual analysis, it is appropriate to convey it to them in its historical setting. With these precautionary notes of explanation, therefore, let me now take up some of Wittgenstein's examples in order to show what is their relevance to the study of the concept of belief.

II

The obvious case to begin with is that of games, an example which has acquired a near-classic status in modern philosophy. Wittgenstein introduces the topic in the *Blue Book*, as we have seen, and later develops the theme in *Philosophical Investigations*. This paradigm case should best be presented in his own words (1953, secs. 66–67):

Consider for example the proceedings that we call 'games'. I mean board-games, card-games, ball-games, Olympic games, and so on. What is common to them all?—Don't say: 'There must be something common, or they would not be called "games"'—but *look and see* whether there is anything common to all.—For if you look at them you will not see something that is common to *all*, but similarities, relationships, and a whole series of them at that. To repeat: don't think, but look!—Look for example at board-games, with their multifarious relationships. Now pass to card-games; here you find many correspondences with the first group, but many common features drop out, and others appear. When we pass next to ball-games, much that is common is retained, but much is lost.—Are they all 'amusing'? Compare chess with noughts and crosses. Or is there always winning and losing, or competition between players? Think of patience. In ball games there is winning and losing; but when a child throws his ball at the wall and catches it again, this feature has disappeared. Look at the parts played by skill and luck; and at the difference between skill in chess and skill in tennis. Think now of games like ring-a-ring-a-roses; here is the element of amusement, but how many other characteristic features have disappeared! And we can go through the many, many other groups of games in the same way; can see how similarities crop up and disappear.

And the result of this examination is: we see a complicated network of similarities overlapping and criss-crossing: sometimes overall similarities, sometimes similarities of detail.

I can think of no better expression to characterize these similarities than 'family resemblances'; for the various resemblances between members of a family: build, features, colour of eyes, gait, temperament, etc. etc. overlap and criss-cross in the same way.—And I shall say: 'games' form a family.

The kinds of number, Wittgenstein continues, also form a family in this way. We call something a number because, perhaps, it has a direct relationship with several things that have hitherto been called number; and this can be said to give it an indirect relationship to other things that we call by the same name (1953, sec. 67). Then, the illuminating metaphor:

And we extend our concept of number as in spinning a thread we twist fibre on fibre. And the strength of the thread does not reside in the fact that some one fibre runs through its whole length, but in the overlapping of many fibres.[5]

With the general idea now established, we may better appreciate

[5] Also, in *The Blue Book*: 'What ties the ship to the wharf is a rope, and the rope consists of fibres, but it does not get its strength from any fibre that runs through it from one end to the other, but from the fact that there is a vast number of fibres overlapping' (1958: 87).

the crucial importance of Wittgenstein's analysis of the constitution
of a class, in relation to our present inquiry, by reviewing some of his
observations on a number of verbal concepts standing for activities,
experiences, or inner states, and culminating with further adversions
on his part to the concept of belief itself.

First, seeing. 'The concept of "seeing" makes a tangled impression' (1953: 200) and indeed, says Wittgenstein, it is tangled. If we
look at a landscape we see all sorts of distinct and indistinct movement; one feature makes a sharp impression, another is quite hazy.
What we actually see can appear 'completely ragged'. We see
things, too, under variable aspects, and it is possible to bring about
in ourselves an effortless transition from the seeing of one aspect
to another according to the interpretation that we put upon the
object, or the dimension in which we see it. 'There is not *one
genuine* proper case of such description.'

Next, if we look closely at a number of instances of comparing,
it is very easy to see a great number of activities and states of mind,
all more or less characteristic of the act of comparing. 'We know a
vast number of such processes, processes similar to each other in a
vast number of ways. . . . The more such cases we observe and the
closer we look at them, the more doubtful we feel about finding
one particular mental experience characteristic of comparing.' If it
were conceded that a specific mental experience might be isolated
as the experience of comparing, such that the word 'comparing'
would be used only in cases where this peculiar feeling had occurred,
there would still remain to be accounted for the vast number of
other cases from which the definitive instances had been isolated,
and the point of looking for the real comparison would be lost.
For the 'specific experience' we were looking for turns out to be
just one among a number of more or less characteristic experiences.
A careful scrutiny of the actual uses of the word 'comparing' shows
that 'what connects all the cases of comparing is a vast number of
overlapping similarities, and as soon as we see this, we feel no
longer compelled to say that there must be some one feature
common to them all' (1958: 85—7).

Being guided in a certain course sounds a straightforward enough
business, observable and clearly describable. But just what does this
experience consist in? Here are some cases. Being led by the hand,
blind-folded, and responding to the tug of the guide's hand, turning
to left or right and taking care not to stumble at an unexpected tug.
Being led unwillingly by the hand, by force. To be guided by a

partner in a dance, making yourself as receptive as possible in order to sense the partner's intention. Someone takes you for a walk; you carry on a conversation, and you go wherever he goes. Or you walk along a field-track, simply following it. 'All these situations are similar to one another; but what is common to all the experiences?' If the response is made that surely being guided is a particular experience, the reason is that one is thinking of a particular experience of being guided, not of the class of such cases (1953, secs. 172–3).

We tend to think of experiences of this kind in terms of feeling, but the concept of feeling also is various. If a water-diviner says that he can feel in his hand that there is water three feet under the ground, one may answer that one does not know what this means. 'But the diviner will say: "Surely you know what it means. You know what 'three feet under the ground' means, and you know what 'I feel' means!" But I should answer him: I know what a word means *in certain contexts*.' If one is not a diviner one does not know how to interpret his report, for it hangs on questions of mensuration, tactual sensation, and the correlations of different phenomena which are obscure to the uninitiated and which are not immediately conveyed by the ordinary terms of description. A new context implies a new use of the word 'to feel', and it cannot be presumed that the meaning in this case will have anything in common with its employment in other contexts (1958: 9–10).

To expect something is one of the commonest events in consciousness and in everyday report, but what happens in a state of expectation? Suppose you expect someone to come to tea between 4 and 4:30. This description does not refer to one process or state of mind going on throughout that interval, but to a great many activities and states of mind. For example, you may look at your diary and check that the person is coming on that day; you prepare tea for two; think for a moment whether the visitor smokes, and then put out cigarettes; feel impatient as 4:30 approaches, imagine how the guest will look when he arrives, and so on. All this is called 'expecting' someone from 4 to 4:30. There are endless variations on this process, all of which we describe by the same expression. 'If one asks what the different processes of expecting someone to tea have in common, the answer is that there is no single feature in common to all of them, though there are many common features overlapping. These cases of expectation form a family; they have family likenesses which are not clearly defined' (1958: 20).

Similar analyses can be carried out on other verbal concepts such as 'reading' (1953, sec. 156; 1958: 119), 'understanding' (1953, secs. 139–54), and 'wishing' (1958: 19). The very concept of 'similar', on which depend both the activity of comparing and the search for common features, is itself susceptible to this kind of critical treatment (1958: 135).

Now it is deporable that the examples that I have sketched out here have had to be so much reduced from the full effectiveness of their originals; but even such compressed indications as these should have given some idea of the consequences of Wittgenstein's analyses for the conventional acceptation of a concept as a class of objects. With this background, therefore, we can next take up his examination, in *The Brown Book* (which was dictated in 1934–5), of the concept of belief. He starts by dealing with belief together with the concept of meaning what one says (1958: 144–5). Here also:

... Many different criteria distinguish, under different circumstances, cases of believing what you say from those of not believing what you say. There may be cases where the presence of a sensation other than those bound up with gestures, tone of voice etc. distinguishes meaning what you say from not meaning it. But sometimes what distinguishes these two is nothing that happens while we speak, but a variety of actions and experiences of different kinds before and after.

It is possible for some feeling to accompany meaning what we say, but it is also possible for the feeling characteristic of meaning a certain utterance in a certain situation not to accompany meaning another utterance in another situation. 'It is even possible while lying to have quite strong experience of what might be called the characteristic for meaning what one says' (1958: 146). Whatever justification we may have in associating a specific experience with meaning what one says, because of certain situations in which we think we can discern it, there are yet other circumstances which give the lie to this association.

Similarly, then, 'If by "believing" we mean an activity, a process, taking place while we say that we believe, we may say that believing is something similar to or the same as expressing a belief' (1958: 146). But: 'If I [say]—what I do not believe—that there exist superhuman beings of human form who can be called gods, and if I say "I fear the wrath of the gods", this shows that I can mean something by doing so, or can express a feeling, which is not necessarily connected with any belief' (Wittgenstein 1967b: 240).

We therefore cannot say that believing is a specific experience which accompanies all expressions of belief. The meaning of an expression of belief depends on the context in which it is uttered, and there is no necessity to postulate a specific experience of believing in order to interpret the context. We use the word 'believing' in such a way that it refers to 'certain acts, states of mind, given certain circumstances' (1958: 147).

This does not mean that there is *no* difference between speaking, believing what one says, and speaking, not believing what one says (1958: 152).

But the pair 'believing'/'not believing' refers to various differences in different cases (differences forming a family), not to one difference, that between the presence and the absence of a certain mental state.

III

The investigations of Vygotsky and of Wittgenstein thus give us sound reason to think that belief is not a concept in the sense of a class of phenomena defined by a common feature.

Vygotsky shows that this mode of definition is not necessarily, or perhaps even generally, the pattern on which concepts are formed or apprehended, and Wittgenstein shows that it is not the way that verbal concepts are actually employed. Belief, in these genetic and pragmatic respects, is thus comparable with many other concepts; it is subject to the same method of explication or resolution, and loses something of its apparent singularity. But before we try to interpret the concept of belief by reference to 'family likenesses',[6] it is advisable to construe this analytical notion a little more minutely.

Let us take an example, from *The Brown Book*, in which Wittgenstein comes unusually close to an explicit statement of the matter (1958: 117). He is considering the vast network of family likenesses which connects the cases in which the expressions of possibility 'can', 'to be able to', etc. are used:

Certain characteristic features, we may say, appear in these cases in different combinations: there is, e.g., the element of conjecture (that

[6] If this phrase were not so well established, they might perhaps better be termed, more formally at any rate and with less chance of sociological ambiguity, 'serial likenesses', 'sporadic likenesses', or something of the sort.

something will behave in a certain way in the future); the description of the state of something (as a condition for its behaving in a certain way in the future); the account of certain tests someone or something has passed.

These features are distinct from various reasons which induce us to look at the fact of something being possible, someone being able to do something, etc., as the fact that he or it is in a particular state.

We can grasp well enough the grounds for this distinction, but there remains a possible uncertainty about the incidence of the 'characteristic features', and it is this which (if I have understood the point correctly) it is important to construe. It might be thought, namely, that these characteristic features defined the class of cases, so that they would in effect be properties common to members of the class. Expressions of possibility would then be those which comprised the element of conjecture, description of a state, and so on; and these features would thus appear to be essential to the concept. It is necessary, however, not to fall into this interpretation. It is true that the adjective 'characteristic' is a temptation to do so, but it is a reading which radically conflicts with Wittgenstein's constant concern and with the outcome of his several analyses. The clue is that these likenesses are 'more or less' characteristic of the cases in question. In looking at cases of comparing, for instance, 'it is very easy to see a great number of activities and states of mind, all *more or less* characteristic of the act of comparing' (1958: 86; original emphasis). The features can occur sporadically and in 'different combinations'; they can 'disappear' (1953, sec. 66); their incidence is literally incidental, not essential. Thus there are what can be called 'characteristic experiences' of pointing to the shape of something, e.g., following the outline with one's finger or with one's eyes as one points; but this does not happen in all cases in which I 'mean the shape' (rather than the colour, for instance) of what I point to, 'and no more does any other one characteristic process occur in all these cases' (1953, sec. 35). Similarly, 'there is not one definite class of features which characterize all cases of wishing' (1958: 19), and so on. Besides, even if one characteristic feature did recur in all cases, the interpretation of the act or state would still depend on the circumstances (1953, sec. 35).

When, by contrast, Wittgenstein looks for what is usually supposed to be definitive, in the sense of an attribute common to all members of the class (all cases covered by the concept), he writes instead of a 'specific' feature or experience. And this is exactly what in one concept after another he demonstrates to be lacking: 'We never wanted the specific experience to be just one among a number of *more or less* characteristic experiences' (1958: 86; original emphasis).

It might, then, be feasible in principle to abstract the characteristic features of believing, but this procedure would be quite distinct from the isolation of a specific feature that would constitute the real and essential significance of the concept of belief. And in any case, even supposing we could find something that happened in all cases of believing, why should that feature be the believing?[7]

IV

The best that we in our turn might hope to do, therefore, would be to discern the characteristic features of believing, and to take this fluctuating set of features as the grounds for the concept.

But whereas we can find such features in the instances of comparing, for example, the search for criteria carried out in chap. 6 gives no occasion to think that there are any which are characteristic of believing. I need not try to demonstrate this negative conclusion, with special reference to characteristic features, since to do so would entail a tedious recapitulation of the arguments for and against the supposed criteria, only in differing combinations of factors considered and with different emphases, according to the features selected as characteristic. We can however usefully take up a separate question of the kind.

Wittgenstein suggests that the differences between the various cases of believing/not believing form a family, as though these differences could be thought of as characteristic features; but he does not elaborate this view, and it is not at all evident in what respects they do form a family of likenesses by difference. Let us consider the following typical statements of belief: 'I believe in God', 'I believe what he says', and 'I believe she is coming to tea'. Then let us contrast with them the several denials of these expressions. Obviously, to say 'I do not believe in God' is quite different from the first assertion; 'I do not believe what he says' is similarly different from the second; and there is a like difference again

---

[7] Cf. Wittgenstein (1953, sec. 153): '. . . even supposing I had found something that happened in all those cases of understanding,—why should *it* be the understanding?'

between the statements about believing and not believing that some-one is coming to tea. But there is, so far as I can make out, no family resemblance among these differences other than the similarity—which is in fact a precise identity of construction—among the grammatical forms by which the believing/not believing pairs of statements are contrasted. The same grammatical recourse for formulating the denial of belief, in different contexts, does not however yield any characteristic feature by which a non-grammatical difference between believing and not believing can be determined.

If this conclusion is right, nevertheless, it remains in accord with Wittgenstein's view that there is no single difference, namely that between the presence and the absence of a specific mental state, between believing and not believing. The distinction is to be found in the facts of language, not in experience.

V

The conventional force of expressions of belief is that they are taken to report a distinct and specific experience; yet the cumulative results of our investigation argue insistently that we get this idea, not from experiential introspection and observation, but from a word and from the linguistic conventions by which its use is governed.

Ordinary discourse and the common-sense psychology that is in part its product tend to induce us into two capital errors: first, the assumption that there must be something in common to all instances of believing; second, the assumption that there must be a mental counterpart to the expression of belief. An equally fallacious inference derives from the conjunction of these two assumptions, namely that what is common (and thus essential) to all instances of believing is the manifestation of the mental event or state. Wittgenstein offers (1958: 41–2) a rule of thumb for the removal of such temptations:

If you are puzzled about the nature of thought, belief, knowledge, and the like, substitute for the thought the expression of the thought, etc. The difficulty which lies in this substitution, and at the same time the whole point of it, is this: the expression of belief, thought, etc., is just a sentence;—and the sentence has sense only as a member of a system of language; as one expression within a calculus.

We are tempted to imagine this calculus, he says, as a kind of permanent background to every sentence that we say, and to think that although the sentence stands isolated in writing or in spoken words, the calculus exists as an entity in the mental act of thinking, etc. 'The mental act seems to perform in a miraculous way what could not be performed by any act of manipulating symbols.' But when the idea that the whole calculus must somehow be present at the same time vanishes, there is no point any longer in *postulating* the existence of a peculiar kind of mental act alongside the expression. 'This, of course, doesn't mean that we have shown that peculiar acts of consciousness do not accompany the expressions of our thoughts! Only we no longer say that they *must* accompany them' (42).

In the case of belief, there is no denying that a peculiar kind of mental act, or a distinct state, has normally been thought to correspond to expressions of belief. This idea has been most explicit in theology, but it is general in all types of discourse and over centuries of learned debate and philosophical disquisition. Perhaps, therefore, there will be some resistance to the suggestion that the erroneous assumptions isolated by Wittgenstein are at the root of our puzzlement over belief. Nevertheless, as far as the supposed inner state is concerned, we have been able to discover absolutely no evidence of its existence; and even those who are most convinced of its reality are forced in the end to concede that they cannot give any account of it.

On the other hand, there is no reason to think that the expressions of belief are so remarkable or singular that the concept deserves a special status. 'Belief' is indeed a word of extremely ramified and extended uses, but there is nothing essentially unusual about it in these respects. Its use often appears confused, also, but in this regard it is merely like other psychological verbs; 'nor', with such verbs, 'can we expect anything else' (Wittgenstein 1967a, sec. 113). We find it difficult, or even impossible, to provide a description of its regular employment; but, as Wittgenstein says of the word 'thinking', it is not to be expected of this word that it should have a unified employment. We are not at all prepared for the task of describing its use, for there is no reason (outside philosophy) and no purpose for which we need to do so (1967a, secs. 111–2). 'In general, we don't use language according to strict rules—it hasn't been taught to us by strict rules, either' (1958: 25).

If we find it difficult to circumscribe the concept of belief, this is not because we do not know its real definition but because it has no 'real' definition (cf. 1958: 25). If it has no such definition, it is the more unlikely to denote a real and specific experience.

VI

To speak of the real introduces an illuminating parallel drawn by Waismann in his remarks on the concept of 'reality', and these will enable us to get a still clearer view of the concept of belief.

He calls into question the assumption that there is a clearly bounded domain called 'the real', and the implication that it is one of the tasks of the philosopher to define it sharply. In fact, he maintains, the evidence that there is such a domain is very slender. 'Not that I deny for a moment,' he continues, 'that a word like "reality" is a blessing; it definitely is.' Its usefulness is demonstrated by such phrases as 'A tautology does not say anything about reality', 'Pure mathematics is not concerned with reality', or 'In reality it was not Smith I saw but his brother'. The word is very convenient, and if it were not already in use we should have to invent it. 'On the other hand, when a philosopher looks closely at it, tears it from the context and asks himself, "Now what *is* reality?" he has successfully manoeuvred himself into a fairly awkward position' (Waismann 1968: 57). Here Waismann is developing a point made by Wittgenstein in *The Blue Book*, and one which enables us to see better how it is that the word 'belief' has shown such persistence and has maintained such a prominence in so many varied contexts; also why it causes so much trouble when we analyse it.

Wittgenstein makes his case by way of certain observations on the concept of 'meaning'. This, he writes, is 'one of the words of which we may say that they have odd jobs in our language' (1958: 43–4):

It is these words which cause most philosophical troubles. Imagine some institution: most of its members have certain regular functions, functions which can easily be described, say, in the statutes of the institution. There are, on the other hand, some members who are employed for odd jobs, which may nevertheless be extremely important.—What causes most trouble in philosophy is that we are tempted to describe the use of important 'odd-job' words as though they were words with regular functions.

This point is taken up, and made rather more explicit, by Waismann (1968: 59), who employs a different metaphor and puts the matter in this way:

There is a group of words such as 'fact', 'event', 'situation', 'case', 'circumstance', which display a queer sort of behaviour. One might say of such words that they serve as pegs: it's marvellous what a lot of things you can put on them. . . . So far they are very handy; but as soon as one focuses on them and asks, e.g., 'What *is* a fact?' they betray a tendency to melt away. The peg-aspect is by far the most important of all.

Now if there is one substantive which performs a great number of important odd-job functions, or serves as a peg for the support of an extraordinary variety of types of proposition, it is the word 'belief'.[8] It is in fact precisely this aspect of it that has repeatedly frustrated every attempt at a unitary or regular interpretation. Again and again we have found that as soon as we focus upon it and ask 'What *is* belief?' the concept disintegrates.

An immediate inference, therefore, is that belief really is not likely to be a discriminable inner state, and that we were right to conclude that phenomenally it has no specific features. We have been taken in, it appears, by one of the great sources of philosophical bewilderment: 'a substantive makes us look for a thing that corresponds to it' (Wittgenstein 1958: 1).

[8] Cf. above, chap. 4, sec. I. It is a distinct problem why the Sanskrit *pratyaya* should have an even more variegated range of meanings (chap. 3, sec. II).
Waismann himself actually alludes to belief under this aspect (though as a matter of fact I did not notice that he had done so until I was well into my own inquiry and had got this lead from Wittgenstein). In discussing the concept of understanding (1965: 351), he writes: 'We do not use "understanding" to refer to any *one* process, which accompanies reading or hearing, but to various combinations of processes more or less akin, and namely those of the actual use of language. Although saying that understanding is a "mental process" describes correctly the use of the word in a number of cases, this description becomes a source of confusion if it is applied to all cases. It likens understanding to a definite *process*, e.g. the occurrences of a series of characteristic experiences; and it suggests similar analyses for thinking, knowing, believing, wishing, fearing, etc. We see in all these cases that what we naïvely should give as the sign of a psychic process is not characteristic for all or even the majority of cases. From this the next inference is that the essential feature of the process is something as yet undiscovered, and difficult to apprehend.'

VII

Writing about the concept of imagination, Wittgenstein argues that one ought to ask, not what images are or what happens when one imagines anything, but how the word 'imagination' is used. 'But that does not mean that I want to talk only about words. For to the extent that my question is about the word "imagination", it is also about the nature of imagination' (1953, sec. 370).[9] Thus, 'Grammar tells us what kind of object something is' (sec. 373).

Does this mean, then, that what is needed in the present case is an improved grammar of belief? Hardly, for in a literal sense it is our minute knowledge of the grammar that makes our investigation so difficult, and reveals to us the full intricacy of the concept the grounds of which we are trying to understand. As Wittgenstein (1953: 192) maintains,[10]

When you say 'Suppose I believe...' you are presupposing the whole grammar of the word 'believe', the ordinary use of which you are master.—You are not supposing some state of affairs which, so to speak, is clearly presented to your view by a picture, so that you can then tack on to this supposition some use other than the usual one.—You would not know at all what you were supposing here (i.e., what, for example, would follow from this supposition) if you were not already familiar with the employment of 'believe'.

We can thus be masters, as we are, of the practical grammar of belief-statements, yet remain wholly unconvinced that these rest on any objective foundations in psychic experience. Indeed, one of the most powerful factors in the persistence of many crucial problems in the analysis of belief is the fact that it is a mastery of the grammar that has provided philosophers with their very terms of discourse. This is a prime reason why there can be such unresolved contradictions among them. Each philosopher adopts, more or less

---

[9] 'Denn soweit in meiner Frage vom Wort "Vorstellung" die Rede ist, ist sie's auch in der Frage nach dem Wesen der Vorstellung.' The published translation does not make clear sense: 'For the question as to the nature of the imagination is as much about the word "imagination" as my question is.'

[10] Translation slightly modified. (I should state at this point that in quite a number of places below I have departed from the printed translations of Wittgenstein, but have reported that I have done so only when there is a significant discrepancy of sense.)

arbitrarily, a different acceptation of belief from among the kaleido-
scopic representations in current usage; and because they write
about the same word, or about similar statements, they then sound
as though they were advancing different theories about the same (if
complex) thing. It is against this background that our investigation must certainly be in part a grammatical one. As Wittgenstein
(1953, sec. 90) contends,

Such an investigation sheds light on our problem by clearing misunderstandings away. Misunderstandings concerning the use of words, caused,
among other things, by certain analogies between the forms of expression
in different regions of language.—Some of them can be removed by
substituting one form of expression for another. . . .

In our present inquiry, we can see that analogies among the
forms of expression of belief, in many quite different contexts, have
conduced to the assumption that belief is a distinct and unitary
phenomenon; and some of the misunderstandings implicit in this
amalgamation can certainly be removed by substituting one form of
expression for another. This is what Braithwaite, in expounding an
empiricist's view of religious belief (1955: 32), has in fact done in
one type of context:

I have . . . taken my task to be that of explaining the use of [religious]
assertions, in accordance with the principle that meaning is to be found
by ascertaining use. In disentangling the elements of this use I have
discovered nothing which can be termed 'belief' in the senses of this
word normally applicable either to an empirical or to a logically necessary
proposition.

We need not rehearse the course of the investigation by which
Braithwaite arrives at this conclusion, especially since he confines
his attention to what is distinguished as religious belief. The central point is that in effect he is claiming that the verbal concept of
belief can be, as it were, translated away. Doubtless there will be
dissent from this outcome, particularly on the part of religious believers in the western tradition, but there is undeniably a serious contention to argue about. According to an able and responsible philosopher, the very word 'belief' is not essential to the language in
which religious beliefs are expressed: whatever is asserted by means
of this word can equally be expressed, from logical and empirical
points of view, by other words. I am not sure to what extent, outside
the limits of his own inquiry, Braithwaite would wish to maintain this position; but there is no doubt that in many of its

K

non-religious uses as well the word 'belief' (and its inflected forms) can very well be translated away, and it is a question whether there is any belief-statement which cannot be treated in the same way.

If this is so, the presumptively specific experience of belief will once more be shown to have no basis in fact—this time, in the facts of language. We cannot however draw this inference directly, and without qualification, for 'We speak of understanding a sentence in the sense in which it can be understood by another which says the same; but also in the sense in which it cannot be replaced by any other' (Wittgenstein 1953, sec. 531). So whereas we can in many types of context translate belief away by rendering it as assent, expectation, supposition, confidence, uncertainty, and so on, there might still remain a specific significance that could not at all be conveyed by any other verbal means. This is certainly a position adopted by theologians, but they then resort to a supposed spiritual faculty for which there is no independent evidence, as we have seen, and which they themselves concede is in the end indescribable in words. It is also the position taken by philosophers, such as Kant, who seek to reform the grammar of common usage by framing a technical connotation of belief, but this also is no argument in favour of an irreducible character in belief. Moreover, whereas it is true of a sentence that it can have a meaning which cannot be rendered by any equivalent sentence, the situation is not necessarily the same when the meaning of a word is in question. In the case of belief, if there is a specific content which cannot be verbally expressed at all, let alone be translated by any other word, then no object of critical attention remains. On the other hand, the word certainly has a variety of connotations such that the notion of belief is in fact progressively translated away as these separable meanings are serially isolated; and at no point in our repeated analyses have we been able to discover a central or ultimate meaning. In either event, the conclusion holds that a word does not entail the existence of a thing that corresponds to it.

But it must at once be admitted that the converse does not obtain: i.e., we cannot infer from the absence of a word that a certain thing does not exist. There may be what Whorf calls a 'covert concept' or a 'cryptotype', namely a latent notion that can have 'a very subtle meaning, and . . . may have no overt mark other than certain distinctive "reactances" with certain overtly marked forms' (Whorf 1956: 70–1). According to Whorf, the most impressively penetrating logical discriminations in some African and North

American languages are often those that are revealed by analysing to the covert or cryptotypic level; and such 'covert categories', moreover, are 'quite apt to be more rational than overt ones' (80). It may even be, he suggests, that many abstract ideas arise in this way, and that only later may a covert idea be 'more or less duplicated in a word and a lexical concept invented by a philosopher, e.g., causation' (80, 81). These contentions have consequences for the argument suggested above (chap. 3, sec. III), to the effect that the experiential reality of belief is called into question by the existence of languages in which there are no exact lexical equivalents to the word 'belief'. If the concept can exist as a covert category, then the absence of an overt denotation in the form of a separate word is not evidence that the concept itself is lacking. For that matter, there might even be a specific experience of belief, after all, only one that corresponded in certain languages to a cryptotypical discrimination rather than to a specific verbal denotation.

We have in fact already encountered a possible indication of the existence of a covert concept of belief, as demonstrated by the inheritance and distribution throughout the Indonesian archipelago of a Sanskritic word for 'believe'. It could be that the far-scattered and culturally diverse peoples who all adopted this word (*pratyaya*) into their languages showed thereby that they had previously no distinct terms of their own to express belief. The inference proposes itself that the superiority of Sanskrit, in the discrimination of psychic states as in much else, then gave the Indonesians the lexical facility to recognize in themselves a discriminable mode of consciousness for which their languages provided various indications but no precise denotation. Otherwise, it might be asked, why should this particular word have had such a widespread, thorough, and tenacious reception? This question is practically impossible to resolve etymologically, after such a great lapse of time and in the case of mostly unwritten languages. Dempwolff, for instance, does not include 'believe' in his reconstructed vocabulary of 'Uraustronesisch' (1938), and there is no ready means of determining the existence, forms, or application of any original Indonesian words for this concept. However, a wider examination of the issue argues against this interesting conjecture. Gonda's extensive survey (1961) displays the very great effect of Sanskrit, throughout the archipelago and in a very large number of respects, and this knowledge of the general influence of the language, in respects other than belief, permits a better estimation of the possibility in question. Against this background, Maxwell's sketch of the Sanskrit element in Malay (1888: 41–5) is of particular value of (cf. Marsden 1795). He sets out, in a list which is not professed to be complete, a total of no fewer than twenty-seven Malay words for emotions, moral characteristics, and qualities of various kinds (25–6), all of which words have Sanskrit origins; and he also supplies parallel examples from Javanese, Sundanese, 'Dayak', Batak, Makassarese, Tagala, and Kawi, all of which have the same derivation from Sanskrit. The list does not include, strangely enough, the word for 'believe' (*perchaya*), but it does include such items as joy, sorrow, anger, hope, happiness, and thought. Now the Indonesian languages in question may have been philosophically unsubtle (as Penan, for instance, still is) before the incursion of Sanskritic influence, but it cannot readily be supposed that they lacked words for these cardinal features of human experience. It can be assumed, indeed, that they must have made lexical denotations of these features, and that their own words were superseded by Sanskritic forms. In Malay, the further accretion of terms of philosophy and religion, later taken from Arabic and introduced with the spread of conversion to Islam, shows historically that the prestige of a powerful faith or a great civilization can well modify the designation of even the most fundamental aspects of life. The fact, therefore, that early Indonesians adopted a Sanskritic word denoting belief is no proof that they previously had no equivalent word and had hence failed to discriminate this state of mind.

Whorf's notion suggests, however, that there is still a further possibility. Belief might be a special kind of cryptotypical concept, and exceedingly subtle in an unexpected way; that is, it might be a hidden and indefinite concept which nevertheless was actually marked overtly by the very word 'belief', but the essential significance of which could not be determined except by tracing its boundaries through its 'reactances' against other linguistic forms. One or more of the separable connotations of the word 'belief' might thus partly overlap, as it were, with the covert concept and serve indistinctly merely to indicate its subliminal presence. This would account for something of the range and variety of meanings that the word has in English, and also for the fact that even languages which seem to recognize belief nevertheless employ denotations that do not much coincide with the semantic scope of the English word. More importantly, it would account for some of the difficulties met with by theologians and philosophers in their attempts to locate or circumscribe belief; for it could then be seen that they were trying to do so at an inappropriately overt level and in terms that were too crude for the purpose. It may be thought that these suggestions go altogether too far—especially when the validity of Whorf's notion of a cryptotype is by no means indisputably established by his own examples—but in an investigation of this kind it is clear that we have to go to any lengths, and adopt any analytical recourse, if we are to satisfy ourselves of the true status of belief. In the event, however, I have to admit that this extreme hypothesis offers no more than a formal possibility, and that I have been able to detect no positive evidence whatever in favour of it. In our search for criteria of belief, moreover, we have drawn no lexical or arbitrary limits to inquiry, and we have in fact been led by the philosophers' confessed bafflement to look beneath linguistic forms in search of the grounds of the concept. We might therefore have got a glimpse of what we are now calling a covert concept of belief, even one that was paradoxically camouflaged rather than revealed by the word itself, but nothing of the kind has been discerned and we have no cause to think that it is to be found.

We are thus confirmed in our conclusion that the phenomenon of belief consists in no more than the custom of making statements about belief. 'We are not analysing a phenomenon . . . but a concept . . . , and therefore the use of a word' (Wittgenstein 1953, sec. 383). Yet if the meaning of a word is found by ascertaining its use, there is no necessity that any particular use shall be exclusive to that word. The odd-job uses of 'belief' can be separately rendered by other words or by the substitution of other forms of expression, and the word can be so far translated away that the concept must disintegrate in correlation with the dispersal of its connotations. If grammar tells us what kind of an object something is, then the grammar of belief tells us that there is no such object.

VIII

In this case, nevertheless, the comparative testimony of language acquires even more interest.

In order to fix our position in the terrain of human experience we turn to other languages;[11] for not only do these sometimes lack,

---

[11] Not only real languages, either. See the stories by Borges: 'Tlön, Uqbar, Orbis Tertius' (1965: 17–34) and 'The Library of Babel' (72–80).

instructively, certain features that we have taken for granted in our own, but they enable us to take back-bearings. Of course, the features on which we take our readings are themselves words, so that in this conceptual cartography there are no absolutely fixed points of reference, for each word may on closer inspection lose its sharp contours or dissolve like a mirage. But it is none the less disturbing to our sense of location to find that from the vantage-points of other languages our redoubt of belief cannot be plotted. That is, we have in English the verbal concept of belief but have not been able to delimit any grounds for the expressions by which we refer to it; and other languages accentuate this failure by evidently not needing to mark any such lexical or conceptual feature in their own charting of human capacities.

Hampshire proposes that 'we can explain and justify our use . . . of language, or of part of a language, as involving variations of those most general principles of differentiating elements in reality that we find in all types of dicourse' (1959: 14); but by this test we can neither explain nor defend the use of the word 'belief'. We cannot plausibly maintain, either, that we have a superior power of psychological apperception, conveniently expressed in the English word (i.e., in certain carefully selected senses of it); and it is quite plain that we cannot justify the word as a precise descriptive device that happens to possess advantages of which the speakers of a great many other languages are simply oblivious.

The question of belief confronts us, rather, with alternative linguistic conventions for classifying states of mind, pronouncing judgements, declaring expectations, and so on. When someone says that he believes, he is resorting to a convention appropriate to a given situation (one given, that is, by a certain cultural past and the resultant ideology and forms of social life), but he is not reporting his experience of a distinct inner state or capacity. When we say of him that he believes, similarly, we are not observing any signs of a specific mental process but are describing a feature of that social situation as it is represented in a certain language. The evidences, positive and negative, that are supplied by other languages and the associated forms of life are therefore crucial, if not decisive, for our inquiry.

Wittgenstein has suggested that 'being acquainted with many languages prevents us from taking quite seriously a philosophy which is set down in the forms of any one'; but he cautions us that we are still blind to the fact that we have strong prejudices for and against certain forms of expression, and his own conclusion is that 'this very piling up of a lot of languages results in our having a particular picture' (1967a, sec. 323). Doubtless it is true that we labour under such unrecognized prejudices, but it does not follow that a comparative acquaintance with a number of languages has any prejudicial effect on our thought. On this score it is noteworthy, rather, that Wittgenstein does not resort to the abundant materials of natural languages, and does not test what actually is the effect on our conceptions when this is done explicitly. Thus when he distinguishes two interpretations of 'expecting'—one describing a state of mind and the other not—he merely conjectures that 'we could imagine a language in which different verbs were consistently used in these cases' (1953, sec. 577). He even proposes that similarly more than one verb might be used, in the imaginary language, where we speak simply of 'believing', and he suggests that perhaps the concepts of such a language might be more suitable than those of our own for an understanding of psychology. But he does not embark on an empirical investigation in order to find out, as we have tried to do, how believing is actually represented (or if it is) and what can be learned by a comparison of other linguistic usages.

Now we do not have to imagine other languages, and there is no apparent advantage in doing so when they offer so volubly to speak for themselves. In the event, it turns out that we need not form any 'particular picture' by considering a number of languages, but can give up many of our conceptual prejudices and begin to comprehend (as an ethnographer does) in what different ways the psychic constitution of man can be conceived. Again, Wittgenstein merely speculates that 'an education quite different from ours could also be the foundation for quite different concepts' (1967a, sec. 387); but it has long been a lesson of comparative ethnography that different cultures do in fact inculcate classificatory concepts which, in some regards, are quite different from our own.[12] The problem then is

[12] For a recent survey of primitive classification, see Lévi-Strauss's *The Savage Mind* (1966). If it should be wondered at, by the way, that I have elsewhere in the present investigation paid no attention to that work, I should perhaps explain that it has simply not proved relevant to my problems. The main reason for this fact is that what Lévi-Strauss writes about is restricted precisely to classification; that is to say, he deals with the forms of collective representations rather than with the operations by which these are articulated and with the inner states of those who do so. In any case, I have to agree with Chomsky's judgement of Lévi-Strauss's book: 'I do not see what conclusions can be reached from a study of his materials beyond the fact

how to choose among this spectrum of concepts in order to arrive at a less parochial and better substantiated view of human powers.

A relevant instance, and a proof that it is feasible to select empirically from among the varied psychological classifications constructed by mankind, is to be found in Wittgenstein's example of studying the concept (and the nature) of imagination by asking how the word 'imagination' is used. This word is open to the same method of analysis as we have applied to the word 'belief' and its usage. It also has a distinct idiomatic history, and forms part of an intricate and unique conceptual tradition; it fulfils a large variety of odd-job functions, severally interpretable in different contexts, and can similarly be regarded as a very useful peg on which to hang numerous types of proposition; it possesses no specific and essential feature that is common to all of its uses; no one could suppose, either, that the concept of imagination was simple or that any definite and comprehensive account of it could well be given (cf. Sartre 1936); and in other languages, perhaps the majority, there is no lexical equivalent to the English word. But, all the same, I do not think anyone would deny that the word 'imagination' does refer—in certain contexts—to an introspectible activity or state of mind. We can produce sharp images, bearing all the visual tokens of reality, before our inner vision, and we can manipulate such images at will; it is the force of imagination that enables art to procure participation and commitment to the point of 'belief'; dreams provide a more spontaneous and independent display of that mode of experience; and a vivid and continual aspect of our lives is framed by this ready and discriminable power—'cette superbe puissance', against which Pascal, in the *Pensées* (1964: 95), directed some of his most eloquent and apprehensive warnings in defence of reason.

In the case of 'imagination' also, of course, it is certainly grammar that in part tells us what sort of an object it is, and the analysis of propositions about the imagination can give rise to philosophical problems, but at least the phenomenology is well founded. Under-

that the savage mind attempts to impose some organization on the physical world—that humans classify, if they perform any mental acts at all' (1968: 65). The materials in question tell us, at any rate, nothing for sure about the inner states of individuals with regard to the classifications they employ, and certainly nothing at all about the nature of belief. (One would give much to have Wittgenstein's views on *The Savage Mind*, if that had been chronologically possible, instead of his remarks [1967b] on *The Golden Bough*.)

lying the varied uses of the word, defined by a vast number of more or less similar (and dissimilar) contexts, there is a complex but resourceful concept; and underpinning certain characteristic features of this verbal concept there are specific and recurrent phenomena of psychic experience.

Now Hampshire says that 'the phenomenology of belief is very various' (1965: 101), Wittgenstein states that 'psychology observes the phenomena *of* . . . believing' (1967a, sec. 471; original emphasis), and Price concludes that 'belief is a complex attitude which may manifest itself in many ways' (1969: 487)—in each instance as though belief were an entity with properties. But the great difference in this latter case, in contrast with the lively manifestations of the imagination, is that we have not been able to discover any experiential grounds to the supposed phenomena 'of' belief. To put the outcome very bluntly: imagination is real, belief is not.

8

Resemblances

I

To say of belief that it does not exist as a discriminable mode of consciousness raises the question whether there are any experiential discriminations at all that are universally made by men among their states of mind.

The case of imagination certainly makes a useful contrast with the supposed experience of belief, and shows that recourse to the test of reality is feasible so far as these particular concepts are concerned, but it is only one counter-example. It does not establish those most general principles of differentiating elements in reality that we find, according to Hampshire, in all types of discourse, but merely indicates that there may in certain cases be an empirical basis to such differentiation. In assessing the phenomenal status of belief, however, what is ultimately implied is that there are standard discriminations that are made everywhere among modes of consciousness, whatever the language or the forms of social life. It is this tacit premise, suggesting that there exists an absolute basis for the appraisal of conceptions of states of mind, that now requires justification.

The idea of universal criteria of psychological classification seems intrinsically suspect, and to go against the relativity that increasingly qualifies the combined findings of science (Waismann 1968, chap. 6), modern philosophy, and social anthropology. 'There are no criteria that anything must satisfy in order to be called a thing in the wide sense of the word' (Hampshire 1959: 25). Men classify according to the conventions of their languages, and these conventions are differently shaped over time by an innumerable variety of contingent circumstances and purposes. 'The institutions of language are always developing, and the history of their development is the history of the human mind' (Hampshire 1959: 13). The mind is not a condition of language but a construct from language. The states of mind characteristic of mankind can be conceived only through the categories of language, and no language can enjoy a universal privilege as a standard authority on the discrimination of inner states. There are indeed, as Hampshire maintains, certain 'most general principles of differentiation which, as far as we can see, are used in *every* application of language to reality' (13), but these ultimate categories are, it is argued, conditions of thought: they are not particular descriptions of experiential (psychic) reality. The question, then, is whether there are any comparable constraints or predispositions which will everywhere shape men's psychological vocabularies and incline them to the common recognition of inner states.

The difficulty is that 'the vocabulary of emotions, attitudes, moods, states of mind and feelings requires that we identify our thoughts and feelings at least partly by reference to the public occasion and the circumstances of [our] situation at the time' (Hampshire 1959: 64). These occasions and circumstances are largely contingent and, especially in a comparative setting, practically in-numerable. They are differently identified by varied and changing social forms, and by means of linguistic classifications which similarly are variable cultural conventions. It would seem therefore that in order to assess the reality of any discrimination of states of mind we need somehow to stand outside both society and language. As in philosophy, the social anthropologist is 'trying to survey the human situation from some more independent standpoint, dividing that which is in some sense given in the nature of things and is necessary from that which is contingent upon changeable human convention' (Hampshire 1959: 68). But in what sense, if at all, can the things presently in question, namely states of mind, be regarded as given in nature?

II

The first and most obvious objection to the notion of natural re-semblances, in connection with inner states, is factual, and has to do with the kind of things that in this case are to be noticed and recorded. It is simply that belief and other presumed states of mind are internal and not open to direct observation in others.

There is an approximate and conditional sense in which such external objects as human beings, topographical features, and manufactures can be said to be given to the observer, and in fact all languages apply distinct designations to large repertories of things of this external kind. Every ethnographer knows that such appellations are usually very simple to learn, whereas the psychological vocabulary is a quite different matter: there is an extreme contrast between 'This is a blowpipe' and 'I believe. . . .' Yet states of mind are constant and indispensable referents in human discourse; they have to be described and their peculiar qualities communicated. As Hampshire writes, to find more and more effective ways of describing them is the most serious of all the necessary refinements of language: 'Every variety of analogy and metaphor is called into play, and, in this use of language we cannot be sure in advance that we will succeed in communicating, in making ourselves understood' (1959: 65).

But analogies and metaphors are not descriptions, i.e., they are not records of observations that can be checked. A similarity of figurative expression between one language and another, with respect to a state of mind, would show an interesting correspondence in the conception and representation of an inner experience; but the similarity would not in itself provide confirmation that there was such a distinct state or experience, or that it should be characterized by certain features. There would be a linguistic resemblance, in other words, but this would not constitute or establish a natural resemblance. In that it was linguistic, moreover, and thus a matter of convention, it could not by definition qualify as natural, so that it would merely present all the more clearly the logical difficulty in positing natural resemblances: 'How can we say what resemblances we would still notice and wish to record if we did not have any of those conventions of language, of drawing and of many other modes of representation, that we do in fact have?' (Hampshire 1959: 34).

The search for natural resemblances among states of mind, such as would be required to substantiate the notion of standard or universal discriminations, would thus appear to be empirically unfeasible and logically invalid.

III

This is a perturbing conclusion, but it is not a final obstacle; for 'there may be *some* resemblances in appearance that are in fact noticed and recorded in all known languages' (Hampshire 1959: 33), and there may similarly be some resemblances in inner states that are equally recognized.

I want to maintain, indeed, that there is one specific kind of natural resemblance among men that all human beings recognize, and which permits effective comparison across the divides of culture and language. The locus of this resemblance is provided by the human body, the one thing in nature that is internally experienced, the only object of which we have subjective knowledge.

Not that this is a novel suggestion, for the facts have long been well observed. 'There are mystically in our faces certaine characters,' wrote Sir Thomas Browne, 'which carry in them the motto of our Soules, wherein he that cannot read A.B.C. may read our natures' (1643, pt. II, sec. 2; 1955: 78). Dunbar more widely referred to such characteristics, including also tones of voice, as 'natural signs', certain of which, 'independently of art, by an inexplicable mechanism of nature, declare the purposes of man to man' (1780: 67, 80, 382-3). Dugald Stewart further took up 'the interpretation of natural signs', finding that there seems to be in man a power of understanding immediately 'certain expressions of the countenance, certain gestures of the body, and certain tones of voice'; in these respects, he concluded, there are 'natural signs of the operations and passions of mind, which are interpreted instinctively by all who see them', and this to the extent that there is even an 'agreement of different ages and nations in the employment of various signs which seem at first to be quite arbitrary' (1792–1827, vol. 3 [1827]: 6, 9, 17–18).

There are many natural resemblances of these kinds which obtain among all men everywhere, and by such signs an 'inexplicable mechanism' permits direct inferences about certain inner states of other people. There is always room for error, of course, and the expressive conventions of different cultures can variously mask or transform the manifestation of such states; but there remains a general fund of sentiment and apprehension which allows an intuitive communication, and the means by which this is effected are not conceptual but are natural signs of a common human condition. Concepts of the human being and his capacities differ greatly, from one civilization or period to another, but not the bodily intuitions of being human. The conception of pain, for instance, is a changeable cultural convention that is variously stated in language (cf. Wittgenstein 1967a, sec. 380), and to understand and translate an alien concept of pain is a formidable ethnographical task; but neither familiarity with convention nor power of analysis is required in order to grasp something essential to the inner state of a man who is actually in pain. The spectacle of a man whose leg has been broken is, in the categories peculiar to his culture, a social situation like any other: it presents all the familiar difficulties of description, causal analysis, judging of circumstances, prediction of consequences, and so on which are part of any attempt to understand an event in a foreign society. But preceding all of these objective considerations there is a subjective response that is not mediated by cultural concepts. The observer himself need not ever have suffered a broken leg, or even have experienced any painful injury to that part of his body; he need not be inspired by any moral or sympathetic concern, or put any particular interpretation on the situation. He has at once an intuitive apprehension, cumulatively prepared by the experience of his own body,[1] of the general phenomenon of physical pain, and this is prompted in him by natural signs of pain evinced by another human being.

Now it may seem that this elementary mode of apprehension is at too far a remove from 'belief' to be considered instructively, together with belief, as a state of mind, but there is a useful comparison to be made. We have concluded above (chap. 6, secs. IX, X) that there is no specific behaviour or physiognomy of belief, so that we cannot seek natural resemblances among men in this regard. But there are natural postures, gestures, and facial expressions, discernible whatever techniques of the body are customary (cf. Mauss 1935) and whatever the psychological vocabulary employed, which are intuitively recognizable and which regularly accompany certain inner states. For example, there is not only physical pain, the direct cause of which is some bodily hurt such as a broken leg; there is also moral pain, the direct cause of which is an event in human intercourse. A man who is broken by the death of his son exhibits externally the distinctive signs of grief, and no human observer needs to learn the prevailing expressive conventions of the culture, or the social interpretation of the situation, in order to recognize

---

[1] As Condillac wrote about 'the language of action', i.e., those gestures and facial movements which constitute 'the first means that men had for the communication of their thoughts' (1780, 1: 4–13), 'Ce langage n'est . . . pas si naturel qu'on le sache sans l'avoir appris' (6). It is formed, moreover, of both 'natural signs' and 'artificial signs' (7), and the latter in particular have to be learned.

that state of mind. A woman looking with dancing eyes at her lover may be inspired by a medley of emotions and thoughts, compounded of erotic recollections, defiant collusion, trust, plans for the future, and so on, but an observer uninstructed in the circumstances of the relationship, cultural and individual, will nevertheless be able to give a confident description of her state of mind. The observation of these situations will necessarily be phrased in the words of some language (an English ethnographer would, one presumes, describe the former as one of 'grief' and the latter as one of 'love'), but the recognition of the inner states in question will be based on natural resemblances among men in the association of certain states of mind with certain bodily experiences and manifestations. As Wittgenstein (1967a, sec. 225) has remarked:

We do not see facial contortions and make inferences from them (like a doctor forming a diagnosis) to joy, grief, boredom. We describe a face immediately as sad, radiant, bored, even when we are unable to give any other description of the features.—Grief, one would like to say, is personified in the face.

There is a wide range of such states, the definition of which will differ according to the language in which they are discriminated; and they vary also in complexity or subtlety, so that to characterize them in any language may be more or less difficult. There can be no finite list of them, for to posit such a complete repertory would involve the fallacious premise of an absolute classification and would presume an unreal limit to the resources of language. But it is not hard to make a preliminary and partial register of psychic states that have bodily concomitants. We can say, for instance, that a man *looks* hurt, fearful, worried, angry, surprised, intent, suspicious, disgusted, happy, and so on. I do not want to extend this brief list, since to do so would divert attention to the psychological adequacy of the English language, and also because the longer the list the more it prompts the invalid question of its approach to completeness. All I want to do is to establish and exemplify a ground of differentiation in any classification of states of mind, a principle based upon natural bodily resemblances.

In addition to the lessons of common experience, there are two main sources of justification for this kind of differentiation. Both have to do particularly with the emotions, rather than with states of mind in general, but they provide a more extended support to the argument. It can be said that these resemblances are natural, in the first place, because in so many observable bodily respects (posture, movement, facial expression) there is a striking similarity between human and primate behaviour and in the reactions of other animals. This does not mean, of course, that human states of mind are merely animal qualities, or that such apprehensions are thereby to be attributed to other species, but it does serve to confirm that some at least of the bodily states which among humans are connected with states of mind have a phylogenetic origin (cf. Darwin 1872).[2] In the second place, there are specific physiological and chemical concomitants to certain major emotions, e.g., anger, anxiety, fear (Cannon 1929). Emotional states may be signalled physiologically by changes

[2] Darwin sent out a questionnaire designed to discover whether expressions of the emotions were innate or conventional (1872). The thirty-six responses demonstrated, in his opinion, that 'the same state of mind is expressed throughout the world with remarkable uniformity' (17). Cf. Schlosberg 1952.

Grant, in drawing up a check list for the study of human facial expression (1969), distinguishes 118 elements of behaviour. 'An important question that will be asked,' he continues, 'is whether the elements described here are species behaviour or are in some way culturally determined. The final answer to this is not known as the necessary studies have yet to be made but such evidence as is available . . . indicates that many of the elements described here are common to all cultures. It is to be expected that cross-cultural differences will exist in the frequency with which elements are shown . . .' (535).

More recently, and while the present work was in preparation, Eibl-Eibesfeldt has surveyed the position in an authoritative chapter on 'The Ethology of Man' (1970, chap. 18). Referring to Darwin (1872), he observes that in spite of the subsequent lack of research 'many present-day psychologists are aware of the basic agreement in mimic expression among different peoples' (408). He rejects the contentions by R. L. Birdwhistell that no expressive movement has any universal meaning, that they are all the products of culture and are not in-born; 'such far-reaching generalizations are certainly unjustified. . . .' Eibl-Elbesfeldt himself thinks there is a widespread agreement in 'the international language of facial expressions' (409, 411). He has made investigations, with photographic records, in Europe, Kenya, Tanzania, Uganda, India, Siam, Hong Kong, New Guinea, Japan, Samoa, the United States, Mexico, Peru, and Brazil, with the conclusion that: 'Some of the more complex human expressions can be traced back to the super-position of a few fixed action patterns which do not seem to be culturally determined' (416); 'The assertion of R. L. Birdwhistell that there are no culturally independent expressions and that everything is learned is disproved by these results' (420). 'To communicate emotions we do not necessarily require language even today, because our innate expressive behavior repertoire is quite sufficient' (462). See also his account of the many similarities between humans and animals (426–31). (I am indebted to Dr. Vernon Reynolds for this important reference.)

in respiration, heartbeat, distribution of the blood, sugar release, the secretion of adrenalin and noradrenalin, etc.; and conversely an emotional state such as acute anxiety can be artificially induced in a human subject by the injection of a certain chemical. These bodily changes in human beings may be conditioned responses to situations as conventionally defined by society,[3] but they cannot be ascribed genetically to cultural convention or to linguistic differentiation. They are natural kinds of response, common to man as a species and in some instances shared by man with other animals. It is this fact which permits external resemblances to be established among the formalized expressions of emotion in different societies.

Emotions, however they may be defined and classified, are not coterminous with all states of mind; and it is evident also that there is no direct connection between physiological conditions and the discriminations that are made by any society (e.g., Nuer) in its psychological vocabulary. But the observable, and perceptible, bodily signs of affective apprehensions nevertheless provide an objective basis for the comparative appraisal of conceptions of inner states.

IV

Some states of mind, then, have bodily concomitants which conduce to overt natural resemblances among men, and these states can be mutually recognized independently of their social and linguistic forms.

This fact provides us initially with a methodical security similar to that present in the study of colour categories,[4] in which undertaking the physical components of colours can be measured and recorded by instruments, the readings of which supply a standard against which cultural discriminations can be marked. This is an encouraging advantage but not sufficient for our purpose, for not all natural resemblances are isolable in the same way. Human beings possess certain less obvious and less determinate capacities, and others which although characteristic of man are recalcitrant to both description and analysis. There are hence some psychological

[3] The social organization of the emotions is to be treated in a separate study.

[4] 'In any discussion of classification, one returns always to colours' (Hampshire 1959: 35).

L

discriminations, even universal ones, which have no clear physical correspondences, and others which refer to capacities that may have no such immediate and specific manifestations at all. These have a more hidden character, and need to be discerned inferentially in modes of human action and social intercourse.

For instance, it is generally taken to be a distinctive trait of man (though Hume indeed maintained that it was not exclusive to him) that he is a thinking animal, and this essential feature must surely be considered a kind of natural resemblance; yet there is no natural sign of thinking and it certainly has no specific physiognomy. In this quite fundamental respect there are no bodily phenomena that can be recognized intuitively as signs of the capacity to think, or of the operation of thinking, but there are nevertheless many complex indications that signal this characteristic feature to all men and thus constitute a ground of communication among them. This type of natural resemblance is hard to define and, as Wittgenstein observes, the use of the word 'thinking' is itself confused: 'Nor can we expect anything else,' he continues, 'and that can of course be said of all psychological verbs' (1967a, sec. 113). But not all psychological verbs occasion the same degree of confusion or present the same kind of descriptive difficulty. For example, to attempt, to want, to regret are modes of consciousness that are fairly readily identified and differentiated; they are characteristic of human thought and feeling, marked on occasion by tone of voice and less surely by facial expression and by posture, and there can be, it seems, no language which fails to provide for their conventional recognition. These also are kinds of natural resemblance among men.

A cardinal concept in any account of such essential capacities, universally discriminated in all traditions of discourse and logically indispensable to human understanding, is that of intention. Dunbar writes significantly that natural signs declare the 'purposes' of man to man; and according to Hampshire, in a passage that has a particular relevance here, 'The often quoted fact that human beings are essentially thinking, and therefore symbol-using, animals is a special case of the fact that they are essentially intentional animals' (1959: 135). There are, admittedly, conflicting views on how intention is best to be represented: e.g., Wittgenstein holds that intention does not have 'genuine duration' (1967a, sec. 45); whereas Hampshire maintains that intention 'is not a momentary occurrence' (100), and refers explicitly to the 'guiding intention' within the continuous trajectory of an action (126). The concept of intention is indeed a notorious focus of argument in philosophy (Anscombe 1963), and this demonstrates that it is a matter for philosophical opinion, not solely observation; but the notion is none the less ineluctable, and intentional action (in some sense of 'intention') is ineliminable from our notion of experience (Hampshire 1959: 119). Hampshire goes so far as to write that intentions and beliefs together actually 'constitute thought' and, at any particular time, a man's present state of consciousness (158, 101). Moreover, intention and belief are said to be similar: 'to express an intention, or to impute an intention to do something to someone else, is in many ways like expressing or imputing a belief' (100).

This proposition returns us to the specific concept, indistinct and confused as it assuredly is, that we are trying to assess. The sense in which Hampshire writes of 'belief' is exceedingly general and inclusive, and he does not subject it to a critical analysis; yet this highly accommodating acceptation, by which belief holds with intention a complementary place in the very constitution of thought and consciousness, leads us to a clearer realization of the logical and experiential status of the concept.

Social life entails directed conduct, and the regular forms of action by which it is made up cannot be understood wholly apart from the play of intention. In everyday life, people in any culture declare their own intentions, ascribe intentions to others, and order their common affairs in part by reference to the myriad vectors of intention that are thus plotted. Generally the law anywhere presumes that men act intentionally, and the estimation of legal responsibility rests on the idea that there are degrees in the ability of individuals to appreciate their intentions or to carry them out with due judgement. This distinct capacity may find various expression in other languages, in the form of equivalent words or phrases or inflections, but the possibility of making statements of intention cannot be absent from them. 'It is logically impossible that there should be beings who have a means of communication, properly to be described as a language, and who can be said to make statements to each other, but who do not act with intention' (Hampshire 1959: 135). Not only do we carry on our affairs in society by constant reference to this essential feature, but we have an immediate apprehension of intention within ourselves. If we intend something, we know that we do so, and we can actually feel the intention: there is an inner tension, as it were, an impression of tightening resolve, sometimes even a bodily stirring like that which is preparatory to action. In these respects we can say that intending can be experienced. The concept of intention cannot be argued or translated away, and no consideration of alien social forms and linguistic conventions could undermine empirically its necessary character or its universal application in the study of human conduct. It is thus a natural resemblance, and the concept is hence entirely apt to the description and analysis of both social and individual life. It is for these reasons that intention, under one or another linguistic guise, forms part of all traditions of discourse.

But in all these regards belief makes an extreme contrast. It is not a necessary concept, and it is not a distinct capacity or inner state; other languages make no recognition of a mode of consciousness of the kind, and other peoples order their lives without reference to any such capacity. Whereas intention, together with other inner capacities, is logically necessary and experientially discriminable, belief is neither.

V

Another ground of natural resemblances is to be sought among the necessary conditions of social life. The presumption is that there are certain constraints which are absolutely requisite to the conduct of human affairs, and that these will everywhere be embodied in institutions. Men governed by these institutions will then, it can be expected, so conform in their behaviour as to appear similar by virtue of some innate capacity.

A prime example of this type of case is the promise. Hume thought the performance of promises to be one of the three 'fundamental laws of nature' on which the peace and security of human society entirely depended (1888: 526); and, since a promise is characteristically a declaration made by an individual, there would seem a reasonable supposition that its performance corresponded naturally to an act of the mind. But, as Hume proved, it is not in itself a natural phenomenon. A promise is not simply a resolution, for that alone never imposes any obligation; it is not a desire to perform what is promised, for we may bind ourselves without such a desire or even with an aversion; nor is it, he argued, the willing of the action that is promised, for a promise always concerns some future time, whereas the will has an influence only on present actions. Therefore, Hume concluded, the act of the mind that enters into a promise 'must necessarily be the *willing* of that *obligation*, which arises from the promise' (516). We need not follow Hume in his subsequent argument about moral sentiments, but may come directly to his conclusion: 'A promise . . . is *naturally* something altogether unintelligible, not is there any act of the mind belonging to it' (517). Moreover, if there were any act of the mind belonging to the promise, it could not naturally produce any obligation, for promises have no force antecedent to human conventions. Thus 'promises are human inventions, founded on the necessities and interests of society' (519). The necessity comes from the fact that society depends on the mutual performance of services, but since these cannot be finished at the same instant, it is unavoidable that one party be contented to remain in uncertainty. A special form of words is hence invented by which we bind ourselves to the performance of any action, and on which the other party can rely: this form of words constitutes a promise, 'which is the sanction of the interested commerce of mankind' (522).

By Hume's account, therefore, a type of declaration which might seem to be the expression of a distinct state of mind, and intrinsic to the individual, is no such thing. It is instead the expression through the individual of a social institution, and it exists and has a special force because it is intrinsic to social life. The natural act of the mind which promises express is resolution (522), but the expression of a resolution is not commonly supposed to entail an obligation; so 'we *feign* a new act of the mind, which we call the *willing* an obligation' (523). Nor is there only one right form of a promise, but 'as the obligation of promises is an invention for the interest of society, 'tis warp'd into as many different forms as that interest requires . . .' (524). Promises, then, are not natural but are 'mere artificial contrivances for the convenience and advantage of society' (525).

Here we have an excellent case to set beside that of belief. Like belief, a promise is not a discriminable type of experience; yet unlike belief it is nevertheless held to be essential to human society and thus to constitute a kind of natural resemblance among men. In order to assess the concept of belief against this type of resemblance, I shall briefly suggest certain respects in which the institution of the promise can be contrasted with that supposed capacity.

A promise is quite distinct from an inner state or experience: the whole point is that it must be public and conventional. It is a performative utterance, and there is no implication that it must be accompanied by any special emotion, etc. Sometimes a particular

inner state is in fact appropriate to what happens to be promised—
e.g., a man who promises to love and cherish a woman may be presumed, if he is sincere, to be in a corresponding mood as he does so
—but this state pertains to the contingent circumstances and not to
the act of promising. The promise can be accompanied by various
intentions, also, e.g., to do as one promises or not to do so; or it may
be accompanied by no intention at all other than merely to cope with
a situation to which the promise offers a solution. To make a
promise, moreover, implies nothing about the continuance of the
state one is in when one makes it: there is no promissory disposition.
The commitment, though made at a certain time and having a
present significance, focuses on a future action and does not
characterize the intervening period; a promise marks the beginning
of a length of time that is to be terminated by a stipulated occasion
but which imposes no special state on the promiser. The occasion
itself, finally, which accomplishes what was promised, is only
whatever it happens to be: it does not necessarily have a particular
character deriving from the inner state of the person who made the
promise. At no point, therefore, is there an inner state specific to a
promise. While there are indeed many aspects under which a
promise is unlike a belief, the institutions are decidedly comparable
in that neither is an experience.

On the other hand, whereas belief does not constitute a natural
resemblance among men, the promise does appear to be universal
among human societies. Hume's argument that it is a necessary institution is cogent in its own terms, but its premises are uncertain
and there is room in any case to examine the conclusion a little more
closely. One means of doing so is to consider whether a society
would be possible in which there were no promises or anything
equivalent to them: i.e., a society in which no one freely committed
himself to some future action. A hypothetical case would be a social
situation (whether it would be a society or not is a separate matter)
that was characterized by anarchy: there would be no individual commitments, no undertakings of one to another, no deferred
reliance upon anyone. The participants might have come together
on some quasi-contractual basis, e.g., on the agreement to establish
a new mode of life; but under utter anarchy no one would be
bound, or need bind himself, to any particular undertaking. It is
difficult to know by what criteria one might say that this would be
impossible, but it certainly seems unfeasible in many regards which
enable us to understand why no human aggregate of the kind is

represented in ethnographical literature. A contrary case is that of a totalitarian regime, in which there would be no rights but only duties: in this situation, no individual would have the liberty to promise anything but would do only as he was told. There would be no individual rights but instead only those pertaining to status and premised on subordination. In place of promises there would be orders and their unevadable fulfilment. Certain types of religious and military organization approximate these conditions, even though they are actually founded on an initial promise in the form of a vow or an oath of obedience: a novice cannot promise his superior that he will do something that he is told, and a subaltern cannot promise his colonel that he will carry out an order. But these are artificial segregations within societies that do observe promises, and it is not at all sure that a viable mode of social life is generally possible without the institution of the promise. Fascist dictatorships have not yet gone so far as to attempt this extreme deprivation of liberty, and even in *1984* the characters arrange meetings and make other forms of promise. It is hard therefore to conceive a society from which the promise was eliminated, and the indications are that the institution is not only universal but necessary.

Given, then, that every society requires (or at least has) this institution, there is still the question whether the promise must be named. In a great many languages it is, though such contrasts as *promettre* and *versprechen* point to possible disparities in the ideas behind the formation of the words (see Buck 1949, s.v. 'promise'), but a separate word or phrase may not be universal. For instance, I do not think there is a word for 'promise' in Penan (*jaji*, which I have heard in the lowlands, is probably a loan from the Malay *janji*), and Dr. Rivière tells me that so far as he knows there is no equivalent in Trio. One needs to be more certain than this, of course, and a definite answer calls for a specific inquiry on the spot; but these examples indicate at least that the word may be neither common nor obvious. In any case, it seems clear enough that no separate word or phrase is actually needed, but only some means of public commitment to a future action. In English there are many ways of making a promise without using the word 'promise', and this is recognized in the saying 'A word is a promise'. There are in addition non-verbal promises in the forms of conventional gestures, such as hand-slapping at a horse-fair or nods and other signals at an auction. A promise can therefore be named or not, and that it may not be distinctly named says nothing against the necessary character of the institution. But belief cannot be belief unless it is named as such; and that belief may be named says nothing in favour of its reality.

Like the promise, belief is an artificial contrivance for the convenience and advantage of society, and to the furtherance of these interests men have indeed 'feigned' a new act of the mind.

VI

It is therefore possible to determine, logically and empirically, certain human capacities which are real and universal, as contrasted with others that are the artificial constructs of various cultural traditions. These capacities provide (to the extent that they are individually established) a useful basis for the appraisal of collective representations of inner states. As natural resemblances, these capacities permit us to stand somewhat outside the bounds of any individual society or language, and to assess the reality of psychological discriminations that in part are always contingent on changing cultural convention. It appears, moreover, that correspondingly there are hence certain standard discriminations among modes of consciousness that are everywhere made by men, whatever the variations otherwise in their forms of ideation. These constitute conceptual resemblances to which men are naturally inclined in the collective elaboration of psychological classifications.

Certain of these natural resemblances have their focus in the human body, and a sympathetic observation of human conduct in any culture yields notions such as anger, grief, fear, surprise, and so on. Other resemblances are displayed in subtler and more complex ways, often finding their specific manifestation in modes of social interaction, and these are to be isolated not physically but by the critical interplay of introspection and rational inference. We find such capacities in ourselves, and conclude that they are (and in some instances logically must be) present in other people also, so that we can confidently ascribe to any human beings the power to think, to imagine, or to intend.

What the full or characteristic range of such natural resemblances may be is a matter for extended investigation, but those so far indicated establish well enough the possibility of finding criteria, descriptive and logical, that are independent of particular social forms and types of discourse. What designations they should bear is similarly a matter for further determination, but it appears (as ex hypothesi ought to be the case) that the lexical concepts of English, appropriately delimited and qualified by context, are matched by practical equivalents in the discriminations of thought and verbal expression that are made in other languages.

We may therefore conclude that there are in fact conditions which can be regarded as normal and as specific to mankind. Gauged against these standards, the notion of a state or capacity of belief stands out as a quite idiocratic concept. It is not the recognition of a bodily phenomenon, it does not discriminate a distinct mode of consciousness, it has no logical claim to inclusion in a universal psychological vocabulary, and it is not a necessary institution for the conduct of social life. Belief does not constitute a natural resemblance among men.

9
Ideation

I

To view the concept of belief as an isolated and artificial alternative among the innumerable cultural classifications of human powers, the arbitrary product of an intricate and unique historical tradition, draws our attention back to the study of the collective representations by means of which men think. To undermine the presumed reality of the state of belief by recourse in part to logical considerations, in a comparison of that alleged state with certain better established inner capacities, raises again the question whether there is a logic that is as universal as are those abilities which in other respects constitute natural resemblances among men.

Both of these topics—collective representations and natural logic —have for some decades been central issues in social anthropology; but a point on which I think we have all consistently fallen short, whether as ethnographers or as comparativists, is in not realizing the full implications of our task of interpreting alien modes of experience. This is not to say, of course, that no progress has been made, or that the advances effected have in themselves been disappointing, for on both counts the contrary is true, but only that there is a further stage to which this theoretical development must be pressed. What I have in mind may best be indicated, especially for the sake of non-anthropologists, by a brief retrospect on certain prominent researches and lines of inquiry that have brought us to where we are today in the development of a comparative study of ideation.

The anthropological analysis of individual concepts has taken, necessarily, two distinct forms. On the one hand, ethnographers have examined the setting and uses of alien ideas upon which their investigations have led them to focus; e.g., *mori* among the Manggarai (Verheijen 1951), *kwoth* among the Nuer (Evans-Pritchard 1956), or *kamo* in New Caledonia (Leenhardt 1947). In this kind of interpretation there are no rules or techniques, but everything depends on the investigator's personal qualities of intelligence, sympathy, erudition, and so on. There are more and less impressive examples of such ethnography, but no general development of a theoretical kind is to be looked for. The intensive analysis of one indigenous concept provides no direct advantage in the study of another; and the cumulative comprehension of a series of such concepts, which in any case is a practically endless procedure, does not in itself compose a method of analysis or supply instruments to carry it out. On the other hand, there has been considerable theoretical accomplishment in the analysis of those terms (chiefly in French and in English) by means of which foreign ideologies are objectively understood and explained. Prominent examples are furnished by Mauss's essay on the gift (1925) and Lévi-Strauss's monograph on totemism (1962). These two cases, separated by more than thirty years, make an instructive comparison. Mauss's essay had the effect, in part, of invalidating the common word 'gift' as a descriptive or explicatory term, and substituted the more neutral and abstract concept of 'exchange' which has since held such a cardinal position among the analytical notions of social anthropology (cf. Needham 1963: xlii–xliii). Lévi-Strauss, instead of examining the technical applicability of a word of everyday use and reference, concentrated his attention on a quasi-technical neologism which had been thought to possess a firm and singular value in the description of tribal cosmologies. In this case the analysis similarly demolished the standard acceptation of the term, and reduced it to a particular illustration of certain very general modes of thought. The argument proposed a method of comparative analysis (which the essay on the gift had not attempted), but it did not replace the discredited notion with anything more specific than a redirection of theoretical interest toward the topic of classification. Clearly, therefore, an explicit method is not essential to the establishment of a valuable analytical notion; and the employment of such a method does not necessarily lead to a new terminological instrument of analysis. Yet in spite of the contrasts between them these two investigations both made definite theoretical advances: one has long had a great effect on ethnography, comparative studies, and academic instruction; and the other seems likely also to produce changes, even if not exactly those that the author apparently had in mind, in anthropological thought and practice.

Research into isolated concepts is thus well established, and makes increasing progress as ethnographers refine their inquiries and comparativists bring into problematical focus their scrutiny of social facts. But alien concepts do not present themselves singly, and, whether they are studied directly in their own idioms or by translation into objective terms of analysis, an obviously related necessity is to study ideologies systematically and in their full context of use.

II

This integrated style of investigation was inaugurated sociologically by Durkheim and Mauss, in their pioneering essay on primitive classification (1903). They wished to explain the very genesis of categories, or what they called 'the classificatory function' of the mind, by showing to what extent classificatory concepts were solidary, in primitive societies, with forms of social grouping. The first logical categories, they argued, were social categories, the first classes of things were classes of men, and the relations uniting classes to one another were those that composed society itself.[1]

The premises on which this argument was founded were unsound, and the manner in which the analysis was pursued was not satisfactory (Needham 1963), but the theoretical inspiration of the essay was genial, and it had scholarly effects that far outweighed the invalidity of its specific argument. In the Netherlands, especially at Leiden, it led to a series of interconnected investigations into the total structure, ideational and social, of Indonesian societies; and in France and elsewhere it furnished a model for an impressive range of studies, in philosophy and linguistics as well as in sociology, of concepts and society in Australia, China, classical Greece, pre-Columbian Mexico, and ancient Persia.[2] In particular, Hertz and

[1] Durkheim later took up this theme again, in a greatly expanded ethnographical context and with certain qualifications and elaborations, in *Les Formes élémentaires de la vie religieuse* (1912).

[2] Something of the extraordinary influence of Durkheim and Mauss's essay has been set out in the introduction to the English edition (1963: xxxi–xxxiii). In addition to the works listed there I should particularly like to cite Cornford's *From Religion to Philosophy* (1912), a work that shows to a remarkable degree the extent to which a profound scholar working in his own sphere of competence can be governed by a radical sociological suggestion (see especially Cornford's pp. viii, 51 n. 1, 53–4, 71), and van Wouden's *Sociale Structuurtypen in de Groote Oost* (1935), in which social categories

his theoretical successors made a decisive advance in isolating for comparative analysis the principle of opposition, most prominently denoted by lateral symbolism but more variously expressed also in institutions and rites, as a universal and seemingly essential relation in the constitution of symbolic classifications (Hertz 1909; cf. Needham 1960; 1967a). Latterly, these several lines of inquiry into categories and their social concomitants have been brought together in a series of analyses of societies that are organized by prescriptive alliance (see, e.g., Needham 1962, chap. 4; 1971b, sec. VII). Since prescriptive systems approach most nearly to Durkheim and Mauss's paradigm, and permit the clearest formulation of the problems they raised, they call for some special attention. Also, they have become the occasion of some controversy in modern social anthropology, and it is advisable therefore to explain something of the theoretical importance that has been claimed for them.

The central interest of a prescriptive system is that in it the relatively distinguishable realms of symbolism and jural organ- ization can be studied together, by total structural analysis, as complementary aspects of one and the same classification. This concordance (as analytical convenience leads us to interpret the matter) does not at all confirm the theory advanced by Durkheim and Mauss, which they based on similar correspondences; but it has the singular advantage of displaying the radical importance of those principles of order, expressed in cultural categories, which serve to articulate the system of thought and action. These prin- ciples, or what Hampshire has called organizing notions (1959: 223), are few and simple, and they can be discerned equally in both symmetric and asymmetric systems of prescriptive alliance. Typi- cally, the conceptual order in systems of this kind is constituted by three modes of relation: opposition, analogy, and homology. These relations, and the specific form of classification that they compose, are themselves the prime objects of analysis.

The real purpose behind working on prescriptive alliance is thus not to study 'kinship',[3] but to investigate, in a distinct and privileged sphere of evidence, certain ultimate and constant features

and their expression in affinal alliances are held to be the model for cosmic classifications (xii, 2).

[3] This obfuscating term is used only in order to match the vocabulary of the textbooks and of common anthropological discourse, not because it has any precise value as a technical designation (cf. Needham 1966: 31–2; 1971b; 1971c, sec. II).

of classification. It is true that here some knowledge of descent systems and rules of marriage is called for, and a certain technical facility also in the analysis of relationship terminologies, but these minor anthropological skills are employed simply in order to delineate the contours of those conceptual features that one desires to explore.

That it is the classificatory principles which are crucial, and not the social forms that they happen to assume, can be demonstrated furthermore by the study of symbolic classification, as expressed primarily in rite and myth, in societies where prescriptive alliance is not practised and without any technical or systematic reference to the descent system, rules of marriage, or other jural institutions (Needham 1967a). The intention is not sociological, but to isolate aspects of classification which are so general as to appear natural proclivities of the human mind, and certain features perhaps which are universal and essential to thought. In other words, the resources of comparative ethnography are put to the service, just as Durkheim and Mauss proposed (1903: 1–7, 72; 1963: 3–9, 88), of an empirical philosophy of mind.

III

Whether one is analysing a single concept or a system of cultural categories, there is a distinction that needs to be clearly observed, namely that between the formal properties of collective representations and the mental operations, on the part of the individual human being, that may be carried out and expressed through the given categories. There is no necessary connection between a system of received ideas and the particular association of ideas in the process of thought. Thus from the fact that a society subscribes to a dual classification, for example, which is analysable systematically by reference to a general relation of complementary opposition, it does not at all follow that the members of that society shall individually conceive their experience in oppositional terms. That an equally general relation of analogy is also analytically necessary in order to compose the pairs of opposites into a system does not entail, either, that the thoughts of any individual shall perpetually follow a dialectical zig-zag between the two sets of opposed cultural categories by which the ideology can be schematized (see, e.g., Needham 1962: 96; 1967a: 447).

This distinction, between the categorical forms of thought and the process of thinking, was emphasized by Durkheim (1898b), and it remains as crucial today as when he formulated it. But the distinction is qualified nevertheless by certain resemblances which Durkheim also noted and which have been better established by more recent researches. Once the heterogeneity between the social and the individual has been recognized, he wrote, the question still remains whether there may not be resemblances between collective and individual representations, by virtue of the fact that they are equally representations, and whether there are not certain abstract laws which are common to both spheres of thought. Myths, legends, religious concepts, and moral beliefs express a reality other than that of the individual; but the way in which they attract or repel each other, unite or separate, may be independent of their content and be related solely to their common quality as representations. It is conceivable that contiguity and resemblance, logical contrasts and antagonisms, may act in the same way whatever the things that are represented. 'Thus we arrive at the idea of an entirely formal psychology which would be a sort of common ground for individual psychology and for sociology' (1898a; 1947: xviii). This formal psychology would include a comparison of the ways in which 'social representations', in myths, legends, traditions, and languages, attract and exclude one another, fuse together or are distinguished, and so on. The task, in other words, would be to establish 'laws of collective ideation' (1947: xviii). 'There is a whole part of sociology which ought to seek the laws of collective ideation and which remains entirely to be carried out' (1898b; 1951: 45 n.). Until such laws were discovered, however, it would be impossible to know for sure whether or not they repeated those of individual psychology (1947: xix). In the absence of such empirical demonstration, Durkheim presumed that certain 'laws of social mentality' might in fact resemble the laws of individual psychology, but not simply because the former were simply a particular instance of the latter. There would remain important differences between collective and individual representations, and what the hypothetical laws might establish would be not identities but certain similarities isolated by abstraction (1898a; 1947; xix).

Durkheim did not himself indicate further what such similarities might prove to be, but instead concentrated his research on the social contexts of systems of collective representations, and on the genesis, as he thought, of categorization in the formal groupings of society. He even suggested that the relation between collective and individual ideation really belonged to philosophy and to logic rather than to the scientific study of social facts (1898a; 1947: xx). But if the systematic combinations of collective representations are social facts, so also are the collective modalities in accordance with which members of society actually relate these categories in their individual trains of thought.

This realization brings us to a fundamental and disturbing issue. If individual ideation is in part contingent on changeable cultural convention, there can be no prior guarantee that it will be comprehensible to men whose representations are framed by other traditions; for it cannot be simply presumed that the manipulation of concepts which are social facts is nevertheless based on a universal logic that is independent of social variation. This issue falls, initially at any rate, within the scope of empirical determination, and can be referred to the test of comparative ethnography; but the very grounds for a factual inquiry could still be undermined by a reliance on unjustified premises about the uniformity of human reason.

There are indeed at least two possible sources of differentiation among men in their modes of thought. Human beings show considerable variation in genetic traits such as skin colour, skull form, blood group, and a whole range of perceptual and physiological differences; so it is conceivable that their brains also could have evolved differently, with the result that modes of thought dependent on the brain might correspondingly differ from one physical variety of man to another or in accordance with the distribution of more minute genetic traits. Mental differences of this origin would not coincide with any typology of races, or with the lines of distinction between systems of collective representations, however these might be circumscribed, but they could have introduced into cultural modes of reasoning a genetic, and thus natural, factor of differentiation. This factor would presumably be variously confined or exploited by different cultures, but it would still remain constantly latent, by genetic transmission, and would thus provide a natural ground for the elaboration of disparate cultural logics. We do not know that any such physical factor has in reality intervened as a source of rational differentiation, let alone what logical variations might be connected with what genetic traits, but it is clearly a possibility. The other possibility is cultural, and also more evidential. Modern logicians have constructed artificial logics, and these demonstrate that not all modes of reason are immutably given by nature or by the categories of natural languages. It is possible therefore that alternative rules of inference and canons of validity might have been worked out in different cultural traditions, and have been collectively prescribed, to the point at which the members of certain societies might reason (in some regards, at least) by means of peculiar logics which they would consider the only right forms of thought. Whether such logical variations have been elaborated into collective representations in any actual societies is again a matter for empirical determination, but the point for the moment is that it is quite conceivable that disparate cultural logics should exist.

Neither of these possible sources of logical differentiation can be ruled out *a priori*, and the question whether man's reasoning is or is not everywhere the same can be decided only by comparative ethnography. In the absence of a demonstrated uniformity, any talk of 'the human mind' can be only presumptive, and will reflect no more than our partial knowledge of styles of rational discourse in the long register of traditions and forms of social life.

IV

As a matter of fact, reports from many regions of the world have long given apparent evidence that other peoples could not be reasoning in accordance with the Aristotelian tradition of Europe, and it has seemed to some of the most careful observers and liberal scholars that there must be logical differences among men—if not fundamentally, at least in the discrimination of matters to which strict reasoning was to be applied.

It was therefore a task of the very highest intellectual importance to ascertain whether there were irreducibly disparate kinds of mentality, in which case the understanding of mankind would be immeasurably complicated; or whether logical operations were invariant, in which case cogitational differences would be the results merely of different cultural premises. It was this disquieting and unresolved issue that even Durkheim excluded from sociology and left to the philosophers to deal with. It was certainly essential, however, that someone should deal with it, for if human thought were not everywhere intelligible and comparable the very notion of humanity, not to speak more trivially of sociology, was at stake. Nevertheless, it was perfectly feasible to proceed pragmatically, and not to contemplate this fundamental question until the analysis of more particular matters made it necessary to do so. This, in fact, was the easier course that for the most part sociologists and anthropologists happened to take. The differences between western societies and those taken to be primitive could be ascribed simply to the low stage of development at which the latter had succeeded in arriving: savages were potentially capable of civilization, and of the correct rationality characteristic of this achievement, but at their actual point of evolution their thoughts were, as Morgan for example concluded, feeble in degree and limited in range, and their intelligence was infantile (Morgan, in Fison and Howitt 1880: 12). Frazer, it is true, did not take so derogatory a stand, and he based his analyses of primitive modes of thought, as displayed in magic and religion, on intellectualist premises which in principle applied to all men; but it was still rather awkward to posit a rationalistic primitive man who, as the late Lord Raglan ironically put it, 'is always asking himself questions and giving himself the wrong answers' (Raglan 1964: 4).

Looking back, it is easy to assert that the question of the logical unity of mankind was utterly crucial, and that the fate of the humane disciplines ultimately depended on the answer. Seen in the perspective of the history of ideas, the issue seems not only obvious and inescapable but to possess an absolute importance such as far outweighs any other conceivable question in the study of man. We therefore have cause to be grateful indeed that it was taken up by a man of such intelligence, erudition, and liberality of mind as Lucien Lévy-Bruhl.[4] It is all the more dejecting, however, that for the most part he vainly saw his views traduced and the problems he discerned largely ignored by the ethnographers and others, mostly British, who were in a position to profit from them in their observations. One prominent and encouraging exception to this general prejudice was Evans-Pritchard, who as early as 1934 wrote that it was difficult to understand why Lévy-Bruhl's ideas had met with 'so great neglect and derision among English anthropologists', and who, while preparing his own classic work on primitive thought, *Witchcraft, Oracles and Magic among the Azande* (1937), found Lévy-Bruhl's researches worth the additional labour of a

---

[4] For a good introduction to Lévy-Bruhl, comprising a biographical note, exposition of his chief views, bibliography of his major works, extracts from his writings, and a list of commentaries on his theory, see Cazeneuve (1963). Cf. also Davy (1950, pt. 4).

long and respectful exegesis (1934; cf. 1965, chap. 4).[5] This commentary was written, as Evans-Pritchard has since explained, because
he thought that 'a scholar should be criticized for what he has said,
and not for what he is supposed to have said' (1965: 81); but there
has nevertheless persisted in the received ideas of social anthropology
what can only be regarded as a travesty of Lévy-Bruhl's theory
which seems likely to induce others to continue to ignore or
belittle him.[6] Yet one need do no more than read carefully what he
actually wrote in order to see the degree of justice in Mary Douglas's
judgement that 'it was he who first posed all the important questions
about primitive cultures and their distinctiveness as a class', and to
agree with her expostulation that 'he has not deserved such neglect'
(1966: 74–5). Against this background, then, it is advisable to recount something of the inception of Lévy-Bruhl's ideas and, more
rapidly, their subsequent development and transformations.

The turning point in Lévy-Bruhl's work as a philosopher was
1903, the year in which 'De quelques formes primitives de classification' was published in the *Année sociologique*. He had received
from a sinologist, Chavannes, a translation of an historical work
by a Chinese scholar, and he was puzzled to find that however
often he read and re-read it he could not discover how the ideas of
the author hung together. This led him to wonder whether the
laws of Chinese logic were the same as those of the European
tradition; and he saw that if they were not the same it would be
a philosophical task of the first importance to investigate the causes
of the difference. Practical and methodological difficulties persuaded
him to give up the intention of working on Chinese evidence, or
else on the great civilizations of Assyria, Egypt, and India, which
would have presented the same scholarly difficulties as China. So he
turned to the indigenous societies of America, Africa, and elsewhere
in the non-European world, in the expectation that if there existed
a logic different from ours he would have more chances of finding

[5] The original paper, published in Egypt, is exceedingly difficult to get hold
of, but it contains a more profound and detailed critique than the briefer
account later given by Evans-Pritchard in his survey of theories of primitive
religion.

[6] Thus one textbook, which purports moreover to represent the theoretical
viewpoint of the majority of social anthropologists in Britain, asserts that
Lévy-Bruhl's views 'are now out of date', that he thought the symbolic,
non-inferential quality of much human thinking was 'restricted . . . to
"primitives",' and that he overemphasized the 'irrationality' of primitive
thought (Beattie 1964: 28, 67).

it among them and could more easily analyse it (Lévy-Bruhl 1923: 20–21). In the same year, also, he published his conviction that it was no longer possible to think of all humanity as being effectively similar, psychologically and morally, to that part of mankind that we (in Europe) know by our direct experience. He suggested that sociology might one day determine what precisely was common to the individuals of all human groups, but short of that time he proposed a preliminary and less ambitious task, namely to analyse with the utmost rigour the rich diversity that could be observed and which there was no present means of drawing together into a unity. Societies studied by anthropologists constantly presented difficulties of a logical kind which could not be resolved by common sense or by any speculation aided merely by current knowledge of human nature: 'The facts that disconcert us must obey certain laws, but what are they?' His proposal, citing the precept of Comte, was that the higher faculties of man should be studied in the historical development of the species. Considerations of individual psychology would not serve: 'The theory of the higher functions (imagination, language, intelligence, under their various aspects) demands the employment of the sociological method' (Lévy-Bruhl 1903; 1937: 75–6).

These were the beginnings of an investigation into human nature that was to occupy Lévy-Bruhl until his merciful death just before the Second World War. Since I hope that not only social anthropologists will read this monograph, and since even anthropologists may not all know what Lévy-Bruhl actually wrote, it will be useful to set out in a paragraph or two those of his conclusions that are characteristic and which are also of the most relevance for my own argument.

The chief book to result from his studies was *Les Fonctions mentales dans les sociétés inférieures* (1910). In this he demonstrated that 'the collective representations of primitives differ ... profoundly from our ideas or concepts; nor are they the equivalents of them' (30). Not only this, but such representations are not interconnected in the mind of the primitive as they are in ours; and there is not even any proof, moreover, that the connections among collective representations must depend solely upon laws of a logical nature (68). In fact, Lévy-Bruhl argued, the law in force is the 'law of participation,' an expression that he made up (for want of a better, as he says) to designate the apparent fact that in primitive collective representations things could be, in a mystical fashion incomprehensible to us, both themselves and something other than themselves. 'In other words, for this mentality, the opposition between the one and the many, same and other, etc., does not impose the necessity to affirm one of the terms if the other is denied, and vice versa' (76–7). The law of participation is difficult to formulate in abstract terms, but clearly it does not resemble any of the laws of formal logic. Indeed, primitive mentality can be described not only as mystical but equally well as 'pre-logical': it is mystical if one concentrates on the content of the collective representations, pre-logical if the attention is on the connections among them. But 'pre-logical' does not mean that this mentality constitutes a sort of anterior stage, prior in time to the appearance of logical thought. We do not know if there were ever human beings, or pre-humans, whose collective representations did not obey logical laws, and it is very unlikely that such ever existed. The pre-logical mentality, as it can be found in primitive societies, is not anti-logical or a-logical: 'In calling it prelogical, I mean only that it is not compelled above all, as our own thought is, to abstain from contradiction.' This characterization is subject to an important qualification, namely that it applies only to collective representations and to their interconnections. To the extent that it is possible for an individual to act independently of his collective representations, a member of a primitive society will usually behave in the way we should expect. In particular, the inferences that he draws will be precisely those that would appear reasonable to us in the circumstances. But it does not follow that the mental activities of primitives shall always follow the same laws as do ours. They have in fact laws of their own, and the first and most general of these is the law of participation (78–80).

Lévy-Bruhl pursued these ideas through a series of books over the next twenty-eight years, but this quick outline of his first views on the distinctive features of 'primitive mentality' is enough to indicate that he made a very arresting case. If there really were human beings who characteristically tolerated contradictions, lacked a sense of the impossible in certain situations, admitted that a person could be in two or more places at once, conceived that a thing could be simultaneously itself and other, and were intellectually satisfied by affective participations among phenomena which they had no care to scrutinize critically, then indeed these were cognitive and logical distinctions among men for which the Aristotelian tradition had made no provision. It was not so much 'laws of social mentality' that Lévy-Bruhl had discovered but, so he inferred, a distinct type of mentality better defined by its very indifference to what had been regarded as the laws of thought.

V

Between 1910 and 1938, however, Lévy-Bruhl gradually gave up most of what he had taken to be the distinctive features of primitive mentality. By 1931, in fact, he had long abandoned for any exact purpose the use of the very phrase: he found that 'primitive' was an unfortunate word that led almost inevitably to confusions, and he abjured 'mentality' as a vague term introduced and popularized by journalists (1931: 6–7).

He had never denied for a moment, as he then affirmed, that the 'fundamental structure of the mind' was everywhere the same (10), so he was not contending that there was an intrinsically different primitive type of mind. What he was concerned to show was that in spite of the structural identity of all human minds, as he put it, there were certain principles of primitive thought which differed from our own to such a point that our traditional psychology and logic were powerless to explain them (11). This was a position that to some degree he continued to maintain, and which a widening survey of ethnographical evidence continued to impress upon him; but what he had isolated as the distinctive factors at work proved not to be such as he had supposed, and the corresponding terms of analysis, which had meanwhile passed into common usage, had to be severely qualified.

He resolved, then, no longer to speak of a 'pre-logical' characteristic, for it had become clearer than ever in the course of his literary investigations that 'the logical structure of the mind is the same in all known human societies' (1949: 62, 70).

From a strictly logical point of view, no essential difference has been established between primitive mentality and our own. In everything that has to do with ordinary everyday experience, transactions of all sorts, political life, economics, the employment of numbering, etc., they [*sc.* primitives] behave in a way that implies the same use of their faculties as we make of our own.

He had never maintained that the adjective 'pre-logical' meant anything more than that primitive mentality was not compelled, above all, to avoid contradiction (1931: 21). Yet even this distinction had to be rephrased as an indifference to incompatibilities, i.e., physical impossibilities (1949: 9–10)—'I used to say contradictions, which seemed to imply logical contradictions such as in reality do not exist' (63). Primitives, Lévy-Bruhl came to realize, 'reject contradiction, just as we do, when they perceive it'; only for them there is an immense domain of the supernatural in which generally they do not recognize contradiction, and are therefore not shocked by it (73). More fundamentally, i.e., from an epistemological standpoint, the cultural facts which had been interpreted as neglect of the law of contradiction were not really such. To conceive a person as being in two places at once, or a thing as being simultaneously what it is and something else, does not entail, strictly speaking, any contradiction (112). What is at issue, rather, are different cultural premises, not different modes of reasoning; and from such alternative premises the members of primitive societies nevertheless draw inferences, and avoid contradictions, just as westerners do. Still, this does not mean, as Lévy-Bruhl had originally assumed, that we could understand the thoughts of primitives simply by putting ourselves in their place. The peoples in question have modes of thought elaborated by quite different traditions, and they speak languages which are inapt to the expression of concepts, so that it is a problem whether they have nevertheless the same mental habits as we do and the same psychological orientation as our own. 'It seems at least probable,' Lévy-Bruhl came to suspect, 'that if we, *as we actually are*, were in their place, we should not at all think as they in fact do' (1931: 12–13).

In the end, Lévy-Bruhl concluded that there was not one primitive mentality, distinguished by two properties that were peculiar to it —namely that it was mystical and pre-logical—but that there was a 'mystical mentality', more marked and more easily observable among primitives than in our own societies, but present in every human mind (1949: 131). What was essential, he thought, to any mystical experience was the sentiment of the presence, and often the action, of an invisible power; the sentiment of a contact, usually unforeseen, with a reality other than the reality given by the actual circumstances. The mystical experience, he surmised, was not a matter of knowledge but was essentially affective, and marked even by a 'characteristic emotion'. In responding to phenomena, the primitive felt that he was not dealing with a uniform and homogeneous reality, but with a complex reality, composed of ordinary apperceptions of the environment to which he had adapted interlaced with what he was accustomed to see as manifestations of the mystical. Although felt as qualitatively different, these two modes of apprehension nevertheless constituted a single and unique experience; and the fact that the two realities were continually intermingled was shown by the sentiment of 'participation'. In the interpretation of what we regard as two experiences, the positive and the mystical, visible and invisible, there is a connective participation between objects belonging to one realm of experience and those belonging to the other (1949: 133–4).

This is an objective, or at least external, way of expressing the fact that man, for as long as we can discover, has had 'the revelation that reality as it is presented to him is at once what it is and other than it is' (1949: 135). Primordially, as preponderantly today in primitive societies, the interconnections, or participations, were almost exclusively felt, but in the course of time they have been more and more consciously represented as relations that called for some logical justification; and this enterprise has led, as is abundantly proved by the history of religions and of metaphysics, to insurmountable difficulties (136–7). Yet the conviction that there are two orders of reality has never vanished, and the compulsion to account for the participation between them remains a characteristic feature of the human mind in any period and in any society (1931: 26–7).

In every human mind, whatever its intellectual development, there subsists an ineradicable fund of primitive mentality. It is not likely that it will ever disappear, or become weakened beyond a certain point, and surely we ought not to wish that it might do so. For with it would disappear, perhaps, poetry, art, metaphysics, and scientific invention—almost everything, in short, that makes for the beauty and grandeur of human life.

This special mode of cognitive concern, expressed though it may characteristically be in forms not approved by traditional western epistemology, is a kind of 'fixed element' that persists throughout the changes and successions of societies and institutions. It is indeed to be found 'constantly around us, and even in us', and we need not look far to discover what appear to be the most primitive beliefs and the most extraordinary mystical experiences. In these respects primitive mentality perpetually makes itself apparent, and thereby 'represents something fundamental and indestructible in the nature of man' (1949: 187).

VI

Lévy-Bruhl's main theoretical merit was thus that he took seriously the possibility that 'the fundamental identity of human nature', a premise on which he quite explicitly based his investigations, might nevertheless be 'compatible with the existence of mentalities that were sharply different one from another' (1931: 8). Methodologically his crucial advance consisted in concentrating analysis on the most general logical articulations of alien ideologies rather than on their component meanings and their social contexts. He formulated precisely what appeared empirically to be the characteristic and problematical features of certain modes of thought; and then, with an admirable care and subtlety unhindered by any self-regard, he scrupulously disproved practically every proposition in the theory of primitive mentality for which he had become so renowned.

But his substantive failure was none the less an admirable analytical achievement. He had carried out an ultimately indispensable investigation into the rational unity of mankind, a source of resemblance which hitherto had been merely presumed or skirted; and he had largely succeeded, in the event, in eliminating those apparent logical disparities among cultural ideologies which threatened otherwise to subvert any comparative proposition about human thought. The scope of his inquiries, and the sharpened sense of problem that he brought to the study of collective ideation, made possible a far more critical analysis of alien modes of thought than had ever been practised before. If his initial and particular ideas about primitive mentality turned out in the end to be untenable, this very result provided nevertheless a confidence in the interpretation of foreign ideologies that could not have been justified so long as the ethnographical obscurities that he examined remained unelucidated. His protracted investigations led him in particular to the isolation of what he regarded as a fixed element, fundamental and indestructible, in the nature of man; and this radical type of proposition about human thought, surely in principle the epitome of anthropological theory, could not have been responsibly arrived at except by the style of comparative analysis exemplified by his still unparalleled researches. And if, finally, he was wrong in his general conception of primitive mentality, it must occasion the most immense relief that he was wrong. Man, it would thence appear, is everywhere governed by an informal logic that is characteristic of his natural species; and he exhibits also just as close resemblances in those modes of thought by which he departs from that logic. These conclusions are crucial to the study of mankind, and the extent to which they can be relied upon is due in the main to the labours of Lévy-Bruhl.

Naturally, his work is still not immune to criticism or rectification, and even the ideas that he latterly recorded in his *Carnets* leave considerable room for critical qualification. The chief issues are by no means yet decided, and in the intensive comparative study of natural logic practically all remains to be done. For the present, however, let us simply grant the advantages that Lévy-Bruhl has secured, and extract from his work certain points touching especially on the analysis of belief.

The first has to do with the relationship between society and concepts. Lévy-Bruhl based his theory on the literature about the simpler societies, and he began by subscribing the central assumption of Durkheim and Mauss (1903) about the isomorphism of institutions and representations at that level of social development (Lévy-Bruhl 1910: 20). As late as 1938 he still thought that in some way there was an immediate association between the two: e.g., 'we are dealing with elementary societies, and consequently with different [types of] consciousness' (1949: 105). It is clear enough by now that the connection between social forms and modes of thought is not so simple or direct, and that immediate inferences from one to the other cannot well be drawn, but there is still a real inter-relation. Thus MacIntyre correctly states, in an example that pertains to our central theme, that 'for a sceptic to grasp the point of religious belief . . . he has to supply a social context' (1964: 132); and this necessity is well shown in comparative researches also (cf. chap. 3 above) and particularly by the inevitable difficulties that are faced by translators of the Bible. Belief-propositions implicate, in part at least, jural features of the social world—statuses, moral obligations, norms of co-operation, etc.—and this means that socio-logical analysis is required if the propositions are to be correctly construed. This analysis, in its turn, cannot be confined entirely to local significations but will need ultimately to be cast in terms of abstraction derived from the comparative study of institutions. In construing statements about belief, therefore, it is necessary to com-bine formal analysis, the linguistic translation of cultural singu-larities, and general sociology (cf. Needham 1971a; 1971b), in order

168

to comprehend the setting to which such statements relate. To represent a member of a simple society as declaring 'I believe in God the Father' is an unfeasible venture unless one knows the connotations in that culture of the term that we render as 'father', and this understanding cannot be achieved short of a systematic analysis of the social classification to which the status in question belongs. More fundamentally, to construe an indigenous statement as expressing belief, in the sense of (for instance) confidence in another person, similarly calls for a command of the scheme of rights and moral expectations prevalent in that culture; and this too cannot be had except by a comprehensive study, informed by external comparison, of the laws, customs, and values of the society. The consequence, then, is that belief-statements relating to different societies or traditions cannot be directly correlated in isolation from their original contexts, as though they were propositions in a general psychology, but only by reference to the disparate social connotations that they severally possess in their local settings.

To adumbrate this essential procedure leads to the second point to be established on the basis of Lévy-Bruhl's work. Whatever the precise method followed, or the characteristics of the idiom under study, the quandaries involved in the elaboration of an analytical vocabulary will sooner or later be inescapably encountered. This is a source of difficulty on which Lévy-Bruhl placed particular and instructive stress. In his last notebooks he once again took up the problem, in connection on this occasion with his intention to develop the positive aspect of his findings about abstraction, generalization, and classification in primitive thought. The necessary alternatives of method, he wrote, were two: either to employ the vocabulary of western philosophers and psychologists, or to forge a new vocabulary. The former course leads perpetually to misunderstandings in the description and analysis of the facts, since the reader cannot be asked to strip the words of their 'atmosphere' and of the associations that are universally attached to them. The latter course, on the other hand, demands from the reader a constant and excessive effort that fatigues and repels him, and it recalls distractingly the traditional senses of terms to which new meanings are ascribed; so that however carefully the terms are defined, confusions and misreadings are inevitable, and misunderstandings are thus produced which the most energetic and explicit rectifications will never suffice to dissipate (1949: 82–3).

Lévy-Bruhl confessed that he could see no satisfactory solution to this problem, and resigned himself to choosing the lesser of the two evils, namely to avoid neologisms above all, and also as far as possible the use of common words in uncommon senses. If the work were to take a dialectical form, he recognized, this would not leave much to hope for, and verbal distinctions would be incapable of preventing confusion; rather, they would engender it. But there was, he thought, a possibility of salvation: to apprehend the facts exactly before expressing and formulating them, 'to feel and understand the mental activity in question before framing it in the categories to which our own thought has so accustomed us that they appear to be necessary' (83).

Now whether we can actually feel a mental activity (however this vague allusion may be better defined) as the subjects under investigation do, or whether we could know that we did so even if we were persuaded that we could feel in such a way, is a difficult and perhaps intractable matter. Lévy-Bruhl, for his part, was undoubtedly led to write of feeling, in this connection, by two factors: first, that in his view 'participation' was essentially affective; second, the patent probability that the exercise of pure thought, unmixed with feelings about the object of thought, is a logical abstraction that has no counterpart in the inner reality of thinking individuals. We can concede, in these terms, the grounds for the inclusion of feeling in his injunction, but need not try to specify here what the phenomena might be or how the method could be justified. The other component, referred to as understanding, looks rather clearer but faces us with the graver question how it is that we can apprehend alien thought immediately in its own categories, without influence by our own.[7] There is no doubt that we can in fact do so, for ethnographers thus reach such a point of understanding that they then have to confess themselves unable to translate the indigenous concepts back into their own languages. Yet to grant as much, without answering the question how it is done, does not at all resolve Lévy-Bruhl's difficulty; for the ethnographer (or even an interpreter of the literature, when this is rich enough) is still obliged to render the alien terms, however deficiently, into those of the language in which he communicates his findings. In this event, not only is there an uncertain likelihood that individual verbal concepts will be neatly matched by single words in another language, but it is a question how well the most circumstantial explication of an alien

[7] It is very different indeed from the case of a child learning its first language.

concept will reproduce in the reader the accreted comprehension that the ethnographer has and wishes to convey.

Perhaps, therefore, it is not so much a clear road to 'salvation' that Lévy-Bruhl indicates, but instead a more critical view of the dialectic of translation. In this process, accordingly, we should scrutinize our own verbal concepts with as much deliberate objectivity as, concomitantly, we explore and circumscribe the alien means of thought that we desire to understand and formulate.

VII

In this venture the concepts of belief and experience have a special relevance, and they were touched on very effectively, if in a rather particular context, by Lévy-Bruhl.

The line between belief (*croyance*) and experience (*expérience*) is, he wrote, shifting and fugitive in primitive thought, and may even be obliterated. A Saulteaux Indian may act, to the danger of his life, on the belief that a bear can understand human speech; or an Australian aborigine may feel, to the point of mortal terror, whatever he believes is done at a distance to a detached lock of his hair. Primitives are not indifferent to the distinction between belief and experience, Lévy-Bruhl maintained, but a difficulty remains (1938: 125): How can what for us is indubitably a belief be taken by primitives for an experience?

This is explained, in part at least, by the ambiguity inherent in the use of the terms 'belief' and 'experience', which [to us] seem so clear. They are convenient, and well enough defined, for the description and analysis of our own mental life, but they have recorded, as it were, results gradually acquired by our psychology and our theory of knowledge, and thus bear the mark of our civilization. If they are transported as they stand, together with what they imply, into the study of primitive mentality, they become a cause of hindrance and a source of errors. For in doing so we revert imprudently to the postulate ... that there is a definition of experience that is uniquely and universally valid. ...

These crucial observations bring into focus an issue that is radical to our entire enterprise and, for that matter, to any comparative interpretation of the forms of human understanding.

The concept of experience, which is commonly treated as though it denoted a constant possibility of apprehension and a permanent background to the varieties of categorical thought, is itself an idiocratic and problematical construct. We can infer as much, indeed, from the very word and from the differences exhibited by its formation in comparison with other words that in translation we employ as direct equivalents. The English 'experience' comes from the Latin *experīrī*, try; the original idea is that of making a trial or test, a meaning now obsolete and conveyed instead by 'experiment'.[8] The German *Erfahrung*, by contrast, comes from the OHG *irfaran*, to travel, traverse, pass through, to reach or arrive at; whence the later (15th cent.) adjectival connotations of 'experienced' (*bewandert*), the quality consequent upon being widely travelled, and 'astute' (*klug*), alerted by extended acquaintance to the possibilities in situations. It is true that the distinct English and German words, reflecting different formative ideas, can nevertheless both be traced back to the IE **per-*, to traverse, and can thus be assigned together to a set of related words in Sanskrit and other Indo-European languages; but this common origin serves at once to emphasize the later disparity between them and to make a further contrast with non-Indo-European languages in which there are no words corresponding to either. A responsible demonstration of this latter point would entail a long and intricate investigation, but it appears that there are many languages in which there exist no verbal concepts that are at all equivalent to the acceptations of 'experience' upon which we have relied in assessing the status of 'belief'. The very notion of 'experience', in other words, is itself a singular and complex concept among others, not a neutral and undifferentiated background against which cultural concepts can be set up for inspection.[9]

Lévy-Bruhl's own gloss on the traditional nature of this notion was intended particularly to make the point that we should not arbitrarily exclude the mystical from our definition of experience, on the ground that what primitives regarded as real could not be objectively verified by an observer who did not share their mystical premises. From the standpoint of the primitives themselves, he maintained, the experience that we distinguish as mystical is as real as the other, and it would not be good method to embark on a study of their ideas by contesting the legitimacy of what for them has an

---

[8] The French language still compounds both senses under *expérience*, a word that has thus become a '*faux ami*' to neophyte translators into English.

[9] 'The word "experience" is one of the most deceitful in philosophy' (Whitehead 1927: 16).

unchallenged validity. What we have to do, rather, is really to adopt their attitude and to try to 'procure in ourselves the experience of their mystical experience' (1938: 8–9). But in doing so, and in formulating our task in such terms, an important qualification has to be kept in mind:

Our current notion of experience bears the mark of certain mental habits that are peculiar to the civilizations of the West. Since classical antiquity it has been elaborated over the centuries by generations of philosophers, psychologists, logicians, and scientists. In their hands it has become, above all, a function of the intelligence. Not that they have failed to recognize the presence of important affective elements, but they have not focused their attention by preference on these. The essential role of experience, as it has been described and analyzed by this tradition, from Plato and his predecessors down to Kant and his successors, is to inform the sentient and thinking subject of the properties of creatures and objects with which it places him in relation, to make him perceive movements, shocks, sounds, colours, forms, odours, etc., and to permit the human mind, which reflects on these data and on their conditions, to construct a representation of the world. The general notion of experience that has been thus developed is above all 'cognitive'.

But this, he continues, is an idea that cannot be applied as it stands to the experience of primitives, which is predominantly 'affective' (9). Of course, primitive experience has also the function of conveying information about the environment to which primitives have to adapt themselves; it is the first condition of existence for human beings, as for other living creatures, and without it they would disappear. Indeed, their practicality in observing and classifying features of their environment is marvellous, as is shown by the Eskimo and by the Australian aborigines. Nevertheless, it is not only as a source of useful knowledge that their experience is important to them: it is also because it provides them with data of another sort which in their eyes have a capital interest, and these have to do with the presence and action of supernatural powers on which their well-being and their survival depend. The existence of this invisible world is not taught to them by experience alone: they are convinced of it in advance by their traditions, and these are confirmed by their experience. In this case, therefore, 'it is very difficult to separate what is properly experience from what is properly belief' (10).[10]

[10] Lévy-Bruhl does not specify, in as much detail as he accords to the notion of experience, just what he thinks is properly to be understood by 'belief'; but it is apparent from his argument that when he speaks of 'what

Lévy-Bruhl later returned to this crucial point, in his notebooks, where he stressed that our ideas of experience and belief are so distinct that confusion seems impossible. According to these, 'what is truly a datum of experience can be checked and verified, and, in identical circumstances, experience is infallibly the same for all human subjects (a sound, a colour, a shock, etc.)' (1949: 161). But for the Saulteaux and the Australian aborigines of his examples, 'and for so many others who have no idea of experience as it is defined in our societies, that distinction is not valid' (162). This cautionary reiteration of Lévy-Bruhl's position contains, as will have been seen, a further qualification that has considerable consequences. Not only is it unjustifiable for an outside observer to presume a distinction between experience and belief, but the analytical validity of the distinction is to be determined by whether or not the people under study actually possess the idea of experience as we define it.[11] This stipulation transfers the burden of judgement from external analysis to internal comprehension: we no longer try to decide objectively whether a distinction is usefully to be drawn between experience and belief in the study of alien representations, but we have to discover quasi-subjectively (from the people's own point of view, as expressed in their language) whether those whose thoughts we wish to understand make in social fact any such distinction. If they do not do so, Lévy-Bruhl contends, we are not justified in imputing to them a categorization of apprehensions that our own tradition and our own language incline us to make.[12] For instance, it is a typical question to ask how other people can believe what we are certain cannot be empirical fact, e.g., that a bear can understand human speech or that an attacking shark is the reincarnation of a

we call beliefs' (1938: 129), as differentiated from experience, he means what is asserted to be the case but cannot be empirically demonstrated. This agrees with one use of the term, but cannot stand for the wide range of connotations that more fully comprise this concept (cf. chap. 4 above).

[11] It would of course be self-defeating to take with minute literalness Lévy-Bruhl's phrase about other peoples possessing the 'idea of experience as it is defined in our societies', for then it would obviously follow that other peoples, not speaking our western languages and not sharing the same traditions of ideas, could not possibly define experience exactly as it has been elaborated in the philosophical tradition of western Europe.

[12] The impression that what primitives regard as real experiences are (mere) beliefs, since they cannot be independently substantiated by western observers, derives, Lévy-Bruhl comments, from our habits of vocabulary: 'We can compare it to those optical illusions that we know to be such, but which are produced all the same as soon as the object meets our gaze' (1938: 129).

deceased kinsman, and the question is in principle a reasonable one. But the very formulation in these terms introduces a conceptual distinction that is not likely to be appropriate to an understanding of the situation as it presents itself to those whose thought disconcerts us; and in that case we are not comprehending their experience, for 'thought is a factor in the fact of experience' (Whitehead 1929: 80). If they do not distinguish, in their own equivalent concepts, between experience and belief, then we are not sharing their apprehension and are not understanding their thought if we foist this typically western distinction on to them. In that case, evidently, we cannot validly answer the question, for our foreign premises will distort the inferences that we draw from the situation in question. Lévy-Bruhl's precept of method has the consequence, therefore, that outside our own culture and ideological tradition we should not rely on arguments that are premised on the familiar but disruptive contrast between experience and belief.

But this does not mean that an investigation into the experiential grounds of belief is undermined. To the contrary, it is precisely the contrast with our concept of experience that gives the notion of belief much of its special character. It is indeed this very source of specificity that makes it a question whether other civilizations have elaborated any such concept, and hence poses the problem whether human beings possess a natural capacity to believe.

We have discovered grounds enough to conclude that the concept of belief is not expressed in all languages, which provides occasion to doubt that there is a universal capacity to be recognized; and Lévy-Bruhl has given reason to doubt, in addition, whether the representation of experience, against which we delineate the contrastive operation of belief, is any more general.

To the extent therefore that the concept of belief depends on that of experience, Lévy-Bruhl's invalidation of 'experience' as a term of universal application, in the comparative analysis of alien concepts, is a further indication that belief cannot be regarded as a natural resemblance among men and is not to be expected among their collective representations. Similarly, to accept the outcome of Lévy-Bruhl's investigations into collective ideation, which is in effect that there is a natural ratiocination that is common to all men, leads to the clearer realization that the logical peculiarities of the concept of belief are unlikely to be paralleled in modes of thought that are cast in other languages and are the products of different ideological traditions.

N

10

Relativities

I

Lévy-Bruhl was a founder, together with Durkheim and Mauss, of the comparative and sociological study of forms of classification and modes of ratiocination; but of even greater importance is the fact that he effectively inaugurated a comparative epistemology.

In order to appreciate this crucial development we need to glance back at the predominant approaches to the study of the cultural varieties of thought, in the nineteenth century and the early years of the twentieth, from which Lévy-Bruhl explicitly distinguished his own. There is a quite simple but fundamental train of theoretical progress to be established.

Comte, who died in the year of Lévy-Bruhl's birth, had clearly announced that man's intellectual faculties should be studied by the comparative method: biology could account for the immediate responses characteristic of the human species, but the greater part of man's mental life was necessarily of a social nature and had to be investigated by the new science of sociology. But this idea brought no direct results, either in the works of Comte himself or at the hands of his disciples and successors. The route was barred, as Lévy-Bruhl was to write, by a piecemeal kind of sociology and by a sociological theory that was in reality a philosophy of history (Lévy-Bruhl 1910: 4). Comte's main contention was that he had discovered a 'fundamental law' governing the advance of reason. The intellectual evolution of man followed naturally a course through three stages, 'epochs', or types of thought: theological (or fictive), then metaphysical (abstract), and finally scientific (positive) (Comte 1830: 3–5). Positive philosophy, in considering the results of our intellectual activities, was to supply the only true, rational means of revealing 'the logical laws of the human mind' (32), which hitherto had been sought by means that were very little apt to the purpose. It was in the study of human society, itself so impregnated

176

with traces of theological and metaphysical ideas, that sociology was to have its great effect, by dragging man and his conceptions of himself into the positivist stage that the exact sciences had already triumphantly attained.

But, objected Lévy-Bruhl, this was to argue as though the evolution of the 'higher mental functions' could be studied in humanity taken as a whole, and equally in any individual society whatever. For Comte, there was hence no need to begin with a comparative study of these functions in different types of human society: the law of the three stages sufficed in itself, since any particular laws would readily be subsumed under the more general types. Moreover, he had built up his theory on the basis of the development of Mediterranean civilization, yet he nevertheless did not doubt that the laws of thought thus discovered were valid for all human societies. 'Comte is thus, in a sense, the initiator of a positive science of mental functions, and to a large extent he deserves recognition for having shown that this is a sociological science. But he did not undertake the factual researches that this demands. He did not even make a start ...' (Lévy-Bruhl 1910: 5).

This empirical task was undertaken instead by anthropologists and ethnographers, headed by Tylor and Frazer. Tylor's *Primitive Culture*, first published in 1871, marked in Lévy-Bruhl's opinion a new era in the history of anthropological science: it led to a great accumulation of ethnographical reports from many parts of the world, and as these were amassed they made it strikingly apparent that there was a certain uniformity in the facts. Not only were there 'extraordinary analogies' among far-separated primitive societies, but often there were resemblances that were exact down to the last detail: the same institutions, the same religious or magical ceremonies, the same beliefs and practices concerning birth and death, the same myths, and so on. 'In this way the comparative method imposed itself, as it were, of its own accord' (6). Tylor employed this method, and so did Frazer in his *Golden Bough*, and they thus laid the indispensable foundations for 'the positive science of the higher mental functions', but they did not establish this science, any more than Comte had done.[1]

How was it, then, Lévy-Bruhl inquired, that the use of the

---

[1] Lévy-Bruhl does not mention here the vast comparative labours of Bastian, e.g., his *Ethnische Elementargedanken in der Lehre vom Menschen*, which had appeared in 1895; nor does he refer to Andree's extensive collections of ethnological parallels (1878; 1889).

comparative method had not induced them to do so? The answer, he thought, was (paradoxically) that they had tried to *explain* the relation between 'savage' thought and 'civilized' thought; and it was precisely this explanation that had prevented them going any further. 'They had it [the explanation] ready-made. They did not seek it in the facts themselves; they imposed it on them' (6). In observing among primitive societies certain institutions and beliefs that were so different from our own, they did not ask themselves whether there might not be occasion to examine a number of hypotheses in order to account for the differences. They took for granted that the facts could be explained in only one way. But this was to ignore the question: 'Do the collective representations of the societies considered derive from higher mental functions that are identical with our own, or must they be related to a mentality that differs from our own to a degree yet to be determined? This alternative never occurred to them.' Instead, they postulated, and indeed adopted as an axiom, a 'human mind' that was logically the same in all periods and in all places (7):

Consequently, the collective representations of primitives, which are often so strange to us, and the no less strange liaisons that are to be found among them, do not raise problems the solution to which might enrich or modify the conception that we hold of 'the human mind'. We know in advance that this mind is no different among them than it is among ourselves. All that remains to be looked for is how mental functions that are identical with our own could have produced these representations and these interconnections.

Now the British intellectualists knew of course perfectly well that savage civilizations employed differing schemes of classification and that in their mystical concerns they followed trains of thought that were puzzling to Europeans; but in their comparative anthropological studies they relied with a most comfortable assurance on their own conceptions, and these seemingly had in their eyes an absolute and unchallengeable validity. These ideas, against which they confidently measured the validity and the evolution of alien ideas, had been authoritatively framed by the long Aristotelian tradition of formal logic and had been tested and proved by the advances of European science. Philosophical scrutiny and empirical application thus appeared to have raised western thought, by the turn of the century, to a supreme vantage point that gave a purview and a clarity that had not hitherto been obtained. After Darwin, the cosmological doctrines of the Christian churches had developed fissures that foretold their eventual downfall, and the prestige of natural science was rapidly superseding scriptural authority and the edicts of prelates. The traces of magical thought still found in folklore, superstitious custom, and vulgar reference could be seen as relics of a world view that had almost finally succumbed to the assault of scientific reason, expectable perhaps in the countryside and among the lower orders but not of lasting interest or intrinsic intellectual value. As for savages, they were characteristically sunk in ignorance and pathetic incapacities of reason, their imaginations imbued with magical prejudices and their rational faculties stunted for lack of occasion, at best, to elaborate the critical concepts of empirical cosmology. Doubtless they possessed innate mental resources that were comparable with those of Europeans, and indeed under the influence of European education they could show themselves apt for rapid and satisfactory improvement, but there was little question that in their common condition they were sadly inferior.

The aim of anthropology, consequently, was to explain how the erroneous conceptions of savages had originated, and by what persuasion they had proved so tenacious and predominant in primitive thought. But it was at the same time desired to demonstrate that the errors were reasonable ones, understandable in the circumstances, such as evolution naturally tended to correct and which could more speedily be eradicated as the savages copied European standards of observation and discourse. Thus Tylor conjectured the origin of the idea of the soul in the naive acceptance of dreams as veridical visions; and the cognate virtue ascribed by animism to the realm of nature could hence be seen to have frustrated the perception of causal relations among objects. Frazer explained the practices of magic as an attempt to adjust cause and effect, only on premises of sympathy and contagion which though comprehensible were the products of apprehensive imagination, of common fears and hopes such as a European might feel, instead of critical and empirical analysis. In each instance, too, an attempt was made to explain the persistence of such fundamental mistakes; for it was so obvious that the ideas in question were wrong, and that the inferential connections among them were unsound, that it was a special problem to understand how it could be that even savages did not realize as much for themselves. Once again, the reasons adduced were entirely recognizable and in some cases even creditable, not gross and incomprehensible perversions of understanding. (To see them as the latter would have subverted both the humanitarian ideals of the anthropologists and their theoretical postulate of a capacity for evolutionary advance.) So the power of magical thought resided in part, it was argued, in a quite natural temptation to emphasize apparent successes and to discount failures, to exploit advantages optimistically rather than call an entire mystical doctrine sceptically and arduously into question. The hold of religion was in part the intensity of hope and in part an effect, familiar enough from our own history, of the political domination of the credulous by priests and medicine-men who unscrupulously furthered their own ends. Such intellectual failures on the part of mankind, in the infancy of scientific growth, were certainly deleterious in themselves and obstructive to the progress of the race; but they were merely childish failings in common human endeavours, appropriate to certain early stages of development and, like children's innocent miscomprehensions, ultimately corrigible.

In this reconstruction of the genesis of error and the advance of reason, as it was taken to be, there were more and less qualified judgements, and different observers or analysts displayed varying degrees of subtlety in their interpretations; but in the main European thought was assumed to possess a decided and very great superiority over the primitive modes of thought under study. Given any ideational disparity, then, between western civilization and primitive culture, the anthropologists' unquestioned task was simply to find out where and why the primitives had gone astray.

The study of primitive mentality could thus be instructive in tracing the mental ascent of man, and also perhaps in isolating certain intellectual weaknesses to which even Europeans remained prone, but the values which defined and inspired the anthropological approach did not readily permit a more philosophical kind of instruction. The approach rested on a number of unanalysed premises, prominent among which were: the universal exercise by mankind, though varyingly developed by different cultural traditions, of certain rational capacities common to the species; a regular course of development by which rudimentary and defective mental operations evolved into a more subtle and accurate logic; and the association of inferior modes of thought with preliterate, non-industrial societies, in contrast with the Aristotelian logic and the theories and methods characteristic of the most spectacular scientific successes of the period. So long as these presuppositions prevailed, as they did in the anthropological profession for decades and still do in many uninformed quarters today, a genuinely comparative study of the forms of human understanding was effectively out of the question. Just as it was hardly feasible to carry out a comparison of ethical notions so long as it was assumed that savages were immoral, or to understand primitive mysticisms from the premise that the peoples in question had no religion, or to found a sociology of domestic organization on the assumption that the Australian aborigines lacked the institution of the family, so it was self-defeating to compare modes of thought in the conviction that the intellectual capacities of man were already known and that the forms of correct reasoning were definitively exemplified in the thoughts of the anthropologist.

It was Lévy-Bruhl, more than any other single scholar, who turned inquiry out of the confined circuit laid down by Comte and his British successors, and who took up a quite new line of advance. Basing himself on the work of Durkheim and the other members of the *Année sociologique* school, he first isolated two major defects in the arguments of Tylor and Frazer (Lévy-Bruhl 1910, Introduction). The first was that they ignored the distinct character of collective representations, and thus were satisfied by arguments drawn from individual psychology instead of being guided by the characteristic features that actually gave primitive ideologies their peculiar and problematical forms. The second was that even this recourse did not permit analysis, but led to purported explanations that were not only arbitrary but in the best of cases were no more than probable. The intellectualist arguments of the British anthropologists took for granted certain notions of the association of ideas and the inevitable chains of causality, and they assumed that from these premises they could retrace the mental routes by which primitives had been led 'naturally' to certain beliefs and certain practices. But nothing, Lévy-Bruhl contended, was more risky than this postulate; and it could not be verified in more than perhaps five cases out of a hundred.

Lévy-Bruhl's constant aim, then, from the very beginning of his investigations, was to question whether the human mind were really the same everywhere, and to demonstrate that in societies of different structures there might in fact be found certain associated differences in 'the higher mental functions' (1910: 20).

We have therefore to give up the *a priori* reduction of mental operations to one single type, whatever the societies considered, and the explanation of all collective representations by a psychological and logical mechanism that is everywhere the same.

This radical injunction expressed in a number of respects a very salutary redefinition of attitude toward the assessment of human powers. In the first place, Lévy-Bruhl's approach started from no assumption of an absolute superiority inherent in European modes of thought. What he was concerned to understand were certain features of ideation in primitive societies that could not be accounted for by the traditional notions of our own psychology and our own logic. This is a point of capital importance. He was not maintaining, and never did maintain, that primitive thought was simply 'irrational', but that it was characterized by a distinct mode of rationality that did not correspond to what we regarded as the laws of thought. It had its own 'general laws' (1910: 20) or 'principles' (1931: 11), and the task was to discover what these were.

Now to maintain that there were modes of reasoning that Europeans just could not account for, by reference to their own traditional ideas, carried in itself no implication that western thought was absolutely superior. On the contrary, it implied that the categories and inferences reported from primitive societies had their own validity. This is well brought out by the attention that Lévy-Bruhl paid to the notion of experience. He concluded, as we have seen, that in primitive thought 'the world of their experience does not coincide exactly with ours' (1931: 13); and it followed therefore that we could not trace the course of primitive thought if we assumed instead (as Tylor and Frazer had done) that it did coincide in some universal and necessary way. In isolating what he took to be the peculiar features of primitive mentality, Lévy-Bruhl nevertheless maintained that they were indeed laws of thought, and that these could be established and retrospectively applied. None of this carried the implication that the primitive categories or laws were intrinsically inferior to those that western Europe prided itself on. In fact, whereas from one point of view the primitive apprehension of experience is much poorer than ours, 'from another point of view, it is richer and more complex' (1931: 13). As for the reasoning by which primitives conducted their lives, it was plain enough that they made very efficient accommodations, and that in applying the 'law of participation' to other situations than the practical undertakings in which they excelled they were in no worse case than were Christians who believed in miracles (cf. 1931: 14). Although they employed different causal concepts, they nevertheless submitted, just as we do, to 'the need', as Lévy-Bruhl significantly phrased it, 'to explain events by their causes' (16). If they did not abstain from contradiction, in all those contexts where our own notions of logical incompatibility or physical impossibility would oblige us to do so, this was not because they lacked the concept or were careless of its rigour but because they reasoned from different premises and with different expectations in view.

The true burden of Lévy-Bruhl's arguments, and the momentous realization that his researches first empirically permitted, was therefore that the strangenesses of primitive mentality were not mere errors, as detected by a finally superior rationality of which we were the fortunate possessors,[2] but that other civilizations presented us with *alternative* categories and modes of thought.

Lévy-Bruhl was so impressed by the remarkable resemblances among the collective representations of non-western societies that he couched his arguments in terms of a simple opposition between 'primitive mentality' and western thought. This was understandable, and to an extent it was quite justifiable as a means of exposition. The resemblances were indeed striking, and the simplicity and the starkness of the polar contrast served very economically to isolate fundamental problems for analysis. But it was questionable, all the same, whether this was the best method to pursue, at any rate so constantly as Lévy-Bruhl did over so long a series of studies. Towards the end of his life he was still trying to determine the essential features of a distinct mode of thought, defined by a combination of certain distinctive features; but as early as 1923 Marcel Mauss, in an incidental but far-reaching comment (1923: 27; 1969, 2: 128), posed the question whether this was really the most appropriate line to take:

> I think it would be better, instead of seeking all at once the general character of all categories in all these primitive societies, to investigate the forms of each one of the categories in order then to arrive at conclusions about this general character.

As we have seen above, with regard to the concepts of belief and experience, Lévy-Bruhl did to some extent take up the problem whether the members of the simpler societies possessed precisely the same categories as we took for granted; but he did not adjust his

---

[2] Contrast, in particular, Comte on the positive phase of thought as the final, 'fixed and definitive' state of human intelligence (1830: 4).

method to the point of isolating for intensive analysis the individual categories, such as Mauss had in mind, that were peculiar to other ideological traditions. If he had done so, in those fundamental respects that occupied him, he would have been led to appreciate more fully the force and possible consequences of Mauss' characteristically genial observation.

The chief effect, namely, is to turn the attention of the comparativist back from the comprehension of alien categories and to direct it into a more critical scrutiny of his own. It is not possible to study, for example, the conception of cause (whether or not there is a lexical distinction comparable to that in English or French) in another culture, without at the same time holding in full view the range of connotations that the word has acquired in western philosophical discourse. To consider whether or not the apprehension of experience in a simple society coincides exactly with 'our own', as Lévy-Bruhl cursorily put it, presents at the same time the question of what is our own concept of experience. More particularly, if we consider it a problem to discover whether and in what senses other peoples can be said to believe anything, then at once—as it has been the intention of the present monograph to demonstrate—the problem turns against ourselves, and we have to determine what exactly are the grounds for our own concept of belief. A comparative study of forms of knowledge is thus transformed into a comparative theory of knowledge.

Lévy-Bruhl certainly recognized something of this implication when he wrote, in the introduction to Les Fonctions mentales, of the desirability of framing for comparative analysis problems the solution to which might 'enrich or modify' our conception of the human mind, and he took up this possible outcome once more at the end of that work. The comparative study of the mentality of various human societies, he wrote, enlightens us also about our own mental activity. 'It leads us to realize that the logical unity of the thinking subject, which is taken for granted by the majority of philosophers, is a *desideratum*, not a fact' (1910: 454). This was a crucial hypothesis, as I have stressed, and it has had very considerable consequences, but it still does not quite match the demands of Mauss's adjuration. For to the degree that it is concerned solely with logic it leaves unanalysed the classificatory concepts that characterize other traditions of thought and which logic, whether or not this varies with type of society, serves to connect up into coherent schemes of interpretation and ratiocination.

Mauss presumably had in mind that Lévy-Bruhl might better investigate individually such ultimate categories as space, time, cause, and so on; but his suggestion may be taken to cover also those cultural categories by means of which men of other ideological traditions take account of human powers. In this enlarged comparative perspective, then, we find that our notion of mankind no longer provides a firm basis from which to judge the capacities of other men. The criteria that we are led to employ in assessing the concepts of other civilizations have a like value in assessing our own; and the concepts proper to other traditions must moreover be accorded an application that can in principle compete with ours. In some regards at least there may thus exist genuinely alternative and comparably valid instruments of thought that challenge those of European civilization.

With this realization the categorical assurance represented by Tylor and Frazer must evaporate, and the methodical doubt that inspires Lévy-Bruhl's work stands vindicated. The premise of an absolute conception of human experience, against which cultural styles of thought and action can be objectively assessed, disintegrates; and its place is taken by an apprehension of conceptual relativity in which variant collective representations of man and his powers confusedly contend. The task of social anthropology thus becomes to determine comparatively what means of resolution can be contrived, and whether there are any constant correspondences that can be made into points of reference for a universal and more reliable cartography of human nature.

II

Wittgenstein, at one point in his philosophical investigations, comments: 'What we are supplying are really remarks on the natural history of man' (1953, sec. 415); and at another point he proposes that 'the common behaviour of mankind is the system of reference by means of which we interpret an unknown language' (sec. 206). These mutually relevant statements seem to answer well to my present intention; but in another place Wittgenstein takes up the topics of natural history and language in another focus and with a different outcome. 'If the formation of concepts can be explained by facts of nature,' he asks, 'should we not be interested, not in grammar, but rather in that in nature which is the basis of grammar?' He

concedes that his interest certainly includes the correspondence between concepts and very general facts of nature, but at once dis-
claims an interest in reverting to these facts as possible causes of
the formation of concepts: 'we are not doing natural science; nor yet
natural history—since we can always *invent* natural history for our
purposes' (1953: 230; my emphasis). If anyone believes, he continues, that certain concepts are absolutely the correct ones, then let
him 'imagine' certain very general facts of nature to be different
from what we are used to, and 'the formation of concepts different
from the usual ones will become intelligible to him' (230).

Here we have to determine a point of method, not by controvert-
ing Wittgenstein's practice in relation to his philosophical interests,
but by making a contrast for the purposes of our own undertaking.
The case is similar to that of the relevance of natural languages. In
that connection, as we saw above (chap. 7, sec. VIII), Wittgenstein
resorted to imagining a language in which different verbs were
used where we speak simply of believing. Whether there were disadvantages in this procedure, as far as his problems were concerned,
is a matter I need not argue; but there have certainly proved to be
advantages in turning instead to the real examples of natural languages when the intention is precisely to do a natural history of
man, i.e., to learn something factual from the different ways in
which the psychic constitution of human beings is conceived in
other ideological traditions. This lesson once more has its effect
here. It is an essential part of our investigation that we distinguish
and compare the various ways in which other languages represent
man and his powers, and in each instance we have eventually to
interpret linguistic categories in relation to their attendant social
forms. 'All interpretations have to begin with detecting the standards of intelligibility established in a society' (MacIntyre 1964:
126), and these are to be detected only in the usages of a language
in a social context, what Wittgenstein calls a 'form of life' (*Lebens-
form*). To the extent that it is useful to determine meaning by
establishing use, it is necessary in construing alien verbal concepts
to take into account the variety of institutions in which the concepts have their uses, as well as those apparent constraints in human
experience which may subtend the institutions. Imaginary contrasts with our own usages of belief might well serve to bring out
more clearly certain facets and depths of the concept, but they cannot expose its foundations or justify its propriety to the description
of human nature. A radical investigation of a concept such as

belief has thus to be comparative, and what in the end is inevitably called for is in reality a natural history of man.

The perspective that is provided (in principle, at any rate) by social anthropology has a number of advantages which, I should like to think, have to some extent been brought out in the preceding investigation. These professional predispositions include, briefly: a universal purview; the habit of assessment of social facts by constant comparison; the equal evaluation of all cultural particulars from whatever form or style of civilization; an immediate consideration of the difficulties of translation; and a realization of the importance of the social setting, i.e., the systematic context of collective representations in their relations to institutions. In these regards social anthropologists have become well versed in the interpretation of individual categories of social classification, e.g., Kuki *pu*, Gurage *däbwa* (Needham 1962: 78, 84–5; 1969: 162–3). Such categories are systematically connected with other categories, and in each case the system makes for intelligibility. Social systems compose recognizable types, also, or are organized by certain recognizable principles, such that it is possible by comparison and abstraction to isolate formal criteria of analysis, and these in turn aid in the comprehension of individual cases. Examples of this dialectic of theory and practice may be seen in the development of studies of jural-mystical diarchy (Needham 1967: 437–8) and prescriptive alliance (Needham 1971a, sec. VII). In addition to the comprehensibility provided by social systems, finally, the analyst has the demonstrative advantage that the categories are embodied in persons and are acted out in social conduct.

But the use of a psychological category, such as 'belief', presents a quite dissimilar task of comparative analysis. The connections of such a notion with other categories in a classification of human capacities do not compose so recognizable a system as in the case of a social classification of persons, groups, and institutions. There are no formal criteria, either, such as are resorted to in sociological analysis, but instead logical and other criteria which may not possess —as Lévy-Bruhl was concerned to argue—the value that we are inclined by our own language and traditions to presume they must have. In fact, as Lévy-Bruhl demonstrated, the criteria themselves may even turn out to be necessarily the very objects of the investigation. In this sphere of comparative analysis nothing at all can be taken for granted, and all our expectations must be suspect.

Nevertheless, social anthropologists have not so far carried fully into effect, in conceptual analysis, the precepts of their own characteristic method or the benefits proffered by the examples of Lévy-Bruhl, Mauss, and Wittgenstein. Whereas ethnographers, in particular, have become alert to the dangers of denotative terms such as 'soul', 'gift', 'family', and so on, they have continued in the main to adhere uncritically to a received philosophy of mind, namely that provided by the categories of European languages and the prevailing 'tone of thought' (Waismann 1968: 65) that these express. They recognize that culture is differentiated, but they conduct their investigations as though the operations of the mind were undifferentiated. That is, they take it for granted (or at least write as though they took it for granted) that human nature is already adequately charted and determined, so that an ethnographer approaching a foreign culture, or an analyst interpreting published reports, can assume that the human beings under consideration will have certain well-known logical and psychic capacities that they share with the observer. The prime objective of the present monograph (cf. chap. 1, sec. II) has been to prove that this tacit presumption is not well founded, and that the essential capacities of man have yet to be empirically determined by comparative research.

III

The specific argument of the investigation that I have undertaken here is that the notion of belief is not appropriate to an empirical philosophy of mind or to an exact account of human motives and conduct. Belief is not a discriminable experience, it does not constitute a natural resemblance among men, and it does not belong to 'the common behaviour of mankind'.

It follows from this that when other peoples are said, without qualification, to 'believe' anything, it must be entirely unclear what kind of idea or state of mind is being ascribed to them. The task of ethnography is to render accurate reports of alien modes of experience and action, but I cannot find that this has yet been done with respect to belief.[3] The word is often enough employed

[3] In this respect Richards is justified when he states that the 'study of the varieties of belief, the natural history of the believings, is . . . oddly neglected' (1942: 170). Whether he is right in his inference that 'the neglect somewhat suggests that men are afraid of the topic' is another matter, and one that obviously would be hard to settle.

in ethnographical reports, and with an assurance which implies the assumption that we can directly and with confidence apply the concept of belief to others, but it does not appear that the reportorial use of this word has in any instance provided a precise or verifiable description.

This is not to say, though, that it could not in any circumstances be useful for this purpose. There are, after all, standards of appropriateness for linguistic conventions, and there are certainly many familiar situations in any society in which the English word 'believe' is quite informative. When someone says, in that language and in a situation moreover that we can otherwise interpret, that he believes something, this statement does in a general way throw light on his state of mind, and conclusions about his conduct can be drawn from his expression of belief (cf. Wittgenstein 1953: 191). It is conceivable, therefore, that there might be other languages and situations that so corresponded to the English case—in those features by which it was decided to define belief—that an observer could find it feasible to employ the word 'belief' as a term of description.

But to do so, even in these hypothetically privileged circumstances, would still not be sufficient to provide an exact and adequate description of any state of mind or disposition in the members of the society under study. The observer would first have to stipulate the particular definition of belief that he chose to adopt, then make explicit the grounds of comparison between that culture and his own, and only thereafter isolate the points of similarity between the alien situation and the English paradigm of belief that he had especially in mind. By this stage, however, he would have accomplished his description, by means of the categories and standards of intelligibility proper to the culture in question, only without deriving any objective benefit from the English word 'belief'.

What he would be doing, in effect, would be merely to construct an occasional definition of belief by reference to alien cultural particulars: namely, to select such connotations of the word as fitted the situation, and conversely to select such features of the situation as fitted the definition. This correlative selection and adjustment of particulars, from among culturally heterogeneous concepts and social facts, could presumably lead to a partial description of a kind, and the use of the word 'belief' could thus be thought appropriate in this decidedly factitious sense. But the English word itself would still not be proved apt to contribute directly to a valid understanding of the alien situation or to the framing of a comprehensive and precise description. From a formal point of view, also, the whole procedure would be at once arbitrary and circular.

In any case, what would be the point in deliberately taking this circuitous and potentially misleading course? 'We can only appeal to established habits and conventions of classification and appraisal,' writes Hampshire, 'if . . . we find reason to prefer them to every suggested alternative' (1959: 234). Certainly the established notion of belief should be appealed to only if we have such compelling reason. But it is hard indeed to accept that alternatives to this notion, obscure and intricate as it is, would not suggest themselves to an ethnographer who carefully scrutinized both his linguistic predispositions and what he was trying to describe as the inner states of other people.

Moreover, in the great majority of ethnographical situations, as I suppose, the postulated similarities of linguistic convention and social context will surely not be present, so that in general a reliance on the notion of belief will be not at all appropriate.

The question remains, however, whether the possibility in principle of some significant similarity of the kind could be made the ground for a better formulation of the notion for comparative purposes. Evans-Pritchard has drawn attention to what he regards as 'the failure to build up an adequate and agreed-upon terminology in Comparative Religion' (1956: vi), and the weight of European tradition and linguistic usage would seem to call in the first place for the inclusion of 'belief' in such a vocabulary, but it now appears that the term is not suitable for comparative employment. On the other hand, even the ideal case considered above shows that to try to redefine belief, or even to recommend a quasi-technical agreement on some sense that the word already possesses, would not improve the position. The connotations of the English word are undeniably far too extensive for unqualified employment, yet each attempt to make its meaning more precise, and hence restricted, would reduce the possibility of establishing significant similarities and would narrow the scope of the resultant description even where these similarities could be established. Furthermore, anthropologists cannot interfere with the actual use of language, and in the case of so profound and historical a notion as that of belief they would do better not to try to do so. In some kinds of inquiry, particularly sociological, certain reforms for practical purposes are indeed possible, and technical acceptations and novel terms (e.g., 'cross-cousin', 'prescriptive alliance') can usefully be contrived; but the notion of belief is so central to the European tradition, and so constantly resorted to in everyday discourse, that it cannot readily be manipulated in order to prevent misunderstandings among comparativists. 'What is or is not a cow,' Wittgenstein is said to have remarked, 'is for the public to decide' (Toulmin 1953: 51). What is or is not belief has been overwhelmingly and irreversibly decided, as it were, by centuries of cumulative and often impassioned linguistic usages and events of social life, and it would be greatly inadvisable to contemplate any tampering with the boundaries of this concept in the public contexts where it characteristically belongs.

What we must do, though, is to give up the received idea that this verbal concept corresponds to a distinct and natural capacity that is shared by all human beings. If we are persuaded to do this, then there remains no further occasion to consider any improvement in the use of the word 'belief' as a term of ethnographical report.

IV

Before we take up some of the major implications of these conclusions, and indicate the larger critical enterprise to which this study pertains, perhaps I should interpolate at this point certain qualifications and the responses to some obvious objections.

The first touches on a point of ordinary courtesy in a humane study, and has to do with an aspect of my investigation that has given me concern at a number of places in the argument. I can well understand that those with religious convictions may have found my assertions about belief repugnant, and I wish to assure them that I do not at all desire to offer the least affront to their views. In denying the reality of belief—in the precise respects examined—I do not by any means deny or call into question those fundamental commitments that are commonly, and properly, known as beliefs. Men are willing to suffer and to die for the sake of passionate and irremovable convictions which they themselves term their beliefs; and out of decent respect one would not wish in any way to derogate their resolution or to attack, in general, the validity of what they firmly hold to be eternal truths and perennial values. The same disclaimer applies also to moral convictions unconnected with the doctrines or forms of religion. We believe, we say, in persons, ideas,

O

principles of conduct, and many other matters of close personal import, and my argument is not directed against this formulation or these particulars either. A great historical treasury of linguistic and social institutions gives an inexhaustible and irreplaceable significance to the word 'belief' (as also to *Glaube* and *croyance* and many other terms in the same tradition), and it is not to be thought that an investigation of the present kind could ever have been inspired by disregard for such a central idea in western civilization. If any readers should remain perturbed, nevertheless, by implications that they may have extracted from the argument, perhaps the asseverations just made may induce them to peruse again what I have actually written, and to consider whether my analysis can really touch (as I am sure it cannot) the substance of their beliefs or the terms in which they express them.[4]

Next, and in order to avert an expectable inference, perhaps I ought to stress that I am not urging the general abandonment of the word 'belief', or a rectification of the vocabulary of belief-statements as these are customarily expressed within our own tradition. (I could not responsibly propose as much without having made an intensive study of the grammar of belief in English.) Thus I do not object, and should not expect any reader who had accepted my arguments to object, to Waismann, for example, when he writes of a philosopher who 'believes' that he has freed himself of certain restrictive notions (1968: 32). There is really no reason to object, for I know the language in which the statement is made and the range of connotations of 'believe'; I can appreciate the context, which helps me to narrow down the connotations possibly intended, and to select from these the most appropriate meaning; and I understand the particular point at issue, the concern that gives the word its value in that place. But when I read an ethnographical report none of these conditions obtains—not even the last—and in this case I can make nothing, with any confidence or certainty, of belief-statements that relate to people speaking another language in a strange social environment. Here we have an instance of the feasibility of a linguistic reform for certain practical purposes, 'the improvement of our terminology in order to avoid misunderstandings in practice' (Wittgenstein 1953, sec. 132); and since the possibilities of misunderstand-

[4] Perhaps I am vicariously over-sensitive in this disclaimer (though it has to be made), for I can well imagine that religious critics will conclude that I do not know what I am talking about, which is in fact what they are talking about—and I have already conceded that (chap. 6, sec. VII).

ing that are inherent in the notion of belief are so great, I do indeed urge that in ethnographical reports, or in comparative epistemology, the use of the word should be quite abandoned. It is true that in another context Wittgenstein has asked, 'Does it matter what we say, so long as we avoid misunderstandings in any particular case?' (1953, sec. 48), and I suspect that some anthropologists will be inclined to protest that in ethnographical practice common usage has served well enough; but it is precisely in particular cases, and the more deleteriously as we try to comprehend cultural particulars, that misunderstandings (and worse) are almost invariably created by the unqualified use of the word 'belief'.

It might be contended, on the other hand, that I have become bemused by the very word, simply by concentrating on it so unremittingly, and that this inordinate degree of attention has itself fabricated difficulties of understanding. It is well known that the mere repetition of a word can eventually reduce it to meaninglessness,[5] and the suggestion might hence be made that my wearisome reiteration of the word 'belief' has had just such a result. But we have not been simply repeating the word: we have repeatedly examined its actual and possible uses in a large variety of historical, social, psychic, and hypothetical contexts, and this perpetual variation of viewpoint and situation has prevented any attrition of significance. The effect, I should like to think, has perhaps been something like that of Wittgenstein's 'sketches of landscapes' in his philosophical investigations: 'The same or almost the same points were constantly being approached afresh from different directions, and new sketches repeatedly made' (1953: ix). In this way the meaning of the word has been traced throughout its limits, and our comprehension of its topography and boundaries has been made increasingly precise, in a great number of traverses, not reduced or nullified. Another objection, of a related kind, is that, as Valéry is said to have written, there is not one word that we can understand if we only go deep enough.[6] The aphorism certainly has a perturbing point, but it applies, as it says, to all words and not specifically to belief. What is being asserted about this particular word, however, is that it belongs to a curious kind of words, and

---

[5] In a *mantra*, it is true, the repetition intensifies a conviction of meaningfulness; but in this case it is not any discrete characteristics of a verbal concept that bring about this result.

[6] 'Il n'y a pas une parole qu'on puisse comprendre, si l'on va au fond'; quoted, without location of source, by Sartre (1936: 76).

that it is the 'odd-job' or 'peg' characteristic—something that we have indeed been able to understand—that in part deprives the notion of belief of a precise application in comparative studies.

Another line of criticism, again, might be that my eclectic approach, casting about all over the place for clearer views of belief, suffers by the lack of a constant set of criteria, and that the inquiry has followed a rather haphazard method that militates against a unified conclusion. There would be some justice in this characterization, but I am not sure that any analytical disadvantages have actually resulted from the procedure. I should like to claim, instead, that the diverse means to which I have resorted in tackling the problem of belief have in themselves demonstrated what a multifarious problem it really is. To adopt a clear-cut procedure, complete with declared axioms and rules of evidence and method, or to concentrate on just one aspect (logical, phenomenal, linguistic), might have led to a more coherent and better integrated exposition, but the argument could well have been impaired or even vitiated by the operational stipulations. The concept of belief has so many aspects, many of which have no systematic connections one with another, that to concentrate on only one of them, or to try to delineate all of them by a method appropriate only to one of them, would have resulted in a very partial account. As it is, a philosopher who approves one part of the argument (e.g., an examination of linguistic sources of misunderstanding) may disapprove another (on the ground, e.g., that it involves an outmoded psychological empiricism); a social anthropologist may agree with a consideration of institutions, and their coercive influence on individuals, but be restless with issues of psychological inference; or a philologist who subscribes an argument about the changing historical connotations of a word[7] may not accord the same value to statements about dreams or bodily intuitions. It is not only that my own relative competence in such different fields of inquiry cannot be of comparable reliability in each, as I have recognized

[7] Perhaps I should be more explicit, incidentally, in recognizing the large degree of uncertain inference that there can be in establishing an etymology and tracing the development of meaning (cf. above, chap. 4). I have in mind, for instance, Benveniste's salutary argument that the shift of sense in a well-known philological paradigm was not from the solidity of 'tree' to the firmness of 'trust', but inversely from *der-w/*dr-eu, firm, solid, to *derwo-, etc., tree (1966: 298–301)'. This cautionary case does indeed illustrate the interpretative hazard, but it also shows that the hazard can largely be evaded by a reliance upon established authority and competence.

from the beginning (chap. 1, sec. VI), but that my readers will be in the parallel position of not being able to make, with much confidence, a unitary assessment of the argument in which all of its parts are taken into account. Nevertheless, it is the problem itself, I maintain, that presents so many disparate issues for analysis; and it is this complexity that conduces to an account that continually changes perspective.

For that matter, my own unease is rather that I have dealt too quickly and superficially with problematical issues which I know are more profound than I have made them appear. What I have tried to do, though, is to present a case, as clearly as I can and with due recognition of its many different facets. My aim has not been to carry out a complete analysis (assuming one could conceive what that might be), but to offer sufficient grounds for the reassessment of the status of the concept of belief. What is called for here is not completeness but a panoptic view. How to achieve so effective a circumscription of the problem of belief is largely a question of literary judgement, and there will be different opinions about this quasi-technical task of presentation. Also, the 'discontinued way of writing, may have occasioned, besides others, two contrary Faults, *viz.*, that too little and too much may be said . . .' (Locke 1690, Epistle to the Reader), and I should have to admit that the book contains such disproportion. But I should not like the defects or lacunae in the style of exposition that I have adopted to be taken for a neglect to realize that certain matters have in themselves, or in other contexts, more importance than I have accorded them.

In the same vein, I should like to make it clear that the sources that I cite, though numerous and quite varied, are not by any means all that I have found relevant to the topic, nor those that alone I wish to commend to others who take up the matter. They are adduced because they convey special lessons, or make my points in an effective way, or simply because they are convenient or offer some other quite occasional advantage. So the fact that, as I realize, I have not discussed the views of James or Buber, Ryle or Hintikka, Wisdom or Black,[8] and many others who have written about belief,

---

[8] Not even, for instance, Black's 'Saying and Disbelieving' (1952; cf. on the same topic Wilks, Deutscher, and Bonney, listed in Griffiths 1967: 166) —in this case partly for the reason that the logical oddity in a hypothetical proposition such as 'Oysters are edible, but I don't believe that they are' (56) does not depend on any particular stipulation of what is to count as belief.

does not necessarily mean that I have not found them valuable or worth quoting. But in even so digressive an inquiry as this has been, there must be some economy, and if Sir Thomas Browne or Lichtenberg makes a point for me there would be no profit in accumulating other observations to the same effect, however cogently they may be put; and certainly there would be none in doing so just to look encyclopedic or to claim the support of a weightier phalanx of authorities. Actually, in this type of undertaking I am not sure that there can be any 'authorities', except naturally those who are experts on specific points in etymology, biblical criticism, and other such matters of exact scholarship; for the problems implicit in the concept of belief are so multifarious that there can be no prior means of knowing what considerations and fields of learning are contingent and what are intrinsic to the undertaking. In fact, a rather makeshift argument is probably the best, even though it may at some places look disorderly or repetitious. If one point can be made in a certain way, and another in a different way, good enough; and if the same point can be made first on some particular grounds and then again on others, all the better. Also, after Locke once more, 'I shall frankly avow, that I have sometimes dwelt long upon the same Argument, and expressed it in different ways, with a quite different Design' (1690, Epistle). In this monograph, as it has turned out, I have not so much presented an integrated and polished argument, neatly articulated and continuously shaped throughout its length, but I have tried to carry out what is precisely speaking an investigation.[9] The itineraries, maps, sketches, bearings, and so on have been registered only to such a point of detail and practical use as will enable other venturers into the territory to find their own way about.

One source of special difficulty in this kind of investigation calls for particular emphasis, for it affects both the evidence upon which I have initially relied and the future inquiries to which the argument may lead. The analysis of belief-statements, or the search for

[9] On this score, however, I might as well admit that on looking back over the preceding chapters I find the argument in general to be rather constrained and over-prudent; that it sometimes halts before a theoretical vista just when a vigorous advance is called for. Partly this is the result of my diffidence in writing about so wide a variety of topics in which I have no special competence, and of course it would have been irresponsible simply to give way to recklessness; but, all the same, a bolder and less conventional approach might have served better at some places to explore this irregular and accidented concept.

the criteria by which these are to be determined, is in the first place
a linguistic task; and in any given cultural context this task
demands a mastery of the language, and a familiarity with the
attendant social forms, as subtle and as profound as the practised
command with which we unravel the grammar of belief in English
in its relation to the institutions of our own historical tradition.
The comparativist, naturally, has not these competences on any
appropriately wide scale, and he has therefore to place his trust in
the quality of the ethnographical reports. But there are not many
of these, either, that record the minute nuances and other linguistic
evidences that ultimately are essential to a proven argument. Not
only this, but in the nature of the case it is not probable that many
reports could ever possess such qualities of detail and reliability.
The best instances are the publications of linguistic missionaries,
those who dedicate their lives to gaining that familiarity with
foreign languages as will permit them to expound their faiths in
alien idioms,[10] but men of this calibre are very few and are likely
only to diminish in number. In their place we are forced to depend
more exclusively on professional anthropologists, and it has to be
admitted that there are inevitably certain hazards in doing so (cf.
above, chap. 2, sec. III). To begin with, ethnographers spend comparatively short periods in the field, and the instructiveness of these
periods, from a linguistic point of view, is very commonly impaired by the fact (far more general, perhaps, than is usually
imagined) that the ethnographer lives among the people under
study rather than with them. Then there are of course variations
among individual investigators in the degree of linguistic preparation they have received, in their own talents of ear and tongue in
learning foreign languages, and in many other respects that bear
upon the quality of their translations. These disadvantages can
scarcely be mitigated very far by even the numerous aids that
modern ethnographers can often count on: grammars, dictionaries,
texts, the Bible in vernacular translation, a local press, or informants
who have been educated in English.[11] These compensations are

[10] I think, with humble admiration, of such as Professor Dr. L. Onvlee
(Sumba), Fr. J. A. J. Verheijen (Manggarai, Flores), Fr. J. P. Crazzolara
(Nuer), and my friends in the Borneo Evangelical Mission.

[11] The example of Mr. Bangot Kier (above, chap. 2, sec. VI) introduces the
point that today there are numerous societies, traditionally of the 'tribal'
kind conventionally studied by anthropologists, in which there are to be
found members whose command of the ethnographer's language far exceeds
any converse competence that the foreign investigator might ever hope for:

most convenient, but they cannot in themselves procure that fluency and sense for allusion that can come, and even then only most arduously, with more protracted residence and constant discourse. Ethnographers themselves are in the main, I trust, sharply aware of these factors and desiderata, if with varying degrees of stricken conscience, but for a medley of understandable reasons their linguistic doubts and deficiencies do not figure in their writings.[12] Anthropological monographs tend to convey, rather, an impression of linguistic confidence and ability that, to judge sometimes by other evidences and indications, is somewhat unexpectable in the circumstances. It is important, therefore, to make explicit the fact that ethnographical reports about alien concepts can hardly ever be accepted as they stand.[13] Admitted, ethnographers sometimes do quite extraordinarily well in their abbreviated attempts to learn foreign languages and strange collective representations, and in certain realms of observation and inquiry their accounts are often reliable enough for given purposes; but in the study of modes of thought their inevitable linguistic weaknesses must qualify the comparative and philosophical value of their reports. There is, moreover, another source of uncertainty in anthropological reports about modes of thought and classification, namely the philosophical ignorance of the average social anthropologist. This is a relative matter, of course, since no educated man is likely to be philosophically wholly naive; and even a philosophical education, also, could be thought the wrong education by a philosopher of a different persuasion. But in general the matter is plain that an ethnographer is unlikely to ask revealing questions about categories, inference, contradiction, and other topics of the kind if he has not prepared himself philosophically to do so. As far as the concept of belief is concerned, at any rate, we have encountered indications enough

one can meet, for instance, educated Dinka and Nyoro whose English is quite exquisitely modulated, and whose thoughts are expressed in that language with admirable subtlety. There can be very few ethnographers whose conversation in the vernacular could at all compare, and in fact I really wonder if there are any such.

[12] One agreeable exception is Gregory Bateson, who with an engaging candour modestly confesses the stumbling and rudimentary character of his speech in Iatmül (1932), and thus clearly forewarns his readers of the precarious linguistic foundations to some of his reports on the intricacies of Iatmül modes of thought and social classification (cf. Korn, n.d., chap. 5).

[13] And all the less, I must add, when the ethnographer asserts without qualification that the people he studied simply 'have no word' for some abstract concept or another. This is a bad sign.

that ethnographers who make belief-statements in their accounts are not translating the epistemological premises or the psychological idioms that are actually prevalent in the languages of the societies they study; and, to judge by the philosophical complexities that we have discovered in our own verbal concept, it seems out of the question that such statements (cf. above, chap. 1, sec. II; chap. 2, sec. III) should have been subjected by the anthropologists to any philosophical scrutiny. Under one aspect, therefore, these conclusions confirm the need for a comparative inquiry of a strictly philosophical kind into the concept of belief; whereas, under another aspect, they also show that the ethnographical evidences from other languages and traditions are generally inadequate to such an inquiry.

These cautionary observations about comparative ethnography bring up a further problem about the analysis of belief, and one that is presented by evidences with which we are much more familiar and over which we have far greater control. This is the question why it is that the family of belief-expressions in European languages has had such an extraordinary and increasing vogue. I have tried to present, in chapter 4, a survey of the traceable beginnings of our concept of belief and its subsequent consolidation and variegation in the European tradition of thought. This account served well enough, I hope, to make the points in question at that stage in the argument, i.e., to exhibit the semantic roots, the historical elaborations, and the idiocratic complexity of a verbal concept that might otherwise be regarded as a simple term of psychological report. But I did not make it my concern to conjecture historically why the concept of belief should have lent itself so readily to this course of development, or why today it should tend to be given an even more extended use. I did not do so because these struck me as questions that pertained especially to the history and forms of European thought rather than to a comparative investigation into a supposed aspect of all human nature. But they are very important issues, calling for the talents of an Onians (1951), and I recognize that no study of belief could be well rounded out unless they too were investigated. That considerations of expository economy should have excluded them from the present monograph argues not at all against their great importance to an understanding of a dominant ideological factor in European civilization.

On the score of economy also there is yet another major ground of criticism that I need to anticipate. It could be claimed by a logical purist that the argument seriously lacks economy, and that the case of belief could have been disposed of far more simply. An extreme exemplification of this point of view could in fact be provided by the quotation of just two passages from Wittgenstein. The answer to the question 'Is belief an experience?' (1961: 89) is: (1) 'The meaning of a word is not the experience one has in hearing or saying it, and the sentence is not a complex of such experiences... The sentence is composed of words, and that is enough' (1953: 181); (2) 'The question is not one of explaining a language-game by means of our experience, but of working out a language-game' (1953, sec. 655).[14] When a language provides no equivalent to 'belief' there is hence no belief; and since it is readily discoverable that many languages make in fact no such distinct provision, it follows that belief is not a conceptual capacity common to all men. This is indeed a highly condensed formula for an argument, and for some it might conceivably make my case, thus dispensing with all the apparatus of historical, philological, behavioural, and other arguments on which I have instead lengthily relied. But this hypothetical class of readers would not need the argument, for they would already so thoroughly have pre-empted the sources, directive ideas, and theoretical ambitions which I have deployed here that they would have needed only to consider the question set in order to decide at once what in their view the answer would have to be. At least, that would be so in principle; but to assume as much would also mean to ascribe to such critics a fund of ethnographical knowledge comparable to that of a social anthropologist, and in addition a command of the linguistic and sociological means by which an anthropologist does in practice work out a strange language-game. These circumstances are not likely to obtain very widely, and such persons must surely be very few.[15] Besides, 'I

[14] '... die Feststellung eines Sprachspiels.' The published translation has merely '... noting a language-game'; whereas the point of the German is, it seems to me, that the usages of the language have to be established, determined, or ascertained—which is a far more demanding adjuration.

[15] For instance, the Wittgensteinian analysis of the constitution of a class has been central to my case (chap. 7), yet in this regard Bambrough, in a publication so recent as 1961, has averred that among modern writings on the problem of universals only two philosophers (John Wisdom and D. F. Pears) have shown 'a complete understanding of the nature and importance of Wittgenstein's contribution' (1961). It should not be forgotten, either, how few years have elapsed since Wittgenstein's views have been given a public circulation, beyond the small circle of his intimates and auditors at Cambridge; and for this reason too there may be more point in my elementary recapitulations of certain of his ideas.

pretend not to publish this Essay for the Information of Men of Large Thoughts and quick Apprehensions', and to 'such Masters of Knowledge' (Locke 1690, Epistle) I can only respond that I have written this book in the conviction that there must be some others who, like myself, stand to gain from a more cursive consideration of belief a degree of correction in their thoughts about men and their knowledge of them. Yet, all the same, there is a kind of reverse aptness to the criticism that I have conjectured. Wittgenstein's statements cannot in themselves make the case that I have argued out in the present inquiry; but my argument can, I think, give more foundation and substance to his conclusions. Likewise with another of Wittgenstein's remarks: 'the expression of belief . . . is just a sentence;—and the sentence has sense only as a member of a system of language' (1958: 42). On the one hand, the whole of my investigation into the concept of belief could be considered as an extended gloss on this single passage; but on the other hand I should like to think that the investigation has buttressed Wittgenstein's observation, radically invaluable though it is, with more evidences and proofs than it could otherwise have had in its support, and has demonstrated that its cogency is as general as its form would claim.

This brings us finally, in this section, to three interconnected points on which I desire especially not to be misunderstood.

First, in trying to find out the meaning of 'belief' I have been guided in the main by Wittgenstein's precept that the meaning of a word is its use in language; but I have not followed this precept with any rigid dogmatism, and I should not wish it to be thought that I overlook Wittgenstein's express caution that meaning is to be thus determined 'for a *large* class of cases—though not for all . . .' (1953, sec. 43).

Second, Wittgenstein's analysis of the constitution of a class has proved crucial in the decomposition of the concept of belief, and I am sure that the consequent procedure can much improve our understanding of other concepts in humane studies,[16] but I do not maintain that this is necessarily the correct example to follow in every case. After all, the formal logicians of the European tradition had a great deal of practical use, as have common men, out of the

---

[16] As I have tried to demonstrate elsewhere, though in a very compressed fashion, in connection with the stock anthropological categories 'kinship', 'marriage', 'descent', 'relationship terminology', and 'incest' (Needham 1971b).

idea that a class is to be defined by the possession of a common feature; and when Hampshire, writing after Wittgenstein and in evident intellectual sympathy with his ideas, states that 'the sense of a classificatory concept is fixed by the contrast between the central and unquestionable specimens falling under the concept and the border-line and challengeable cases...' (1959: 225), there is good occasion to take this definition perfectly seriously. There are many complex and important concepts the meanings of which can be better understood by reference to family likenesses among their uses, or to the odd-job functions that they serve; but there are other such concepts that may respond better to the traditional common-feature definition of their constitution. For that matter, it is to be expected that one and the same verbal concept could be analysed in one way in connection with a certain problem or interest, and again in the other way with regard to some other intention. Moreover, it might be that in some cases a dual approach, looking at a classificatory concept under the two aspects in combination, would yield the most revealing answer to whatever question was put to it. And, in any case, since men can classify as they please, under whatever formative influence they may have been educated and with whatever purpose they may conceive, it must in principle remain admissible that a class may well be constituted by reference to a common feature. As a matter of fact, I take it, men do classify in this way in a variety of circumstances: because, perhaps, they have been taught that logically this is the correct method; or because they wish to find out subsequently what does or does not go with a certain feature; or because in practice, in some technical line of work, it has proved to be useful; or because by the rules of a certain situation, e.g., a psychological test, only that classificatory procedure can score points; or because an artificial class, deliberately based on an arbitrary common feature, makes a philosophically instructive contrast with the classificatory concepts of natural languages; and by virtue of many other reasons and occasions.

My third point is that, although we should not be mistaken about genera and species 'as if they were Things regularly and constantly made by Nature, and had a real Existence in Things' (Locke 1690, bk. 3, chap. 5, sec. 9),[17] there is great variation in the extent to which phenomena may appear to correspond with the ideas of them. Thus Hampshire writes that 'certain resemblances and analogies of feeling seem more "natural" and inevitably noticed than others',

[17] Locke's *Essay* is cited, here and below, in the fourth ed., enl., of 1716.

and that we can expect to find that some resemblances are recorded in every vocabulary (1959: 62). There are many transitions from phenomena to concept that do indeed seem 'natural' (cf. Whitehead 1927: 3–4), and which may be regarded as specific to the operation of the human brain and thus as characteristic of human nature. So that whereas I have repeatedly stressed the conventional character of the concept of belief, and have relied in doing so on the unfettered liberty possessed by men to link one thing with another in the formation of a classificatory concept,[18] I do not wish to maintain an unreservedly idealist position. On the other hand, when I postulate natural resemblances among men, and suggest that these may be recognized in any cultural classification of human powers (chap. 8), I do not maintain, either, a wholly realist position. Just as one might say that certain phenomena approach an autonomous or natural mode of presentation, and that others do not, so we need to appraise our experience now by a realist style of representation and again by an idealist. If we are to concede so much relativity in the apprehension of things as the results of our inquiry into belief have pressed us to do, then we must permit no absolutism in the methods by which we take account of them.

V

Waismann has suggested that the logical form of philosophical arguments screens what actually happens—'the quiet and patient undermining of categories over the whole field of thought' (1968: 21). What I have been working toward in the present inquiry is the standpoint that the first task of social anthropology is precisely this: the undermining of categories throughout the entire range of cultural varieties in the conception of human experience.

Some categories in the description of human nature may, like that of belief, sway and disintegrate as their bastions are sapped. Others,

---

[18] 'Of any two things whatever, there is some respect in which they can be said to resemble each other and not to resemble some third thing' (Hampshire 1959: 31).

Consider, too, the ideal objects in the *Encyclopaedia of Tlön*: one object may be composed of two sense elements such as the colour of sunrise and the distant call of a bird; other objects are made up of many elements—'the sun, the water against the swimmer's chest, the vague quivering pink which one sees when the eyes are closed, the feeling of being swept away by a river or by sleep' (Borges 1965: 23; cf. above, chap. 7, sec. VIII).

it is to be expected, will turn out to be far more resistant, and the result of attempts to undermine them by comparative analysis will prove instead to be a firmer delineation of their foundations and a substantiated estimation of their real sources of strength. But in any instance the conceptual preparation of the comparativist (whether social anthropologist, philosopher, or whatever) will need to consist in an instructed resolution to take absolutely nothing for granted. The categories of experience are infinitely variable, and those that an alien culture has formulated are to be apprehended only by means of a critical awareness that makes as few prior assumptions about human capacities as the necessary coherence of thought and observation will permit. What is thus required of the comparativist is, as Bachelard urged in coming to terms with poetic imagery, a systematically awakened naïvety (Bachelard 1960: 4): social anthropology too ought to be in this way 'a school of naïvety'. We can hence feel ourselves, as Bachelard proposed in consequence of his 'phenomenological' method of literary criticism, 'automatically psycho-analysed' (3), stripped of our conceptual predilections and the traditional constraints of our language.

This is not simply a therapeutic ambition, let alone a destructive conception of social anthropology, for it can have positive effects. On the one hand, it brings us more immediately, with systematically reduced prejudices, into relation with the distinctive features of those alien ideologies that we desire to understand. On the other hand, as we increase our knowledge of the more constant forms that cultural classifications may assume, and successively test their correspondence with our empirical appraisals of human nature, so we can elaborate a set of critical expectations that will prepare our perceptions of alien realities. In other words, comparative analysis can be pursued, by means of this dialectic of observation and self-observation, as a technique of apperception.

The present inquiry has illustrated something of these dialectical advantages. On the former score (the clearer appreciation of the categories of other traditions), we can now see that the problem posed by contradictory statements about belief among the Nuer, with which we illustrated the case for an investigation (chap. 2, sec. VII), has dissolved. At any rate, it cannot be resolved in the terms in which the issue was first stated. The problem cannot be formulated, that is, as whether or not the Nuer possess the concept of belief. Instead, this question must be seen not to constitute an empirically decidable problem. In different acceptations, the Nuer both possess and do not possess a concept of belief. The only recourse is not to seek a decision between the apparently conflicting reports of the missionaries and the ethnographer, but to take account of the linguistic grounds that permit the missionaries to ascribe the concept of belief to the Nuer, together with those that incline the ethnographer to deny the Nuer this concept. This procedure would involve the mutual adjustment of the idioms of Nuer, German, and English; and from it there would emerge, not a decision that the Nuer do or do not have a concept of belief, but a clearer and more comprehensive appreciation of the respects in which this adjustment is essential if a translation is to be made.

The efficacy of the translation, i.e., its dual appropriateness to the idioms and forms of experience registered in Nuer and in a European language, will depend in part on what is being translated. For the rendition of one statement (the description of one kind of social situation) the term 'belief' may be appropriate;[19] for other statements it may not be so appropriate, and it may be judged that an equivalent such as 'think', 'hope', 'trust', 'expect', or 'imagine' will fit the circumstances better. Similarly the premises and the particular intention of the observer will also need to be taken into account; that is, he will be included in the appraisal of the situation, as a component in it, rather than be left outside as though he were a medium through which it could be objectively viewed. One reporter of Nuer ideology may then well say that the Nuer express belief in their god, and within the grammatical conventions of the language in which he says so we need have no difficulty in grasping the particular respect in which he means this; whereas another reporter may equally well say that the Nuer do not do so, and we need have no difficulty in understanding him either. By this view, there is no contradiction between the two reports, but instead an exploitation of different alternatives from among the connotations of 'belief'; and also, probably, the matching of these with different alternatives from among the connotations of whatever word in Nuer is held to correspond, or not to correspond, to 'belief'. In principle, the confrontation of such opposed reports, and then their conflation into a wider interpretation of the circumstances, could lead to a more critical and better founded apprehension of the linguistic forms and the social context in which the Nuer themselves are implicated; but this conclusion would not constitute, either, a

[19] Though see particularly sec. III above.

proof that the Nuer possess or do not possess, a concept of belief. The result, that is, would be a composite view of a segment of Nuer ideology in different perspectives, not an empirical decision between the accuracy of the perspectives.

In either case, the practical problem still cannot be whether or not the Nuer are ever in a particular inner state describable as believing. With this we come to the latter advantage mentioned above, namely the preparation of our perceptions such that we shall better discern alien realities. In the case of the Nuer, the conclusion stands that, on the evidence provided by both parties, we are completely ignorant of what is the interior posture of the Nuer toward their god. We have no idea, factually, whether or not any of the Nuer words under examination (above, chap. 2, secs. IV–VI) denotes a distinct state of belief. This much is just as clear at this point as when we began. But at the conclusion of our investigation we now have overwhelming reasons to doubt that this can be a real problem, i.e., a matter for empirical decision, because the very reality of such a distinct inner state has been so radically called into question. It is not just whether the Nuer are in such a state in association with the use of the word *liaghè*, for instance, but whether it is within the capacity of any human beings to experience a state of belief. My argument has been that belief is not a discriminable mode of experience, and that it does not constitute a natural resemblance among men. If these contentions are right, so that belief can no longer be accounted among human capacities, then the problem about the Nuer—a problem, that is, conceived as an empirical question concerning their inner state in relation to *kwoth* —must be seen to be no problem at all.

By my account, the point is therefore not to demand, or to contrive, a test that will establish whether or not the Nuer experience a state of belief in the respect at issue, but to recognize that they could not possibly experience such a state. In preparing our critical expectations of Nuer life, the forms in which they apprehend and represent their distinctive experience of human existence, the advantage that we now possess in this regard is simply not to expect belief.

VI

I think, then, that the investigation reported here has undermined the category of belief as a term of universal application. If I am right in this,[20] it is a decided and very useful result; and it should have consequences, also, both in the practice of comparativists and in the more general conception of human nature. But even if the conclusion to this particular inquiry is judged correct, it is still only a beginning. There are many other verbal concepts, referring to aspects of experience or to the inner capacities of mankind, that similarly need to be examined comparatively.

The first candidate, perhaps, is a notion that is closely connected with that of the English 'belief', namely the complex of ideas denoted by 'credence' (credit, credible, etc.) and the French *croyance*. Not that credence is a notion of such psychological prominence as belief, for it has in English no verbal form and thus does not so much conduce to the assumption that there is a distinct inner power at issue. To give credence to (or to credit) somebody is to adjudge him worthy of trust, and this is an estimation that belongs to public morality; it focuses on the character of someone else rather than on the attitude that one holds towards him. A creed, on the other hand, is expressly something in which one believes; and this aspect of the notion is directly connected with *croyance*, belief. The use of the French verbal concept calls for a separate inquiry, and it would be interesting then to compare the grammar of belief in French with that in English;[21] but an enterprise that corresponds more effectively with that undertaken here is to trace the notions of credence and *croyance* back to their common root in Latin, and in doing so to compile a separate chapter in the history of European thought.

More fundamentally still, there is the question of the deeper roots of the Latin, traceable through a set of words in Old Irish, Sanskrit, Avestan, and other Indo-European languages. This derivation has already been intriguingly indicated by Benveniste, in his

---

[20] I must admit that I still cannot finally quell the recurrent doubts that afflict me in this matter, the worry that I may have just gone radically wrong. But I should like to think, on the other hand, that these perturbations are really signs of the hold still exercised over me by a Christian upbringing, and by the insistent persuasions of the English language.

There is, too, the factor mentioned by Wittgenstein (one sometimes thinks that that extraordinary man saw everything): 'The problems arising through a misinterpretation of our forms of language have the character of *depth*. They are deep disquietudes; their roots are as deep in us as the forms of our language, and their significance is as great as the importance of our language' (1953, sec. 111).

[21] Also, of course, 'faith' and *foi*.

P

examination of *créance* and *croyance* (1969, 1: 171–9),[22] and the original form has been reconstituted as **kred-dhē*, to place the *kred*. Unfortunately, however, the meaning of **kred* remains obscure (178). Benveniste can offer no more than the conjecture that it was a sort of pledge or stake, something material but endowed with a personal sentiment, a notion vested with a 'magical force' that belongs to all men and which is reposed in a superior being (179). This case is thus likely to remain long undecided, and there is not at present the prospect that the development of the notions of credence and *croyance* will be charted as thoroughly as is possible with 'belief', but it has nevertheless certain interrelated aspects that make it worth special attention. It testifies to a distinct linguistic development that has contributed to the common concept (as it is commonly taken to be) of belief in the European tradition; it exhibits a process of semantic divergence into the English notion of credit and into other related concepts having more or less tenuous connections with various connotations of belief; and, from a methodological point of view, it is interesting in that in explicating the etymology Benveniste relies repeatedly on the meaning of 'belief', i.e., the very concept that we have found so obscure and itself so much in need of explication.[23]

[22] I should like to pay special tribute to Benveniste's work, *Le Vocabulaire des institutions indo-européennes*, and also to urge its essential relevance to the kind of investigation that I have carried out here. Since, as I have argued, we cannot come to terms with alien concepts unless we have a critical understanding of our own, it is the vocabulary of Indo-European institutions that we must first master in our comparative studies. To this end, I should like to see Benveniste's work become one of the basic titles in the education of every social anthropologist. (Within the same tradition, a complementary importance is to be claimed for the great works of Georges Dumézil on the ideological foundations of Indo-European civilization; and also, as has been indicated above [chap. 4, sec. III], for Kittel's theological dictionary to the concepts of that other great and ancient civilization which has so much influenced our own.)

[23] What we are to understand by 'magical force', in Benveniste's concluding conjecture, is a problem that really calls for a serious investigation of the concept of magic, an idea that has been battered almost out of useful recognition. A social anthropologist, at any rate, could not well maintain, I think, that he had any clear idea what in particular this phrase was intended to convey or, hence, what is supposed to have been the central significance of **kred*.

VII

I have sketched out some of the importance of an investigation into credence and *croyance* mainly because there are so many points of connection or overlap with the notion of belief; but there are other concepts, denoting inner states or capacities, which have an independent importance in the history of ideas and in the description of human nature, and these call for at least the extended attention that we have paid to belief.

Some such verbal concepts, which might be made the subjects of comparative analysis, are: knowing,[24] wishing, intending, deciding, expecting. In each of these cases, I propose, a combination of the approaches of Benveniste and Wittgenstein seems, on the basis of our present venture, to offer the most hope of useful results. In a continuation of Lévy-Bruhl's concentration on logic, we already have Waismann's fundamental paper on alternative logics (1968, chap. 3) and Benveniste's demonstration, by means of a comparison of classical Greek with Ewe, that Aristotle's categories reflect 'the structure of classes of a particular language' rather than absolute necessities of thought (1966, chap. 6). These make an exciting and clarifying start, but in the perspective adopted in the present work they are nevertheless no more than a start, and it is for comparativists now to make the most of the headway that has been provided.

I am not claiming, of course, that other conceptual or logical investigations ought to follow the particular example that I have happened to set in making a comparative analysis of the concept of belief, but only that I have presented one kind of example, and that in some respects it may have set a useful precedent. What I should more definitely like to suggest, however, is that this analysis has effected a methodical advance in a line of investigation that has been gradually developed over the past century and more. Comte postulated a universal evolution of very general modes of thought, from the mystical to the positive; Tylor and Frazer tried to explain the genesis and the tenacity of error; Durkheim and Mauss wished to account for the origin of the classificatory function of the mind as implicit in the constitution of society, and for the persistence of categories through their incorporation in social institutions; Lévy-

---

[24] Here too the biblical tradition is crucial; see Bultmann (1952) on *gnosis*.

Bruhl investigated the possibility of alternative cultural logics, and isolated a distinct aspect of non-rational ideation; and Mauss and his colleagues (Hubert, Hertz, van Gennep) made sociological examinations of individual categories and principles of order such as space and time, polarity and transition. Throughout this series of studies there was an increasing concentration of attention, together with some refinement of method. This process of particularization has since been carried on in a number of modern ethnographical studies of individual concepts (cf. above, chap. 9, sec. I); and current investigations into foreign ideologies, on the part of missionary translators, orientalists, historians, and social anthropologists, are continuing to focus more precisely on the classificatory concepts of alien traditions. But typically the attention of the analysts has been turned outward: their examinations have been conducted as though from a position of conceptual objectivity, almost from an absolute vantage point of epistemological certainty. This analytical stance has been a natural concomitant of an unquestioned presumption that the essential capacities of man, the logical and psychic resources that make up a common human nature, were already well known, and that these capacities were already adequately named and discriminated by the rational and psychological vocabularies of European languages.

I have been trying in this investigation to demonstrate that we have not that degree of certainty, and that with particular regard to belief we have not even a substantiated knowledge of ourselves. The grounds of our judgement of other traditions of thought and action are unsure, and our understanding of human nature is greatly defective. It is most necessary, I am contending, to moderate the absolute character, to which we are so much inclined by our language and philosophical tradition, of our categories of human experience, and to admit instead an intrinsic uncertainty in all our premises concerning the nature of man.

This is not to assert a complete relativity in the representation of human existence, but to underline the methodological precept that we should begin our inquiries as though everything were relative. The inquiry into belief has shown with a special clarity that, in spite of the labours of Lévy-Bruhl and Wittgenstein, we are at the very commencement of an empirical understanding of the human condition. The significant dimension of variability is no longer simply in the evolution of thought (Comte, Tylor, Frazer), or in the forms of classification (Durkheim and Mauss), or in the logic of propositions within classifications (Lévy-Bruhl), but in the basic conception of human capacities. These capacities are represented, with immense variation, in the categories of natural languages, and it is to language that we have to look for the formulation of problems and their resolution.

In this regard the partitions of learning by which our universities are organized have, in my view, militated against comparative analysis and have unduly held up the development of a panoptic approach. If the inquiries of social anthropologists have been blunted or diverted by philosophical ignorance, so also have the disquisitions of philosophers been limited or misdirected by an ignorance of the comparative study of social facts. This latter gap in communication is to be seen even in the writings, which otherwise can have such a profound and provocative influence on anthropology, of Friedrich Waismann.[25] For instance, he takes up at one point the idea that 'language, far from serving merely to report facts, is a collective instrument of thought that enters experience itself, shaping and moulding the whole apprehension of phenomena' (1968: 175). He selects as one illustration of this the variation in colour vocabularies from one culture to another, and proposes that to the Romans, who had no words for grey or brown, nor any generic word for blue, the world of colour 'must...have appeared' curiously different. As another example, he thinks that human action as seen through an Eskimo language, from which transitive verbs are said to be lacking, must also *appear* 'curiously different' (176).[26] He remarks thereafter that 'any language contains...certain moulds, designs, forms to apprehend phenomena, human action, etc.', which is undeniable, but then passes directly to the highly disputable inference that 'if we spoke a different language we would perceive a different world' (176). Now the philosophical point that Waismann wishes to make, by reference to the variant categorial forms of different languages, is of capital importance, and we shall come to that presently. But what to a social anthropologist is striking is that he

[25] For one minor indication of this kind of effect on an analysis in social anthropology, see Needham (1962: 122).

[26] Also, in another place and closer to Wittgenstein (cf. above, chap. 7, sec. VIII) in a telling respect: 'If we are disquieted by the peculiar position which the ego occupies in language . . . it is enlightening to *imagine* a language (*and* the possible conditions under which it could be applied) which does without this concept' (1968: 80; emphases added). Consider, too, the implications of Wittgenstein's remark: 'to imagine a language means to imagine a form of life' (1953, sec. 19).

should make no allusion to a large and intriguing literature on the comparative study of colour terms and their symbolism; and also that he should assert that linguistic forms determine perception and interpretation, yet make no mention of the many investigators, from von Humboldt and Mauthner onward, who in linguistics and in anthropology have latterly received prominent notice under the heading (admittedly rather unhistorical and narrow) of 'the Sapir-Whorf hypothesis' (see, e.g., Cassirer 1953; Hoijer 1954; Whorf 1956; above, chap. 7, sec. VII). For all their philosophical deficiencies, anthropologists have after all done quite a lot of serious work on the interdependencies between language and ideation, and it cannot be assumed that their empirical concerns are philosophically irrelevant. Similarly, Waismann deprives himself of valuable evidence when, in his paper (first published in 1946) on whether there are alternative logics, he considers the topic of the laws of natural logic (1968: 68). These laws, he writes, are essentially moulded on the means of expression and the grammatical structure of existing language; and from this viewpoint, he continues, 'it would be interesting . . . to draw upon some non-European languages and to see whether in the languages of Eskimos, Negroes, and Red Indians, the very same "laws of thought" can be found. . . . A thorough study of exotic languages is likely to reveal a much larger variety of logical structures, and we should thus attain a less biassed and more realistic view of these matters.' Well, I need not belabour the point that a number of pretty considerable scholars, including Lévy-Bruhl and Evans-Pritchard,[27] had already long demonstrated that it was indeed interesting to seek the laws of thought implicit in the usages of non-European languages.

Nevertheless, Waismann does make a point of much significance when, in his turn, he isolates a defect in the practice of certain other linguistic philosophers: 'The technique of the ordinary-use philosophers has suffered', he writes, 'from the fact that they restricted themselves to the study of one language to the exclusion of any other—with the result that they became blind to those ubiquitous features of their own language on which their whole

---

[27] The academic lesson is made the more forceful by the fact that Waismann and Evans-Pritchard were both dons at Oxford, where they were contemporaries over quite a span of years. (I at least heard Waismann lecture there, and thought he was marvellous. Cf. Harré [in Waismann 1968: vii] on 'that combination of richness of thought, subtlety of expression and rigour of argument that was so characteristically Waismann'.)

mode of thinking, indeed their world picture, depends' (1968: 188).

It has been a continuing argument in the present work that the concept of belief, which in its recurrent and multifarious uses is certainly a ubiquitous feature of the English language, has in fact blinded commentators to the real status of this notion; and, moreover, that it has led them to ascribe to human nature in general an inner capacity that is in fact only a psychological replication of a grammatical particular. This argument has made an extended demonstration of Waismann's associated contention that:

Certain features of one's own language are noticed and appreciated in their full significance only when it is compared with other languages. . . . The mere *awareness* of other possibilities is, philosophically, of the utmost importance: it makes us see in a flash other ways of world-interpretation of which we are unaware, and thus drives home what is conventional in our outlook.

In adopting this position toward the empirical facts of natural languages,[28] Waismann is, in principle at any rate, decidedly in advance of Wittgenstein's practice. Only, of course, simply to be aware of other linguistic possibilities is not nearly enough: we have to establish them, in their contexts of employment and by reference to the cultural standards of intelligibility that give these situations their proper significance. We have to do so, moreover, not only ethnographically, by comparison among different societies and traditions, but also historically, by reconstructing the successive forms of social life that were the matrices of our own concepts.

VIII

In examining the grounds of the notion of belief we have been dealing in part with, in Hampshire's terms, the boundaries of a very general and essentially disputable concept, and hence with competing possibilities of classification. Here, as Hampshire thinks, 'the natural starting-point is the concept of man itself' (1959: 231); but this too proves to be so general and disputable a concept that,

---

[28] Also: '. . . Our language can be contrasted with an infinite number of other possible languages which may be adapted to other possible empirical worlds. The results of such investigations will be that we shall gradually begin to understand what were the factors which directed our grammar along the paths it has followed' (Waismann 1965: 80).

although it has remained a constant point of reference in our investigation, it has been more a desideratum, an ultimate and ideal hypothetical construct, than a basis of judgement.

This focus of our interest, together with its illimitable refractions, has been characterized and justified by Hampshire (1959: 232) in a striking passage that encapsulates many of our central concerns:

If most classifications of things, other than the disinterested classifications of science, have their grounds mainly in human powers and interests, the distinguishing of these powers and interests, and the understanding of their relations to each other, have an absolute priority in understanding the whole range of our thought and the structure of our vocabulary. For this reason it is possible to characterise philosophy as a search for 'a definition of man'....

By this view, Hampshire continues, we can interpret the great philosophers of the past as each providing a different account of the powers essential to man (cf. above, chap. 5). But the deduction of the essential human virtues will be arbitrary and presumptuous, he maintains, 'if it is not at every point guided by concrete observation of those ordinary divisions of human powers and activities which have been found useful in experience and which are already marked in the vocabulary of our language' (232). Such a philosophy of mind is given sense by 'concrete details ... exemplified in well-known forms of social life' (233), and is framed by the typical method of classifying different forms of language. Hence, Hampshire proposes (233–4):

The different uses of language have ultimately to be understood as acts of communication, and therefore as parts of different forms of social life. The setting and context of use must be illustrated with a wealth of concrete detail before the lines of division in language are understood. Philosophy as linguistic analysis is therefore unwillingly lured into a kind of descriptive anthropology.

This conclusion, reluctant though it may be, provides a metabasis to a recapitulation of the main purpose that has sustained my inquiry into the concept of belief.

This has been in effect a search for the concrete details of one of the most prominent powers that have been accounted essential to humanity. But this division among human powers, although patently very useful within the traditional forms of our experience and clearly marked in our vocabulary, has sense only in relation to our social life and in our own language. So in a way my analysis has provided a negative exemplification of Hampshire's precepts of method, but it nevertheless well accords with his argument.[29] 'The mere fact that, at this time and in this place, a certain specific division of human powers and activities has become normal and customary is not in itself a final justification of this division' (234). In this regard there has been a marked change in philosophical ambitions and expectations. In a traditional metaphysics that showed deductively man's necessary place in a scheme of reality (Spinoza is Hampshire's illustration), it was not unreasonable to claim some finality for the postulated principles of division of human powers.

But if the philosophical inquiry starts from the institution of language, as it has existed in all the variety of its forms, no finality can be claimed for any system of distinction. The nature of the human mind has to be investigated in the history of the successive forms of its social expression. . . .

To this cogent inference I should like merely to add two glosses. One is that it is not only in history, and by tracing successions, that the nature of the human mind should be investigated; but also, and as I have stressed here, chiefly by means of comparative analysis among disparate traditions. The other, and perhaps more important, is to emphasize that the investigation cannot logically have as its aim the justification of any particular powers, however clearly these may be lexically marked and however indispensable their uses in social expression may make them appear. If it is conceded that a classification of human powers can have no necessary finality, then we must be prepared to discover upon empirical investigation that some powers are justifiable as essential human virtues and that others are not.

Even a capacity (such as belief) that has been regarded as undeniably characteristic of man may turn out not to be so; and conversely it may emerge that some other capacity, unmarked perhaps in a particular language or if marked not given much psychological value, has instead an unsuspected range and versatility. Our task, that is, must be not only to establish natural resemblances among

[29] I should like to say that I stress Hampshire's argument, not because I think it is wholly original with him, but because (apart from my admiration of its exposition) I wish strongly to establish links of profitable agreement between the kind of philosophy that he propounds and the kind of social anthropology that I advocate by way of the present piece of work (cf. above, chap. i, sec. V).

mankind but also (and possibly more consequentially in the preparation of our perceptions) to delete from the register those conceptual candidates whose claims prove to be spurious. Only by this
dual procedure of validation and rejection can we sort out what is
constant in the representation of human experience from what is
contingent upon the fluctuating forms of language and social life.

To this end, which is the advancement of an empirical philosophy, there is no recourse other than a universal comparative
analysis of collective representations;[30] 'nor', to take up Dunbar's
adjuration (1780: 436), 'is the detail of the meanest tribes unimportant in [this] philosophy'.

IX

In investigating the topic of belief I have been concerned methodologically with 'fundamental principles of human enquiry' (Wittgenstein 1969, sec. 670).

Ideally, in my submission, it is a proper conception of social
anthropology that it should contribute distinctively, with the unique
professional advantage of its universal purview, to this kind of determination. But I have also wished to bring out the fact that
matters of such general import must implicate in common a number
of what are otherwise academically discriminated as separate disciplines. First among these is philosophy,[31] and Wittgenstein's
clarion phrase calls together the allusions of some of the best
philosophers to an issue that touches all the humane branches of
learning. This is the question whether, in 'the search for a definition
of man', there are to be found any absolute features of thought
and action that are indispensable to an objective conception of
humanity.

Traditionally, philosophy has sought such features under the
aspects of categories of thought, laws of logic, and innate ideas;
psychologically, Jung has urged the recognition of archetypes, and
analysts of other persuasions have formulated various psychic syn-

[30] 'Il faut avant tout dresser le catalogue le plus grand possible de
catégories; il faut partir de toutes celles dont on peut savoir que les hommes
se sont servis' (Mauss 1950: 309).

[31] 'If laying bare the structure of concepts, the analysis of language, the
clarification of meaning is the peculiar task of the philosopher, then we must
say that the philosophic attitude is an essential part of all scientific thought'
(Waismann 1965: 14; cf. Needham 1971a, sec. II).

dromes (such as the Oedipus complex) that are held to be similarly intrinsic to human experience. I myself have coined the designation 'natural symbols'[32] for certain phenomenal and conceptual vehicles of meaning that seem to exert an intuitive influence on man's psyche and the regulation of his thoughts. A term that compendiously refers to capacities, concepts, images, concerns, and intuitions that appear to be recognized in one way or another in all known cultures is 'primary factors of human experience' (Needham 1967a: 449; cf. 1967b: 612–3); and one of my subjacent intentions, throughout the course of this inquiry, has been to discover whether a capacity for belief should be reckoned among those primary factors by which men everywhere take account of the world and of one another.

In this respect the investigation matches the proposal made by Whitehead that 'we should . . . consider the institutions of mankind in the light of an embodiment of their stable experience' (1929: 77); and the conclusion has been that the institutions, linguistic and corporate, of belief do not express a distinct and universal mode of stable experience. In a more precise cast, Frege asserts the possibility of a universal fund or means of knowledge when he writes that, 'for all the multiplicity of languages, mankind has a common stock of thoughts' (1960: 46 n.); but our finding is quite definite that the concept of belief does not belong among such universal and culturally undifferentiated thoughts.[33] Hampshire refers to 'the most general principles of differentiation which . . . are used in *every* application of language to reality' (1959: 13); but the identification of belief among the judgements, declarations, and sentiments of mankind is not entailed by such principles (however they may be formulated) and cannot be derived from them. By none of these philosophical standards and precepts, therefore, can belief be regarded as an elementary constituent in human nature; but the comparative scrutiny of the status of this concept has, I think, helped toward an implementation of fundamental principles of human inquiry.

[32] The paper which, under that title, originally made my case for natural symbols (though see also Needham 1964: 147–8) is to appear in a forthcoming publication, where the topic will be found taken up at length and with suitable demonstration.

[33] Although I need not expatiate on the matter, I should say that I do not overlook the point that Frege's conception of a thought (*Gedanke*) calls for special explication. Cf.: 'Frege regards a "thought" as sharable by many thinkers, and thus as objective' (editors' note in Frege 1960: ix).

Under the main heads of experience, categories, and logic, as well as by very many incidental means of argument and speculation, philosophers have sought what man has always desired in his cogitations about the world: order, certainty, and economy. In these respects the sociological developments that I have traced above (secs. I & VII) can be seen as having provided increasing instruction in the study of collective modes of thought, and in a constantly developing way that exhibits some of the characteristic difficulties in this fundamental kind of enterprise. The evolutionary order of Comte and his successors had to give way to a style of analysis from which sequence was eliminable, and the order of correlation took its place; the order that Durkheim and Mauss found in the determinative influence of institutions was superseded by a conception that saw both society and symbolic classification as refractions of a common source of categorical distinctions in the intellectual proclivities of man; the order that Lévy-Bruhl at first secured, by the distinction of two types of mentality with a differential incidence among cultures, was transformed into a view of the more diffuse pervasion of all thought by tendencies that appeared in combination. The certainty of rational assessment that Comte unhesitatingly proclaimed, that Tylor and Frazer assumed, and that Durkheim and Mauss thought could at last 'liberate' the problems of human understanding from the tautologies in which they had languished (1963: 88) has been eroded to the point at which the real question is whether there are any objective grounds for certainty when we employ collective representations in order to assess other collective representations. The economy achieved by the theoretical ventures that I have cited was the defect of over-simplification, and the analytical discriminations that gave the appearance of economy have proved to be not subtle abstractions but rough empirical generalizations.

Seen in this perspective, the theoretical progress effected since Comte has been a growing awareness, under the shocks of one explanatory setback after another, of the limits and terms within which a comparative theory of human understanding can be empirically worked out. The conceptual improvements brought about have thus been in the main of a negative kind, as unjustified presumptions or convictions have had to be revised or given up; but this succession of retreats has at the same time carried investigators on to higher ground, from which can be had a clearer view of the grounds of lost engagements and a more cautious appreciation of the feasibility of future strategies. From this vantage point the chief weakness to be seen is the 'craving for generality', a constant temptation to try to think on far too large a scale. As the scope of theoretical ambitions has been gradually reduced, so concomitantly there has grown an increasing recognition of the theoretical value of particulars, the individual concepts that are the components in the schemes of interpretation that variously furnish an integrity of experience to those who govern their collective forms of thought and action by them. This recognition has entailed a concentration on questions of meaning rather than on external generalities of sequence, co-ordination, or logical style. The inquiry thus focuses inevitably on language and the conditions of its social use, and the principles that guide the inquiry turn out to be inseparable from those of linguistic analysis.

It is here that the theoretical shift from absolute explanation to relative interpretation leads to a grave uncertainty that threatens to bring down with it the associated ideals of both objective order and explicatory economy. We may be encouraged to think that we are succeeding in elaborating fundamental principles of human inquiry, but it does not follow that we shall thereby be able to isolate the fundamentals of human experience. This theoretical disjunction can be well indicated by referring back to an earlier thinker yet than those who have led us to the present position, and one who set forth a conception of language and reality that our own inquiry has especially confirmed.

Locke was much struck by the relativity in the linguistic partition of phenomena among named classes, and by the consequent difficulty or impossibility of translating the categories of one society into those of another. There are in every language, he contended, many particular words that cannot be rendered by any single word of another. 'For the several Fashions, Customs, and Manners of one Nation, making several combinations of Ideas familiar and necessary in one, which another People have never had any Occasion to make, or, perhaps, so much as take Notice of, Names of course came to be annexed to them'; and where certain customs are lacking there is no notion of any such actions, and hence no use for such combinations of ideas as are united under the terms that stand for them (Locke 1690, bk. 2, chap. 22, sec. 6). 'This could not have happened, if these Species were the steddy workmanship of Nature; and not Collections made and abstracted by the Mind, in order to Naming, and for the convenience of Communication.' Even where equivalent terms among different languages are proposed, as in dictionaries, the difficulty remains; and it is the more evident in the case of complex ideas, such as the concepts of moral discourse, 'whose Names, when men come curiously to compare with those they are translated into, in other Languages, they will find very few of them exactly to correspond in the whole extent of their Significations' (bk. 3, chap. 5, sec. 8).

Leibniz, in his *New Essays on Human Understanding*, handsomely makes a contrary case which joins with Locke's into an excellent theoretical dilemma. He was considerably impressed by Locke's observations on language, and by the demonstration that verbal concepts were quite arbitrarily different from one nation to another. He conceded that this was true 'as regards the names and the customs of men', but maintained that it changed nothing 'in the sciences and in the nature of things'. Yet in his response to Locke he nevertheless put forward a project for a universal grammar, as though this in itself would resolve the conceptual disparities among languages. His grand proposal was that all the literatures of the world should be ransacked in order to compile a universal philosophical lexicon; and that when there remained no more old books to study, the same examination should be made of languages, 'the most ancient monuments of mankind'. In time, he foresaw, all the languages of the world would be recorded in grammars and dictionaries, and would be compared together: 'this will be of very great use, both for the knowledge of things, since names often correspond to their properties, . . . and for the knowledge of our mind and the marvellous variety of its operations' (1961, 2: 171).

This bold suggestion thus presumed a degree of real connection between words and things, and was an absolutist conception in two senses: first, it was based on the tacit premise that the human mind was everywhere the same, to the extent that the languages of the world were mutually comprehensible in their manifestations of its functions; second, it assumed an objective character in the properties of the mind, such that there would be an agreement among different languages of the world in their several testimonies to these properties.[34] Methodologically, Leibniz was thus proposing

[34] These presuppositions were interdependent with Leibniz's doctrine of innate ideas and with his conception of a pre-established harmony in the universe. The ultimate expression of this view of man in the world is to be seen in Leibniz's proposal for a universal ideal language (*lingua characteristica universalis*) in which each simple idea would be represented by a single symbol, and the rules of combination would be so clear that problems could be resolved as by mechanical calculation.

a comparative analysis of the kind that Lévy-Bruhl was to put into effect almost exactly two centuries later, and even in terms that find ready agreement today; but it is his premises, not the type of research that he recommended, that have since been called into renewed question. Underlying his proposal was the conviction that human nature was uniform and fixed, and it is precisely this idea that more recent conceptual analyses have made difficult to accept.

Fundamentally, this uncertainty is the result of investigations into the foundations and the usages of language, which have repeatedly emphasized the contingent connections that characteristically obtain between words and things. If, as Waismann has maintained, language 'enters experience itself' and to some extent determines it, then the stability of experience is in part the grammatical stability of the language by which it is represented; and if, as Hampshire suggests, there are certain general principles of differentiation that are used in every application of language to reality, then there remains the large problem of accounting for the apparently arbitrary significance of linguistic usages that are not so governed. There is a radical division, that is, between the claims to universal validity that are made by any metaphysics (including doctrines, which in essence are moral guides, about human nature) and the autonomy and specificity that we know to be proper to natural languages and to the changeable social circumstances in which they are employed. Affecting our very conception of this contrast itself, moreover, there is the relativity that marks the exercise of our understanding in the forms of any particular language.

Hampshire (1959: 272) has well phrased the predicament in which we find ourselves when we try to make objective judgements:

We know that our minds have been formed by the conventions of our present language and social institutions, and that we can only achieve a certain degree of detachment from them, even by the utmost efforts of reflection and comparison.

Several means of remedy propose themselves, and are to some extent helpful. One is the practice of formal analysis, in which the multifarious details of cultural reality are reduced by abstraction to relational notions such as symmetry, complementarity, and transitivity, or to certain forms of logical possibility. In social anthropology, this recourse has at once deepened analysis and has facilitated wider comparisons (see, e.g., Needham 1967a; 1971b); but the degree of detachment that is achieved comes only at a certain stage within the analysis, and it is conditional upon a comprehension of the evidence, before and after that stage, such as can be had only by the familiar process of translation, i.e., the mutual adjustment of the classificatory idioms of different traditions (cf. Needham 1971a, sec. IX).

The abstractions of formal analysis can certainly help to discern an order among alien concepts of man, society, and the world, but the mode of analysis necessarily remains subject to two main critical qualifications. First, that the formal constructs themselves call ultimately for a validation that is independent of the ideological tradition in which they are framed; and this cannot be done either by meta-formal analysis or by reliance on the traditional concepts that the abstractions are supposed to rectify. Second, that however abstract or purely logical the formal notions may be, they are useful only to the extent that they mediate between the concepts of natural languages; and as soon as these are brought into any connection there rearise all of the stock hazards, of grammar and social circumstance, that attend any attempt to convey meaning from one form of life into the categories proper to another.

A different kind of remedy is the hypothetical construction, as Leibniz proposed, of an ideal language, but this recourse is even less promising than formal analysis. It has long been a philosophical ambition (cf. Rose 1675; Wilkins 1668) but is still without effective results; it is invalidated, as we have just noted, by the unjustified assumption of the homogeneity of human understanding; and, in the context that concerns us more directly, it is self-contradictory. The aim, that is, of an ideal or universal language is to construct verbal concepts that will always bear the same meaning, and this implies that they must be identically comprehensible to speakers of different natural languages and the members of different ideological traditions. Yet (as has in fact been a stock argument against Leibniz's notion of a universal dictionary) this result cannot be attained except on condition that it be already attained: the ideal language is to be the product of a successful comparison and accommodation of differing cultural concepts, but these cannot in the end be objectively and precisely compared except by means of the ideal language itself. There are indeed so many logical and practical difficulties in such an undertaking that it is no wonder the ambition no longer preoccupies philosophers as it once did.[35] Not

[35] It is perhaps a matter for some wonder, however, that in so many re-

that there is no possible advantage to be had from the attempt, for the intensified comparative scrutiny of concepts—ideally, a universal comparison—and the perpetual dialectic of translation cannot but conduce to a certain detachment from one's own; but detachment is simply a precondition of analysis, not a method for the isolation or contrivance of objective categories.

What the comparative analysis of alien concepts does impress upon us, yet again, is precisely the relativity that so largely characterizes the schemes of collective representations by which all traditions (and all humane disciplines) represent and articulate experience. This relativity is intrinsic to linguistic representation, and is impossible to obviate by formal analysis, by an ideal language, or by establishing equivalences among natural languages. There will always subsist, as inescapable factors, an uncertainty and a variability in the categories by which any language whatever secures an order, for one purpose or another and in an unpredictable variety of circumstances, in the organization of collective thought and action.

So it is a question how far we can reasonably hope, in our inquiries into human nature, to be able to identify fundamentals that will be discoverable in any form whatever of social life; for these can be denoted only by means of the categories of some language,[36] and it is a matter for empirical investigation to determine whether there are any categories at all that can have (even by the pragmatic stipulation of qualified and approximate senses) the universal application that in principle is required. In the nature of the case, however, it is clear (on logical and empirical grounds) that ultimately we cannot ever achieve an objective certainty in conceptual analysis. To paraphrase Einstein, as quoted by Waismann (1968: 17), on the laws of mathematics: so far as our categories refer to reality, they are not certain; and so far as they are certain, they do not refer to reality.

The paradox, it might be said, is that the search for primary

gards—in sociological analysis, even, let alone the reporting of psychic particulars—social anthropologists should still so commonly write as though in their own language, and in the technical terms of their profession, they already possessed an ideal language. Cf. Leach (1961: 27) on the failure of anthropologists to realize that 'English language patterns of thought are not a necessary model for the whole of human society'.

36 The intuitive apprehensions of natural resemblances among mankind (above, chap. 8, sec. III) still have to be named, once they become objects of analysis and communication, in the categories of a language, even an artificial one.

Q

factors or fundamental constituents of human experience must be absolute in intention but can be only relative in expectation.

X

The attempt to determine natural resemblances among men, by recourse to comparative ethnographical analysis, is thus unavoidably impaired by the relativity that must affect any linguistic means of representing them.

We may be convinced by analogy and experience, by logic and experiment, that there are such universals of human nature; but as soon as we try to state what they are, our findings are inevitably biassed or given extraneous connotations by the terms of the language in which they are formulated.[37] These are obstacles enough to the success of the enterprise, but there remains yet a further source of hindrance, namely 'the doubtfulness and uncertainty' in the signification of the words of our own language (Locke 1690, bk. 3, chap. 9, sec. 4). These defects have been especially evident in our examination of the concept of belief, and under this aspect the investigation contains a lesson that has a general relevance to conceptual analysis.

Locke drew up lists of the imperfections and abuses of words (bk. 3, chaps. 9, 10) that scarcely need amplification and will classically open the case. Certain imperfections are that the ideas for which words stand may be very complex; that the ideas may have no settled standard existing in nature by which the words may be rectified or adjusted; and that where the meaning of a word is referred to a standard, the standard may not be easily known. So when an idea is complex, as for the most part in ethics (and certainly with belief) the word that stands for it will seldom have the same precise meaning in two different men, 'since one Man's complex Idea seldom agrees with anothers, and often differs from his own, from that which he had Yesterday, or will have to Morrow' (sec. 6). Words that stand for collections of ideas, when such collections are nowhere to be found constantly united in nature and are not exhibited by patterns, are necessarily doubtful in their meaning;

---

[37] This qualification attaches, of course, to my own suggestions and conclusions above, in chapter 8 and elsewhere. (One goes as far as one can, in one's own language, and with whatever degree of detachment can be achieved in the circumstances.)

e.g., 'What the word *Murther*, or *Sacriledge*, &c. signifies, can never be known from Things in themselves. . . . They have their Union and Combination only from the Understanding which unites them under one Name' (sec. 7). It is true that common usage does help to settle the meanings of words, but it is insufficiently precise, 'there being scarce any Name, or any very complex Idea, . . . which in common use, has not a great Latitude, and which keeping within the bounds of Propriety, may not be made the sign of far different Ideas'. Besides, the rules of common usage are nowhere established, so that it is often a matter of dispute whether a certain sense given to a word is proper or not. Hence even when men use a word in the intention of understanding one another, it may not convey the same meaning to each; e.g., many speak of 'glory', but few have the same idea of it (sec. 8). It frequently happens that people learn words without being taught their exact meanings, and without establishing the meanings for themselves, so that the words are 'little more than bare Sounds' in men's mouths; or, when they are given a meaning, it is for the most part 'but a very loose and undetermined, and consequently obscure and confused Signification'. This is so even in the discourse or debate of intelligent and studious men who have paid attention to their ideas, so that they are not agreed on the meanings of words such as 'honour' or 'faith' (sec. 9).[38]

There are a number of other respects in which the meanings of words may be uncertain, and the imperfections are held to vary in

---

[38] The mention of faith calls into view Locke's idea of belief. For him, it is a degree of assent marked by assurance (bk. 4, chap. 16, sec. 9); and to believe is to admit as true a proposition on grounds that persuade one to accept it, but without certain knowledge that it is so. 'That which makes me believe, is something extraneous to the Thing I believe; something not evidently joined on both sides to . . . those Ideas that are under consideration' (chap. 15, sec. 3). Assent, however, is 'no more in our Power than Knowledge'; we can prevent or 'suspend' our assent, but where the consequences matter to us, and we perceive a preponderant probability of truth on one side, we cannot choose to assent to which side we please (chap. 20, sec. 16; cf. above, chap. 6).

Leibniz, commenting on this latter passage, states that we can indirectly 'make ourselves believe' something unpleasant by transferring our attention to a pleasant object, a course which is held to lead us to recognize better which side in the original issue is the more probable. This is indeed an effective psychological trick sometimes, but it does not actually show that we can make ourselves believe, i.e., that belief is an act of the will (cf. above, chap. 6, sec. VI).

degree with the nature of the idea in question, but all words are unreliable. As Locke writes, when he explains why he charges words rather than our understanding with these imperfections (chap. 9, sec. 21),

they interpose themselves so much between our understandings and the Truth, which it would contemplate and apprehend, that like the Medium through which visible Objects pass, their Obscurity and Disorder does not seldom cast a Mist before our Eyes, and impose upon our Understandings. . . .

These occasions of 'great uncertainty' afflict the use of words even among men of the same language and the same country; but there is yet greater cause for care in the interpretation of ancient writings (sec. 22),

when to this natural Difficulty in every Country, there shall be added different countries, and remote Ages, wherein the Speakers and Writers had very different Notions, Tempers, Customs, Ornaments, and Figures of Speech, &c., every one of which influenced the Signification of their Words. . . .

Here, then, in an impressive analysis made in the seventeenth century,[39] we have a marvellously exact and telling account of certain difficulties that we have repeatedly encountered in the analysis of the word 'belief', and an indication of the increased hazards of interpretation when we seek its counterparts among the verbal concepts of other societies and traditions. These, indeed, are characteristic grounds for the assertion that 'Philosophy is a battle against the bewitchment of our understanding by means of our language' (Wittgenstein 1953, sec. 109).[40] If by any word, I have been arguing, we have most certainly been thoroughly and unrelentingly be-

[39] Philosophers and historians of ideas, struck perhaps by the presence of these excerpts from a standard and famous source (though see above, chap. 1, sec. VI), may stand in need of the explanation that not all social anthropologists are entirely persuaded of the relevance of philosophy, let alone that of nearly three centuries ago, to the prosecution of their own studies. As a matter of fact, some of the more pragmatical (and even prominent) among them actually evince some hostility to the idea (cf. Needham 1971a, sec. II).

[40] 'Die Philosophie ist ein Kampf gegen die Verhexung unsres Verstandes durch die Mittel unserer Sprache.' By a slight but consequential omission the published English translation does not render the second possessive (*unserer*), qualifying *Sprache*, so that the remark appears to refer to language in general rather than particularly to our own language and to its peculiar sources of misunderstanding.

witched by the numerous imperfections that are inherent in the uses of the concept of belief: doubt, uncertainty, obscurity, disorder, confusion, loose and undetermined connotations, and much else of the same dilapidated kind.

As for the abuses of words that Locke goes on to isolate (chap. 10), these too are abundantly and precisely exemplified in the employment of the grammatical forms of belief. This word, namely, is used without a clear and distinct idea, and even without signifying anything in particular; it is used inconstantly, standing now for one idea and again for another; it has been made the object of logical subtleties that if generalized would undo logic itself; it has brought perplexity into 'the great Concernements of humane Life and Society'; it has been taken for a real thing in nature, as a representation of 'something that really exists' (sec. 14); it has by its constant use acted to 'charm'[41] men into notions far removed from the truth of things; it has been set in the place of something that it can by no means signify, namely a subtle and essential inner state of man of which we know nothing other than the expressions from which this state is inferred; it has caused the false supposition that nature works regularly in the production of things, namely that in the constitution of man there must invariably be produced that faculty which the word leads us to suppose we possess; its long and familiar use has conduced to the conviction that there is a direct and necessary connection between the word and what it is taken to signify, so that its proponents 'forwardly suppose one cannot but understand what their meaning is', which has led to noise and wrangling without improvement or information (sec. 22); and it has fostered figurative and rhetorical expressions that have insinuated wrong ideas about 'Things as they are', most seriously about the real capacities of man.

As far as the object of our present inquiry is concerned, we have no need for further demonstration of the imperfections and abuses of the verbal concept of belief, though Locke's disquisition on words in general has provided a powerfully apt summation of the predicaments into which we have been led in our investigation of that particular word. What I should like to stress, rather, is the converse, namely the exceedingly salutary effectiveness of the analysis of 'belief' as a paradigm of those mistakes and confusions

---

[41] The metaphorical parallel between Locke's 'charm' and Wittgenstein's 'bewitchment' (*Verhexung*) is again (cf. above, chap. 7, sec. I, n. 4) a correspondence that is hard entirely to ignore.

that are introduced into our thought by words themselves. We cannot think without them, but they make it hard for us to think with them.

XI

These verbal hazards affect every discursive intellectual exercise, yet there nevertheless generally prevails, it seems to me, a confident presumption that we can choose what acceptations we will, from among the congeries of usages that make up the significance of a word, and that by this means we can still manage to formulate our thoughts in a way that is both exact and adequate.

Doubtless we can do so to some extent, and if the thing were in principle not possible we should of course never bother to write about the imperfections of language, or try with great attention to refine the expression of our ideas. But over and above the reasonable conviction that it is feasible to improve our linguistic practice, there exists a more unqualified confidence that we are entirely able in the end to shape words to whatever purposes we may conceive. Thus a renowned authority on language, Benveniste, quite definitely asserts: 'we can say everything, and we can say it as we wish'.[42] But I want to maintain, to the contrary, that the analysis of the verbal concept of belief brings out with a special force (because of the importance of the notion)[43] the fact that in trying to say something about the grounds of our concepts we quite rapidly reach the limits of language. (This is why we are overcome by giddiness.) It is not only that 'language is a deficient instrument, and treacherous in many ways' (Waismann 1968: 175), a point that Locke made abundantly plain, but that even when we think we have a clear premonition of its lures and diversions, along a certain track of investigation, we can still find that it does not permit us to make the advance that we have in view.

[42] 'Nous pouvons tout dire, et nous pouvons le dire comme nous voulons' (Benveniste 1966: 63).

[43] 'Philosophy derives its weight, its grandeur, from the significance of the statements it destroys. It overthrows idols, and it is the importance of these idols that makes philosophy important' (Waismann 1965: 78). Cf. Wittgenstein (1953, sec. 118): 'Where does our investigation get its importance from, since it seems only to destroy everything interesting, that is, all that is great and important? . . . What we are destroying is nothing but houses of cards, and we are clearing up the ground of language on which they stand.'

In considering belief, Hume found that ordinary language was not suitably adapted to the analysis of the operations of the mind, and when he wanted to say what belief was he confessed that he could scarcely find any word that fully answered the case; Kant, though quite clear on the position of belief in relation to truth and necessity, still could not give a speculative account of it; and we have since had proof enough, in one instance after another, that we cannot say anything clearly with this word. Anything that we might please to say, and which in common speech is usually hung on to the handy peg of 'belief', will be better said by recourse to some other word; and if we are clear about what we want to say, we shall find that it can be said clearly only by another word. In this case it is certainly not true that we can say everything, for there is a great deal that even those who most rely on the word cannot say about the meaning of belief; and it is not true that we can say it as we wish, either, for those who wish to explain the essential character of belief generally find that they are much restricted by the resources of the language, and it is the language itself (not, for instance, the conventions of a particular religious idiom) that in their own submission hampers the expression of what they wish to say.

Now in the case of this individual word, we reached the limits of language because we had reached the limits of sense and experience; so it is not to be wondered at that it has afflicted our understanding with so much 'obscurity and disorder'. But there are many other verbal concepts, pertaining especially to our emotional lives, that have great meaning and are poignantly within the realm of experience, but the significance and real character of which we cannot express in words (cf. above, chap. 6, sec. XII). The depths of love, the transports of ecstasy, the sundering pangs of grief, and other such supreme affections in our personal intercourse, are precisely those of which we readily say that they are inexpressible; and the very fact that they are inexpressible is a distinctive sign of their quality.[44] In the arts, too, as the defects and pretensions of aesthetic criticism largely show, we have well founded and exquisite apprehensions that language cannot properly, if at all, convey. Lichtenberg brings together the sensitive and the aesthetic in one of his notes: 'A feeling that is expressed in words is just like music that

---

[44] It is this recognition, though, that gives plausibility to those who would impose on others with the claim that the doctrines they urge, being ultimately ineffable, are thereby of supreme value and even of unchallengeable truth.

is described in words; the expression and the subject are not homogeneous enough' (1958: 63). The difficulty is well enough known, but the fact, as I suppose, is that words and things are not homogeneous at all. It is human beings, with their common capacities, who are homogeneous;[45] and it is they who associate with the words certain varieties of experience which they are persuaded are, in their several contexts, common modes of apprehension. In their general discourse, men quickly learn that in the field of human experience—apart, that is, from the abstractions of mathematics and the disinterested concerns of the exact sciences—there is set such an inevitable gap between words and the apprehensions they denote that no effective communication can be had when the apprehension is lacking. Here, in a paradox that must be a cliché of psychological observation, only that can be communicated which does not need to be communicated, since it is already known; and where communication is called for by reason of lack of that knowledge, in that the apprehension in question has not been experienced, words cannot convey it. In such instances the words serve as reminders that will be premises to a subsequent communication—and how effective they will prove to be then will again be a matter for particular appraisal in relation to the experiences of the interlocutors. I do not maintain, of course, that this is so for all concepts; and I am fairly sure, as I have indicated at a number of points in the preceding chapters, that we can arrive empirically and in other ways at a qualified understanding of the grounds of certain verbal concepts at least concerning the nature of man. But the point that I wish to stress at present is the general inadequacy of words in the explication of experience.

A similar disability afflicts also the expression of our thought. As Lichtenberg wrote, when he found his ideas blunted by the clumsiness of the language in which he was trying to state them: 'The thought has too much play in the expression; I have pointed with the knob of a walking stick, where I ought to have used the tip of a needle' (1958: 150). And Waismann (incidentally an admirer, like Wittgenstein, of Lichtenberg) has recently dwelt at length on the same curious sense of dissatisfaction, the apparently self-contradic-

[45] Again, I do not want to be misunderstood on this score, so let me say clearly once more that the precise capacities in respect of which men are to some extent homogeneous by nature are matters still for investigation, and that their linguistic specification must by any finding pose a problem to which logically there is no evident solution (see chap. 8 above).

tory conviction that we have something to say that cannot be said. The point of great significance that he wishes to make is that 'language is never complete for the expression of all ideas, on the contrary, that it has an essential *openness*' (1958: 199). A philosopher muses on some matter and may notice a subtle yet elusive difference never noticed before; but when he wants to draw attention to it the language fails him. 'There ought to be a word, yet there is none.' Take for instance (199) the various grammatical forms of negation:

You may feel that it makes a difference whether you deny a fact, a mere possibility, or whether you use the word 'not' in the forming of a supposal, etc., and yet if you try to bring out these differences you may find yourself suffering from a sort of speech suffocation as there is only one word to mark these different shades.

Or again the need may be felt to have two ways to describe a state of affairs, one to speak about something absent and another to speak about something present, on the ground that (to abbreviate considerably Waismann's own demonstration) in the latter case what one says about the thing in question is not true or false in the same sense as when the thing is not present. There are, it is suggested, differences between the two situations which call into question the idea of making a mistake, and with it that of a statement, such that there is an 'inflection of sense' according as the object is or is not directly under observation. 'Yet existing language denies you the possibility of stating such conceptual differences, for lack of the requisite words.'

In another example, which again I shall not recount in detail, there may arise a relation between two statements that comes pretty close to an entailment, just as the conjunction is very nearly a contradiction (200):

In such a case you may feel a strong need to have a word for denoting a relation weaker than entailment, yet stronger than implication, or a word to express something that is *almost* a contradiction. This is the sort of situation which occurs time and again in philosophy. We become aware of some subtle difference, or of an unnamed sort of relationship, but in the attempt to impart this knowledge we are hampered by existing language, its paucity of words.

There is, however, a positive aspect to this frustration, Waismann argues. Seeing something in a new light is often the core of a philosophical discovery, or of a new insight, and it is then that the philosopher may feel dissatisfied with existing language: it is seeing a new point, yet finding it impossible to put into words, that goads him on in his search for new means of expression. 'There is a *rational* element in it, the fight of thought with the obtuseness of speech' (201). Thus philosophers and poets (and, one would like to think, social anthropologists and other comparativists) put forth unremitting efforts to express the inexpressible, and it is thanks to these efforts that language becomes an increasingly subtle instrument of thought.

There are different ways of expressing a point that 'the recalcitrance of language' does not allow to be put in a customary way: the writer may cast about for an old word that can be revived for the purpose, or turn to a foreign language, or adopt an expression from popular idiom. 'But the supply of words for the finer purposes of thought is deficient everywhere; and, moreover, it may be that what is lacking is not the words but the grammatical forms' (201).

Now since Waismann is arguing that we can have ideas or apprehensions that existing words cannot express, it might be proposed that the concept of belief actually benefits by this argument; i.e., that belief is after all real enough, only recalcitrant to definition (cf. above, chap. 6, sec. XII), just as are the discriminations that Waismann makes. This is fallacious, but it sounds a plausible inference, so I should quickly dispose of it. The main refutation is that Waismann does manage to convey to us (in the original place) the specific features of those logical situations for which ordinary language fails to provide; we understand, in a discursive fashion, what he wishes to express, and it is only because we do so that we can appreciate his argument.[46] By contrast, the most attentive scrutinies of the arguments for belief have failed to elicit any comparable understanding; however the matter was phrased, and from whatever point of view we looked at it, the outcome proved again and again to be entirely negative. Another decisive difference between the two

---

[46] Naturally, the fact that we can somehow grasp the point in Waismann's account shows that the words and grammatical forms are to that degree adequate to his purpose; so it might appear that all he is complaining of is the discursive character of language, the lack of distinct words for shades of negation and so on—and then it might seem a question what he needs distinct words for when the language can in fact serve his ends by other means. But we should appreciate, I think, that the instances he cites are illustrations, not probative arguments; and what they depict is the sort of logical predicament that may in actual cases provoke dissatisfaction with the resources of language. Certainly Waismann is not trying to convince us by saying in clear words what he wishes to show cannot yet be said.

cases is, moreover, that Waismann lacks words to express new logical discriminations, whereas we have been examining a traditional psychological word in search of an inner state, and this has already been superabundantly testified to by existing language.

The real relevance of the above observations to our inquiry into belief is the realization that words are not only complex, and also very often misleading, but that they are actually inadequate to the precise expression of our ideas. As instruments of thought they are commonly serviceable enough, but some of the handier ones have been so much battered and blunted, by being continually put to one use after another, that they are no longer fit for accurate work. The verbal concept of belief is very much in this condition, and it is not apt to the expression of those humane concerns to which it pre-eminently has been thought rightly adapted. Much the same applies, also, to the words by which in English, at one or more removes, we usually explicate the notion of belief; and then again to the constantly manipulated vocabularies to which we resort when we try to analyse the psychological concepts of other traditions. Far from being able to rely on the simple and definite terms of an ideal or universal language, or on a stock of thoughts (like Frege's hypothetical *Gedanken*) common to all languages, we have to conduct our comparative analyses by means of words that are likely to fail us at every point. And in seeking to translate alien concepts, moreover, we have to appreciate that the foreign words in question are themselves words that may be in the same state as our own; so when the members of a strange society try, in their own language, to explain to us the meanings of these words, they too must be assumed to be the victims of just such linguistic defects, traps, and diversions as are we ourselves when we formulate our own thoughts.

I must stress that this confusing situation is not merely a result of the fact, to which we have repeatedly adverted, that a classificatory concept—particularly perhaps a psychological one—is characteristically composed of numerous connotations bearing family likenesses one to another. It is not just that it is difficult to isolate one distinct or definitive meaning from the concept of 'belief', and then to match it to an equally discriminable meaning isolated from an alien verbal concept that is thought to be somewhat equivalent to the English word. The fundamental source of obscurity and misunderstanding is that the grammar of 'belief' does not permit anything like the precision of analysis and exactitude of expression that ideally we require in the determination of human capacities.

Wittgenstein remarks in another connection that a main source of our failure to understand is that 'we do not command a clear view of [*übersehen*] the use of our words.—Our grammar is lacking in perspicuity' (1953, sec. 122). Yet we do assuredly have a practical mastery of the grammar of belief, and we have now acquired by analysis a 'perspicuous representation' of the anfractuosities of the concept and its myriad sporadically related usages; and it is by virtue of the glaring clarity of this view that we can perceive how flawed and treacherous this concept is, to the extent indeed that for certain tasks it is fit only to be discarded.

In one respect or another, therefore, the words in which we cast our thoughts and communications may not always have the usefulness that we are inclined to ascribe to them. We can only rely upon them, yet often, and perhaps even characteristically, they are unreliable. They lead us to imagine that we can say what we think, and conversely that we think what we say; but neither of these inferences is necessarily correct, and in the case of belief they are both false.

XII

How, then, can we say what we mean, when we do not understand the meaning of the words we say? Or, worse, when we have, as Wittgenstein suggests (1953, sec. 109), a positive 'urge to misunderstand' the operations of our own language? What certainty is there in language when it can so mislead us about ourselves?

The concept of belief certainly seemed, by the great reliance placed upon it in the western tradition, to have an essential and irrefragable significance, formulated over centuries of theological exegesis, philosophical analysis, and its numerous applications in common discourse. Yet the deeper and more minutely we go into the meaning of 'belief', the harder it is to concede it any discrete character or any empirical value as an index to the inner life of men. The closer we peer into its semantic constitution, indeed, the more it resembles an illustration to Lichtenberg's pessimistic aphorism: 'the microscope serves only to confuse us the more' (1958: 137). We need have no urge to misunderstand the operations of this word, for it seems in itself to be recalcitrant to understanding. Under the pressure of rigorous examination it disperses like mercury under the thumb; and if it tends to re-form the scattered significances into its original unity of contour, this is by reason of the form of the word and the grammar by which it is constrained.

Admitted, 'belief' appears to be an unusually confusing and even deceptive word, and this is understandable in a concept that so straddles the border between private states and public appraisal. But its analysis nevertheless strongly suggests that a comparative scrutiny of the real characters of other words, especially those that are taken to denote human powers, is likely to show that their meanings are generally riven by similar flaws. When we turn for guidance to neighbouring concepts, such as 'trust', 'assent', 'imagine', 'expect', and so on, we find ourselves on the verge of other chasms of doubt and obscurity in which it looks as though we should be just as badly lost. If instead we try to take bearings on more distant and prominent features, in the shape of categories that we hope may have been better plotted, we find that these too lose their clarity of outline, wavering in the refractions of the medium, or change form according to the light or perspective in which they are viewed; they become lost to sight behind intervening opacities, or upon magnified inspection turn out to be themselves just as illusory as belief.

Such topographical metaphors, discouraging though they are, may give us the impression that the territory we are exploring has at least some fixed and solid features, and that our difficulty in the search for the true location of belief is no more than a temporary disorientation. But our situation is far worse than that, for the longer we traverse the conceptual landscape that we sketch in our reconnaissances the more it looks like that in a dream. It lacks constancy and continuity, and nothing survives direct attention; we lose faith in our observations, and find it increasingly hard to trust our instruments; and, as we repeatedly criss-cross the terrain and turn back on our own traces, the worsening disorder of our perceptions reduces also our confidence in ourselves and in our ability to direct our own courses. The disorientation is not simply that we do not know where we are, but that a thorough undermining of our leading categories calls into question our judgements of what we are and the sense of the undertaking to which we are committed.

I have resorted to these figurative passages in an attempt to evoke in the reader that sense of conceptual instability and loss of location that I think is inseparable from a serious engagement in this kind of enterprise. In doing so I have been trying to indicate the extent to which the analysis of a psychological concept, if carried out with the widest objective reference, can expose the precarious-ness of our delineations of the human condition. This is perhaps a rather grandiloquent phrase, yet what we have been trying to do in this monograph is to determine our relationship to reality, as this is defined for us by our language and in respect to one of the chief capacities attributed to mankind by the ideology of our tradition, and there can surely be few issues of more humane grandeur than that.

Let us see, though, whether another kind of presentation fits the case better, or is more revealing. Wittgenstein resorts to two meta-phors by which he comes to terms with our predicament. One is to assimilate language to a game, specifically to a board game. We have been inquiring into the character of a word, and Wittgenstein generalizes the problem in this way: 'The question, "What is a word really?" is analogous to "What is a piece in chess?"' (1953, sec. 108). This is certainly apt, in that it stresses the rules by which the game is played and the moves that a piece is permitted; and in this there is a similarity to the grammar of a language and the uses that a word is allowed, as well as a similarity in the fact that the rules of a language permit an infinite number of legitimate moves in the pursuit of innumerable strategies. Of course, there are also in-congruencies such as impair any analogy, but it is not these incidental defects that reduce the impact of Wittgenstein's figure as far as our own question is concerned. What the chess-piece meta-phor does not take into account is that in comparative studies (social anthropology, etc.) we have to consider, not the uses of the various pieces within a single game, the rules of which are (like those of our own language) operationally known, but a large number of games—ideally, all languages, in their social contexts—that differ greatly one from another in the numbers, individual values, and moves of the pieces with which they are played. The game of com-parativism, one might say, is played with pieces that are themselves games.

Wittgenstein's other metaphor refers to the significant combina-tion of words: 'Understanding a sentence is much more akin to understanding a theme in music than one might think' (1953, sec. 527). This idea is effectively glossed by a subsequent passage. After stating that one acceptation of understanding a sentence is that it cannot be replaced by any other, Wittgenstein continues—'any more than one musical theme can be replaced by another' (sec. 531). Clearly there is a revealing analogy here, but in a comparative context we need to expand this allusion also. A sentence in one language accords with a certain style of composition, as it were, and there are rules of harmony, counterpoint, and so on that govern its form and employment. In another language, however, it would of course be largely discordant, and might very well be utterly and totally so. But the comparativist has precisely to hold together in his appreciation of these different styles, not only two languages, but in principle all known and possible languages. From this total comparison there emerges a result that well agrees with the point of Wittgenstein's second metaphor but is most discouraging to the comparativist. Each language is a style of composition, and the style can be appreciated only by reference to a form of life; so that just as in one significant respect a sentence cannot be replaced by any other, so even less can one language ever take the place of another. Different traditions are characterized by disparate themes, each the product of an intricate historical elaboration, and no theme can be replaced by another. The canons of an alien style of composition can to some extent be apprehended, but it is very doubtful that an outsider can ever understand an exotic theme. 'In the end, every language must speak for itself' (Waismann 1965: 363).

Now languages do in another sense speak for themselves, and that is through us. It is well known that we are often unaware of what we have to say (or even, as we put it, 'want' to say) until the act of writing extracts it from us.[47] Any writer, I imagine, will recognize that sometimes he feels as though he were no longer quite in control; that he has suspended his private concentration and that what he is writing is the immediate product of the given rules and forms of the language that he uses—as though the grammar had taken over. Not that this is an unconscious process entirely, for the writer knows that he is to a degree under a kind of formal impulsion, and can appraise the results or arrest the influence whenever he notices what is going on. But there is in fact a more extreme form of the experience that language seems to be writing through us. We may in that case become so detached from our apperceptions that the act of writing has a quasi-automatic quality—at least for as long as

---

[47] 'Writing always brings to light things that previously we did not clearly recognize we had in us' (Lichtenberg 1958: 335). Lichtenberg calls such latent ideas 'dormant systems'. But writing does not in fact always have this effect. Pascal observes in his *Pensées* (Brunschvicg ed., no. 372), 'In writing down my thought, sometimes it escapes me' (1964: 166).

things are going well—and we feel afterwards that the ideas thus expressed, much though we may approve them, had an autonomous origin in the very act of writing. It was not so much that we employed language in order to express what we wanted to say, as that we were under the command of language in the expression of thought. These are curious phenomena, and I do not pretend to understand them. What I am concerned to emphasize is the problematic light in which they cast the relationship between ourselves and language. I do not mean simply that language is a durkheimian social fact, having a generality, independence, and coercive authority over the individual; but that the individual is subject to the influence of an impersonal social fact in even the most personal situation, namely in the expression of his inner and perhaps unique states of mind.

The question prompted by these experiences is how it is that we can compose significant sentences when we do not mean them, i.e., when we do not deliberately intend what we write. Lichtenberg, in a famously aphoristic refutation of Descartes, suggests the answer: 'One should not say "I think", but rather "it thinks" [*es denkt*], just as one says "it thunders" '.[48] In other words, it is the personal pronoun that leads us to infer the existence of a cogitating subject; whereas the facts can be conveyed in a grammatical form that does not carry this implication.

Waismann, commenting on this dictum (1968: 198), phrases the issue in this way:

How far am *I* the maker of my thoughts, and how far do they occur to me? And if they just 'occur', what is there I-ish about them? On the other hand, if there is nothing I-ish about them, why do they choose just *me* for their rendezvous?

His own conclusion is that neither 'I think' nor 'it thinks' is quite apposite, and that the truth lies somewhere between the two formulations. 'Language, in constraining us to ascribe thinking to a grammatical subject, . . . creates the illusion that thinking is a doing that requires a doer. It is, and it is not. In actual fact, there is an interplay between what I do, and what comes to me' (202). Ordinarily, thinking is neither quite ascribable to the conscious subject

[48] Lichtenberg 1958: 458. Also: 'Just as we believe that things happen outside us without our intervention, so also the ideas of them can occur in us without our aid. Indeed, we have also become what we are without assistance from ourselves' (482).

nor to some 'mysterious entity' referred to as 'it'; but language has not quite got the forms to express this.

So language itself, by its indiscriminate employment of the first person singular pronoun, creates an impression which we are then disconcerted to find is not wholly or always correct. We think, that is, that we are entirely responsible for the propositions that we express, and we are then surprised to realize that on occasion we write perfectly sensible sentences that we did not fully, if at all, consciously intend.

Now the grammar of thinking, and the analysis of the related distinction between active and passive, are matters of much philosophical fascination; but I have to skirt these problems in order to get to a point that more directly relates to our investigation. Part of the reason for our surprise or discomfiture at the quasi-autonomous expression of thoughts through us is the distinction that we conventionally make between a word and its intended meaning. 'One thinks of the meaning as a thing of the same kind as the word, if also different from the word. Here the word, there the meaning' (Wittgenstein 1953, sec. 120).[49] We have the idea, then, that if a word is uttered or written there must be a thought behind it; i.e., someone must have intended it to have a meaning. But 'when I think in language, there are not "meanings" hovering in me next to the verbal expression; the language itself is the vehicle of thought' (Wittgenstein 1953, sec. 329). Nevertheless, we are tempted to infer that the concatenation of words in a sentence is evidence of a separate mental process, the inner capacity of which the linguistic formulations are the products. We conceive the meaning that we intend to convey, and then express it in the terms and grammatical forms that the institution of language happens conveniently to provide.

But this mental process is an implicit construct, as Lichtenberg deftly displayed, of the language itself: in this case, an implication of the grammar of 'meaning'. It is partly because of the pressure

---

[49] This is related to the 'delusion' (*Täuschung*) that 'the concepts of proposition, language, thought, and world stand in a line one behind the other, each equivalent to the other' (Wittgenstein 1953, sec. 96).

Lichtenberg, incidentally, makes an ironical expostulation of a similar tenor about the relation between word and meaning: 'I really don't know what man wants. He has got it into his head that certain words have certain meanings which they must perpetually retain. I ask, . . . Who will forbid me to take here a word and there a meaning, and to join them together?' (1958: 198). Cf. the ideal objects imagined by Borges (above, n. 18).

of our grammatical forms that the idea of an inner process, that of meaning the linguistic phrases that we express, is a standing temptation; and we are thereby led also not only to separate the intended meaning from the expression, but hence to conjecture the real nature of the process of meaning something. 'We talk of [mental] processes and states and leave their nature undecided. Sometime perhaps we shall know more about them—we think. But that is just what commits us to a particular way of looking at the matter' (Wittgenstein 1953, sec. 308). This indeed is the way that belief has been regarded. It was apparently a subtle and intricate kind of inner process, if also at times a quite forceful one, and its complexity and elusiveness made it difficult to know anything about. But the repeated attempts to explain it were none the less inspired by the presumption that in time its nature could be decided. None of the attempts was successful, and even the fact that no descriptive progress was ever made still had no effect on the ambition to arrive at last at a clear account of the real character of the inner process or state of belief. As I have been arguing, it was a misunderstanding of the grammar of belief that framed these inquiries, and not until the linguistic forms themselves were called into question[50] was it possible to think clearly about the grounds of the ambition to describe the entity that 'belief' was taken to denote. In the same way, it is a misunderstanding of our grammar that is responsible also for the more general misconception about the meanings that (as we assume) we intend to convey through the words we use. Yet all that we really know when we find sentences forming themselves under our hands, or even when we compose them 'in our heads' without in fact writing them down, is that language is at work and that we are the locus of that occurrence. Naturally, I am not denying that we intentionally chop and change our expressions, alter their construction, add or delete words, and so on; but that is precisely what the employment of language is, and merely to remark that this is what we do is not a justification of any particular theory of the means by which we do it. There is certainly an element of deliberation in our use of language, and we do have a qualified responsibility for what we express (to begin with, we can decide not to express it) and for the forms in which we do so. But we do not therefore have to conclude that there is also at work within us some subtle mental process in addition to what we know we actually do.

[50] 'Distrust of grammar is the first requisite for philosophizing' (Wittgenstein 1961: 93).

Nor, of course, when we find that we have written what we did not know we had in us, should we then further assume that the sentences are the products of a mental process so extremely subtle that it can act, and formulate meanings, without us even being conscious of it.

This conclusion does not follow, either, from an even more common type of experience, namely the realization that our thoughts change over time and independently of a deliberate impulsion to change them or to bring about any particular change or type of change. We find ourselves entertaining or expressing thoughts quite different from those that we held earlier; and we find ourselves also declaring ideas that appear to be spontaneous and unconnected with any previous thoughts on a given topic. Here too we tend to be misled by the idiom of the English language. We say transitively that *we* change our minds, as though it were in our power to foresee a new idea (though without mentally 'seeing' it, in which case our mind would of course already have changed in the sense in question) and then to procure within ourselves a corresponding alteration in a mental mechanism that finally would accommodate the idea as a new accession. Yet all we know, and necessarily only in retrospect, is that we now entertain or express thoughts which are different from those that we were conscious of before. We do not *mean* the changes in our mind (independently of their formulation in language), then determine how they shall be expressed, and end up by saying what we conclude are our thoughts—as though they were the products of a process that we control. We do not change our minds, any more than our minds change us: we change. A different idiom can actually lead us to see this and to put a more valid construction on the issue. Instead of saying that we change our minds, we can say that our ideas *have* changed or even that we have changed *in* our ideas. Empirically, this gets far closer to what happens. Here again, language is at work and we are the locus of that phenomenon.

By this account, then, the query that opened this terminal stage of our investigation into the concept of belief assumes a different aspect. The question was how we can say what we mean, when we do not understand the meanings of the words we use; and one answer is that the question is misphrased—not sophistically, however, but as a reasonable sequence to the preceding section of the argument. To begin with, the formulation confuses two senses of 'meaning': in the first clause this notion stands for an intention to signify something, and in the second it stands for an acceptation that another person may accord to what is expressed. There is no necessary correspondence between these two elements of discourse, and the extent to which in practice there may be a communication of sense is a matter of highly contingent circumstance. Second, when a man utters a belief-statement he is not reporting an inner experience of a discriminable kind, and he cannot intend (mean) to impart to his hearer any distinctive property of such an experience. He is using a word by which he can convey a judgement, supposition, expectation, commitment, doubt, or many another statement about a position that he holds; and in using the word 'believe', in a certain grammatical form and in a particular social situation, he assumes a recognizable part in the play of communication. The meaning that he expresses in a belief-statement is the effect that he intends to procure, and this is an expectation that he has learned by his familiarity with the linguistic and other conventions of the culture. Conversely, the meaning that he is taken to express by that belief-statement is the effect actually produced in a hearer who similarly interprets the situation in the light of his knowledge of the cultural conventions. This act of social intercourse does not depend on the existence of belief as a distinct mode of experience that is reported by the speaker, nor does it require that the hearer shall himself be familiar with such an experience. The situation does not demand, either, that the speaker shall ascribe a distinct meaning to the word 'believe', or that his interlocutor shall accept the word in that precise sense. For 'man possesses an innate capacity for constructing symbols with which *some* sense can be expressed without having the slightest idea what each word signifies' (Wittgenstein 1961: 95).

Indeed, the conduct of social life does not always and in every situation require that the use of language shall be to convey distinct ideas, to declare propositional meanings that a speaker has innerly formulated. As Berkeley long ago observed, 'the communicating of ideas marked by words is not the chief and only end of language, as is commonly supposed. There are other ends, as the raising of some passion, the exciting to, or deterring from an action, the putting the mind in some particular disposition' (*Principles*, Introduction, sec. XX). The mere perception of certain words arouses passions in the mind, 'without any ideas coming between'. In everyday observation there are innumerable instances of this fact. The civil dialogues of daily life are often carried on without any care at all to communicate distinct ideas; and among those who have long been used to each other's company the expressions they utter (comments on the weather, animadversions on the government, references to relatives or to each other, etc.) have typically a repetitious and rote-like quality which shows that the function of language can be something quite other than the communication of discretive sense. Harold Pinter well conveys the habitual and virtually formalized style of such converse, and Samuel Beckett grimly presents the utter meaninglessness that can characterize the interchange of expressions which in themselves are coherent and sensible. These dramatic examples are extreme in the artificial intensity and the explicitness with which they exhibit these features of common usage; but they do not exaggerate the underlying fact that the significant employment of language, even when framed in acceptable grammatical forms and in situations regulated by the institutions of society, requires no propositional content in what is said. The statements of ordinary discourse often do not have use because they communicate distinct conceptual meanings, but they have meaning because they serve indistinct social uses.

At this point in our search for the real grounds of the concept of belief we have thus in another direction approached the limits of language, and nowhere yet have we touched firm foundations or got any reliable bearings. With each step in the analysis, on the contrary, infirmities and obscurities have proliferated, and in nothing have we found any certainty—not in language and not in experience. Every apparent ground of absolute knowledge or judgement has crumbled or dissipated, and only shifting relativities remain. The course of comparative studies, from the confident and universal programme of Comte down to the tentative particularity of the present inquiry, has been a series of setbacks and disillusionments, as ambitions have been reduced and prejudices have been given up. These are certainly achievements of a kind, and in a negative way they give cause for a certain methodological satisfaction; but the advance they effect, instead of achieving some theoretical certainty in the interpretation of human life, consists instead in an increasingly sceptical appreciation of the limitations on our understanding.

We want to discern a constant order in the world, and first of all to make an orderly determination of the true nature of man. We can do so only through language, if at all, yet the perpetual variation and the intrinsic hazards of linguistic representation prevent us in every attempt to work out co-ordinates. Through languages and the schemes of collective representations that they frame we discern one form of order after another; but we cannot now, after the sobering instruction of our quest for belief, reasonably hope ever to attain the order of those orders. It is not to be established by either logic or experiment, and the confused and contradictory testimonies of the numerous cultural traditions argue only against any universal order underlying human affairs and concerns. It is true that in the comparative study of man there is some possibility of ordering those evidences by reference to certain primary factors of human experience, in the form of logical constraints and psychic proclivities; but these are no more than conditions of order, formal and intuitive possibilities out of which men elaborate with untold variety the contingent and arbitrary forms of order that for them are reality itself. Although hypothetically such primary factors are common to all men, they cannot be expected to frame common representations of man in the world. The singularity that is proper to each form of social life cannot be understood by such means alone, any more than what men conjecture about the quandary of their existence can be interpreted by a phonetic analysis of their philosophical statements. The phantasmagoric variegation of the collective forms of significance, in grammar and classificatory concepts and styles of thought, reflects the essential relativity that marks all ideas about the meaning and determination of human experience.

I am not saying that human life is senseless, but that we cannot make sense of it. If only it were at least a tale told by an idiot, we might arrive at some coherent meaning, but the metaphor presupposes criteria of intelligibility and sanity that we do not possess except by convention. Once outside a given form of life, man is lost in a 'wildernesse of formes'.

This might be a situation to which we could somehow accommodate ourselves if only we had some steady means to decide what is a form of life. But the security of discrimination promised by conventional boundaries, such as nation, society, culture, or language, is illusory; and when we consider comparatively, and hence more exactly, the regions and relationships within which communication is held, it proves that there is no means of tracing a sure boundary to any given circumscription of experience. If 'an expression has meaning only in the stream of life',[51] then an inescapable

[51] 'Ein Ausdruck hat nur im Strome des Lebens Bedeutung' (Wittgenstein, in Malcolm 1966: 93).

problem is to chart the stream of human life; but it meanders, changes course, erodes its banks, exposes hidden strata, submerges what had seemed safe elevations, and in every conceivable characteristic it exhibits a perpetual inconstancy.

Not even the concept of the individual can provide any firm delineation of a form of life, for he is not a distinct entity apart from the currents of social existence in which he is carried along. Divided within himself by his very self-consciousness, yet with no real guarantee of his own integrity, he too can maintain no constant and recognizable form independently of the collective representations that frame his being and proffer the means of ascribing significance to human life. He tries indeed to direct his course and plot successive positions in his drift towards extinction, but by acts and instruments (social gestures and linguistic expressions) which themselves belong to the very forces with which he has to contend.

In the formation of the individual, moreover, there are implicit factors which render still more uncertain the postulation of distinct forms of life. MacIntyre has cogently stressed how children, in being educated to the expectations of society, are made not only to assume a type of personality but also to impair their capacity for a more or less direct communication with others. They sometimes learn, he writes, to exhibit behaviour that is symbolically expressive of an emotion before they have learned to feel the emotion: this is often true, as he instances, in the case of gratitude. 'What they have to learn in order to exhibit adult emotions involves them in learning how to pretend, how to be ironic, how to lie, and how to produce those stock responses which sustain fatigued human relationships. In so doing they become, like the adult world, *opaque*' (1971: 242; my italics). Behaviourists, he continues, may not sufficiently have appreciated this fact as standing in the way of the project of scientific inquiry about human beings (243):

They may have underrated the extent to which we are very often opaque to each other a great deal of the time. Misunderstanding and not understanding [is] at the core of human life. . . .

The present investigation has brought out, I think, some of the reasons that we are affected with such obscurity and confusion in our communications. In this case in particular we can appreciate how thoroughly we are induced to misunderstand one another and to misconceive the capacities that can be ascribed to man. The concept of belief is a pattern of the means by which we are subjected to opacity and misunderstanding in taking account of the modes of human experience. But even this realization is cast in terms that are misleading, for they promise an ultimate improvement at which I doubt we can ever arrive. To say that we are opaque to one another may be taken to imply that the achievement of clarity is a feasible aim, and to recognize a misunderstanding suggests a true and certain knowledge that may eventually be attained. Yet our investigation into the supposed capacity for belief, as a premise to social intercourse and as an essential human power, argues corrosively against any such confidence.

Einstein once remarked that 'the eternally incomprehensible fact about the universe is that it is comprehensible' (1938: 6–7). The solitary comprehensible fact about human experience is that it is incomprehensible.

Bibliography

Adriani, N. *Bare'e-Nederlandsch Woordenboek.* Leiden, 1928.

Andree, Richard. *Ethnographische Parallelen und Vergleiche.* Stuttgart: Meier, 1878.

——. *Ethnographische Parallelen und Vergleiche: Neue Folge.* Leipzig: von Veit, 1889.

Anscombe, G. E. M. *Intention.* 2nd ed. Oxford: Blackwell, 1963.

Bachelard, Gaston, *La Poétique de la rêverie.* Paris: Presses Universitaires de France, 1960.

Bambrough, Renford. 'Universals and Family Resemblances.' *Proceedings of the Aristotelian Society* 61 (1960–1): 207–22.

Barr, James. *The Semantics of Biblical Language.* London: Oxford University Press, 1961.

Bastian, Adolf. *Ethnische Elementargedanken in der Lehre vom Menschen.* 2 vols. Berlin: Weidmann, 1895.

Bateson, Gregory. 'Social Structure of the Iatmül People of the Sepik River.' *Oceania* 2 (1932): 246–89.

Beattie, John. *Other Cultures: Aims, Methods and Achievements in Social Anthropology.* London: Cohen & West, 1964.

Beidelman, T. O., editor. *The Translation of Culture: Essays to E. E. Evans-Pritchard.* London: Tavistock, 1971.

Benveniste, Emile. *Problèmes de linguistique générale.* Paris: Gallimard, 1966.

——. *Le Vocabulaire des institutions indo-européennes.* 2 vols. Paris: Editions de Minuit, 1969.

Bergson, Henri. 'Le Rêve.' *Revue scientifique,* 4th ser., 15 (1901): 705–13.

Berkeley, George. *A Treatise concerning the Principles of Human Knowledge.* London, 1710.

Bernardi, B. *The Mugwe, A Failing Prophet: A Study of a Religious and Public Dignitary of the Meru of Kenya.* London: Oxford University Press for the International African Institute, 1959.

Bevan, Edwyn. *Symbolism and Belief*. The Gifford Lectures, 1933–1934. London: Collins, 1962.

Bible, La Sainte. Traduit en Français sous la direction de l'École Biblique de Jérusalem. Paris: Editions du Cerf, 1961.

Bible, The New English. New Testament. Oxford: Oxford University Press; Cambridge: At the University Press, 1961.

Black, Max. 'Saying and Disbelieving.' *Analysis* 13 (1952): 25–33. Reprinted as chap. 3 in Max Black, *Problems of Analysis: Philosophical Essays*, pp. 46–57. London: Routledge & Kegan Paul, 1954.

Borges, Jorge Luis. *Fictions*. London: Calder, 1965.

Braithwaite, R. B. 'The Nature of Believing.' *Proceedings of the Aristotelian Society* 33 (1933): 129–46. Reprinted in *Knowledge and Belief*, edited by A. Phillips Griffiths, pp. 28–40. London: Oxford University Press, 1967.

——. *An Empiricist's View of the Nature of Religious Belief*. 9th Eddington Memorial Lecture. Cambridge: At the University Press, 1955.

Bratcher, Robert C., and Nida, Eugene A. *A Translator's Handbook to the Gospel of Mark*. Leiden: Brill, for the United Bible Societies, 1961.

Brower, Reuben A., editor. *On Translation*. Cambridge, Mass.: Harvard University Press, 1959.

Browne, Thomas. *Religio Medici*. London, 1643.

——. *Religio Medici*. Edited by Jean-Jacques Denonain. Cambridge: At the University Press, 1955.

Buck, Carl Darling. *A Dictionary of Selected Synonyms in the Principal Indo-European Languages: A Contribution to the History of Ideas*. Chicago: University of Chicago Press, 1949.

Bultmann, Rudolf. *Gnosis*. Translated from the German and with additional notes by J. R. Coates. Bible Key Words from Gerhard Kittel, *Theologisches Wörterbuch zum Neuen Testament* [Stuttgart, 1933]. London: Black, 1952.

Bultmann, Rudolf, and Weiser, Artur. *Faith*. Translated from the German by Dorothea M. Barton, edited by P. R. Ackroyd. Bible Key Words from Gerhard Kittel, *Theologisches Wörterbuch zum Neuen Testament* [Stuttgart, 1933]. London: Black, 1961.

Burgin, Richard. *Conversations with Jorge Luis Borges*. New York: Avon Books, 1970.

Cannon, W. B. *Bodily Changes in Pain, Hunger, Fear and Rage*. New York: Appleton, 1929.

Cassirer, Ernst. *Philosophie der symbolischen Formen.* 3 vols. Berlin: Bruno Cassirer, 1923–9.

——. *An Essay on Man: An Introduction to a Philosophy of Human Culture.* New Haven and London: Yale University Press, 1944.

——. *The Philosophy of Symbolic Forms,* vol. 1: *Language.* Translated by Ralph Manheim; preface and introduction by Charles W. Hendel. New Haven and London: Yale University Press, 1953.

Cazeneuve, Jean. *Lucien Lévy-Bruhl: sa vie, son oeuvre, avec un exposé de sa philosophie.* Paris: Presses Universitaires de France, 1963. (English translation by Peter Rivière; Oxford: Blackwell, 1972.)

Chomsky, Noam. *Language and Mind.* New York: Harcourt, Brace & World, 1968.

Clarke, Norris. 'It is compatible!' Response to MacIntyre (1964) in *Faith and the Philosophers,* edited by John Hick, pp. 134–47. London: Macmillan, 1964.

Comte, Auguste. *Cours de philosophie positive,* vol. 1: *Les Préliminaires généraux et la philosophie mathématique.* Paris: Bachelier, 1830.

Condillac, Étienne Bonnot de. *Cours d'étude pour l'instruction du Prince de Parme.* . . . 12 vols. Geneva, 1780.

Cornford, F. M. *From Religion to Philosophy: A Study in the Origins of European Speculation.* London: Arnold, 1912.

Crazzolara, J. P. *Outlines of a Nuer Grammar.* Anthropos Linguistische Bibliothek, vol. 13. Vienna: Verlag 'Anthropos', 1933.

——. *Buk Lam ke Thok Nadh.* Verona: 'Nigrizia' Printing Press School; Yoynyang: Catholic Mission, 1934(a).

——. *Katekismo ke Thok Nadh.* Verona: 'Nigrizia' Printing Press School; Yoynyang: Catholic Mission, 1934(b).

——. *Zur Gesellschaft und Religion der Nueer.* Studia Instituti Anthropos, vol. 5. Vienna-Mödling: Verlag 'Anthropos', 1953.

Danto, Arthur C. 'Beliefs as Sentential States of Persons.' In Kiefer & Munitz (1970): 122–40.

Darwin, Charles. *The Expression of the Emotions in Man and Animals.* London: Murray, 1872.

Davy, Georges. *Sociologues d'hier et d'aujourd'hui.* 2nd ed., rev. Paris: Presses Universitaires de France, 1950.

Dempwolff, Otto. *Vergleichende Lautlehre des Austronesischen Wortschatzes,* vol. 3: *Austronesisches Wörterverzeichnis.* Berlin: Reimer, 1933.

Descartes, René. *Méditations métaphysiques*. Paris, 1647.

——. *Les Passions de l'âme*. Paris, 1649.

Dorssen, J. C. C. van. *De Derivata van de Stam* אמן *in het Hebreeuwsch van het Oude Testament: Een semasiologisch Onderzoek*. Amsterdam: Drukkerij Holland, 1951.

Douglas, Mary. *Purity and Danger: An Analysis of Concepts of Pollution and Taboo*. London: Routledge & Kegan Paul, 1966.

Dumont, Louis. *La Civilisation indienne et nous*. Cahiers des Annales, 23. Paris: Colin, 1964.

Dunbar, James. *Essays on the History of Mankind in Rude and Cultivated Ages*. London, 1780.

Durkheim, Emile. *Les Règles de la méthode sociologique*. 2nd ed. Paris, 1898(a). Reprinted, Paris: Presses Universitaires de France, 1947.

——. 'Représentations individuelles et représentations collectives.' *Revue de Métaphysique et de Morale* 6 (1898[b]): 273–302. Reprinted in *Sociologie et philosophie*, pp. 1–48. Paris: Presses Universitaires de France, 1951.

——. *Les Formes élémentaires de la vie religieuse: le système totémique en Australie*. Paris, 1912.

Durkheim, Emile, and Mauss, Marcel. 'De quelques formes primitives de classification: contribution à l'étude des représentations collectives.' *Année sociologique* 6 (1903): 1–72.

——. *Primitive Classification*. Translated and edited with an introduction by Rodney Needham. Chicago: University of Chicago Press, 1963.

Edgerton, Faye. 'Some Translation Problems in Navajo.' *The Bible Translator* 13 (1962): 25–33.

Eibl-Eibesfeldt, Irenäus. *Ethology: The Biology of Behavior*. Translated by Erich Klinghammer. New York: Holt, Rinehart & Winston, 1970.

Einstein, Albert. 'Physik und Realität.' *Zeitschrift für freie deutsche Forschung* 1 (1938): 5–19. Paris.

Eisler, Rudolf, editor. *Kant-Lexicon: Nachschlagswerk zu Kants Sämtlichen Schriften, Briefen und Handschriftlichen Nachlass*. Hildesheim: Olms, 1961.

Erman, Adolf, and Grapow, Hermann. *Wörterbuch der Aegyptischen Sprache*. 5 vols. Leipzig: Hinrich, 1925–31.

Evans-Pritchard, E. E. 'Lévy-Bruhl's Theory of Primitive Mentality.' *Bulletin of the Faculty of Arts, Egyptian University, Cairo* 2, pt. 1 (1934): 1–26.

——. *Witchcraft, Oracles and Magic among the Azande.* Oxford: Clarendon Press, 1937.

——. *The Nuer: A Description of the Modes of Livelihood and Political Institutions of a Nilotic People.* Oxford: Clarendon Press, 1940.

——. *Nuer Religion.* Oxford: Clarendon Press, 1956.

——. *Theories of Primitive Religion.* Oxford: Clarendon Press, 1965.

——. Comment on Littlejohn (1970). *Bijdragen tot de Taal-, Landen Volkenkunde* 126 (1970): 109–13.

Fison, Lorimer, and Howitt, Alfred William. *Kamilaroi and Kurnai.* Introduction by Lewis H. Morgan. Melbourne: Robertson, 1880.

Flew, Antony, and MacIntyre, Alasdair, editors. *New Essays in Philosophical Theology.* London: SCM Press, 1955.

Frege, Gottlob. *Translations from the Philosophical Writings of Gottlob Frege.* Edited by Peter Geach and Max Black. 2nd ed. Oxford: Blackwell, 1960.

Freud, Sigmund. *The Future of an Illusion.* Translated by W. D. Robertson-Scott. International Psycho-Analytical Library, edited by Ernest Jones, no. 15. London: Hogarth Press, 1928.

Galton, Francis. 'Composite Portraits.' *Journal of the Anthropological Institute* 8 (1879): 132–42.

Geddes, W. R. *Nine Dayak Nights.* Melbourne: Oxford University Press, 1957.

Geertz, Clifford. 'Religion as a Cultural System.' In Michael Banton, ed., *Anthropological Approaches to the Study of Religion* (ASA Monographs 3): 1–46. London: Tavistock, 1966.

Gonda, J. *Sanskrit in Indonesia.* Nagpur: International Academy of Indian Culture, 1952.

——. 'Some Notes on the Study of Ancient-Indian Religious Terminology.' *History of Religions* 1 (1961): 243–73.

Grandsaignes d'Hauterive, R. *Dictionnaire des racines des langues indo-européennes.* 2nd ed. Paris: Larousse, 1949.

Grant, Ewan C. 'Human Facial Expression.' *Man*, n.s. 4 (1969): 525–36.

Grebe, Paul, editor. *Duden Etymologie: Herkunftswörterbuch der deutschen Sprache.* (Der Grosse Duden, vol. 7.) Mannheim: Bibliographisches Institut, 1963.

Griffiths, A. Phillips. 'On Belief.' *Proceedings of the Aristotelian Society* 63 (1963): 167–86. Reprinted in *Knowledge and Belief,* edited by A. Phillips Griffiths, pp. 127–43. London: Oxford University Press, 1967.

Griffiths, A. Phillips, editor. *Knowledge and Belief*. Oxford Readings in Philosophy, edited by G. J. Warnock. London: Oxford University Press, 1967.

Hampshire, Stuart. *Thought and Action*. London: Chatto & Windus, 1959.

——. *Freedom of the Individual*. London: Chatto & Windus; Dunedin, N.Z.: University of Otago Press, 1965.

Hartnack, Justus, 'Some Logical Incongruities between the Concept of Knowledge and the Concept of Belief.' In Kiefer & Munitz (1970): 112–21.

Henle, Paul, editor. *Language, Thought, and Culture*. Ann Arbor, Mich.: University of Michigan Press, 1958.

Hertz, Robert. 'La Prééminence de la main droite: étude sur la polarité religieuse.' *Revue philosophique* 68 (1909): 553–80.

——. *Death and the Right Hand*. Translated by Rodney and Claudia Needham, with an introduction by E. E. Evans-Pritchard. London: Cohen & West, 1960.

High, Dallas M. *Language, Persons and Belief: Studies in Wittgenstein's 'Philosophical Investigations' and Religious Uses of Language*. New York: Oxford University Press, 1967.

Hindley, J. C. 'Salvation and Associated Concepts.' *The Bible Translator* 13 (1962): 102–17.

Hocart, Arthur Maurice. *Kingship*. Oxford: Clarendon Press, 1927.

Hoijer, Harry, editor. *Language in Culture: Conference on the Interrelations of Language and other Aspects of Culture*. Chicago: University of Chicago Press, 1954.

Hudson, W. D. *Ludwig Wittgenstein: The Bearing of his Philosophy upon Religious Belief*. Makers of Contemporary Theology, 7. London: Lutterworth Press, 1968.

Huffman, Ray. *Nuer-English Dictionary*. Berlin: Reimer, 1929.

——. *English–Nuer Dictionary*. London: Oxford University Press, 1931.

Hume, David. *A Treatise of Human Nature: Being an Attempt to introduce the Experimental Method of Reasoning into Moral Subjects*. 3 vols. London, 1739–40.

——. *A Treatise of Human Nature*. Edited, with an analytical index, by L. A. Selby-Bigge. Oxford: Clarendon Press, 1888.

Jonker, J. C. G. *Rottineesch-Hollandsch Woordenboek*. Leiden: Brill, 1908.

Kant, Immanuel. *Kritik der reinen Vernunft.* 2nd ed. Riga, 1787.

———. *Allgemeine Naturgeschichte und Theorie des Himmels.* 2nd ed., rev. Leipzig, 1797.

———. *Immanuel Kant's Logik: Ein Handbuch zu Vorlesungen.* Edited by Gottlob Benjamin Jäsche. Königsberg: Friedrich Nicolovius, 1880.

———. *Kant's Introduction to Logic, and his Essay on the Mistaken Subtilty of the Four Figures.* Translated by Thomas Kingsmill Abbott, with a few notes by Coleridge. London: Longmans, Green, 1885.

Karlgren, Bernhard. *Analytic Dictionary of Chinese and Sino-Japanese.* Paris: Geuthner, 1923.

———. 'Glosses on the Kuo Feng Odes.' *Bulletin of the Museum of Far Eastern Antiquities, Stockholm* 14 (1942): 71–247.

———. 'Glosses on the Ta Ya and Sung Odes.' *Bulletin of the Museum of Far Eastern Antiquities, Stockholm* 18 (1946): 1–198.

———. *Grammata Serica Recensa.* Stockholm: Museum of Far Eastern Antiquities, 1964.

Kenny, Anthony. *Action, Emotion and Will.* New York: Humanities Press, 1963.

Kiefer, Howard E. & Munitz, Milton K., ed. *Language, Belief, and Metaphysics.* Albany, N.Y.: State University of New York Press, 1970.

Kiggen, J. *Nuer-English Dictionary.* Steyl bij Tegelen: Drukkerij van het Missiehuis, 1948.

Kittel, Gerhard, editor. *Theologisches Wörterbuch zum Neuen Testament.* Stuttgart: Kohlhammer, 1932- .

Koper, J. *Enkele Aspecten van het Vraagstuk der Missionaire Bijbelvertaling, in het bijzonder in Indonesië.* The Hague: J. N. Voorhoeve, n.d. [1956].

Korn, Francis. *Elementary Structures Reconsidered: Lévi-Strauss on Kinship.* London: Tavistock, forthcoming.

Kurath, Hans, and Kuhn, Sherman, editors. *Middle English Dictionary.* Ann Arbor, Mich.: University of Michigan Press, 1956- .

Lambooy, P. J. 'Het Begrip "Marapoe" in den Godsdienst von Oost Soemba.' *Bijdragen tot de Taal-, Land- en Volkenkunde van Nederlandsch-Indië* 95 (1937): 425–39.

Lawrence, Peter. *Road Belong Cargo: A Study of the Cargo Movement in the Southern Madang District, New Guinea.* Manchester: Manchester University Press, 1964.

Leach, E. R. *Political Systems of Highland Burma: A Study of Kachin Social Structure.* London: Bell, 1954.

——. *Rethinking Anthropology.* London School of Economics Monographs on Social Anthropology, no. 22. London: Athlone Press, 1961.

——. 'Virgin Birth.' *Proceedings of the Royal Anthropological Institute* 1966: 39–49.

Leenhardt, Maurice. *Do Kamo: La personne et le mythe dans le monde mélanésien.* Paris: Gallimard, 1947.

Leibniz, Gottfried Wilhelm von. *Neue Abhandlungen über den menschlichen Verstand. Nouveaux essais sur l'entendement humain.* Edited and translated by Wolf von Engelhardt and Hans Heinz Holz. 2 vols. Frankfort am Main: Insel-Verlag, 1961.

Lévi-Strauss, Claude. 'Introduction à l'œuvre de M. Mauss.' In Marcel Mauss, *Sociologie et anthropologie,* pp. ix–lii. Paris: Presses Universitaires de France, 1950.

——. *Le Totémisme aujourd'hui.* Paris: Presses Universitaires de France, 1962.

——. *Totemism.* Translated [and edited] by Rodney Needham. Boston: Beacon Press, 1963.

——. *The Savage Mind.* Chicago: University of Chicago Press, 1966.

Lévy-Bruhl, Lucien. *La Morale et la science des mœurs.* Paris: Alcan, 1903.

——. *Les Fonctions mentales dans les sociétés inférieures.* Paris: Alcan, 1910.

——. *La Mentalité primitive.* The Herbert Spencer Lecture, delivered at Oxford 29 May 1931. Oxford: Clarendon Press, 1931.

——. *L'Expérience mystique et les symboles chez les primitifs.* Paris: Alcan, 1938.

——. *Les Carnets de Lucien Lévy-Bruhl.* Preface by Maurice Leenhardt. Paris: Presses Universitaires de France, 1949. (English edition, translated by Peter Rivière; Oxford: Blackwell, forthcoming.)

Lévy-Bruhl, Lucien, et al. 'La Mentalité primitive.' Report of a meeting held 15 February 1923. *Bulletin de la Société française de philosophie* 18, 23ᵉ année, no. 2 (1923): 2–48.

Lichtenberg, Georg Christoph. *Aphorismen.* Edited by Max Rychner. Zürich: Mannesse, 1958.

——. *Schriften und Briefe,* vol. I: *Sudelbücher.* Edited by Wolfgang Promies. Munich: Carl Hanser, 1968.

Littlejohn, James. 'Twins, Birds, Etc.' *Bijdragen tot de Taal-, Landen Volkenkunde* 126 (1970): 91–108; 'Reply to Professor Evans-Pritchard', pp. 113–14.

Locke, John. *An Essay concerning Human Understanding.* London, 1690.

Lonergan, Bernard J. F. *Insight: A Study of Human Understanding.* 2nd ed., rev. London: Longmans, Green, 1958.

Lovejoy, Arthur C. *The Great Chain of Being: A Study of the History of an Idea.* Cambridge, Mass.: Harvard University Press, 1936.

MacIntyre, Alasdair. 'The Logical Status of Religious Belief.' In *Metaphysical Beliefs*, by Stephen Toulmin, Ronald W. Hepburn, and Alastair MacIntyre, pp. 167–211. London: S.C.M. Press, 1957.

———. 'Is Understanding Religion compatible with Believing?' In *Faith and the Philosophers*, edited by John Hick, pp. 115–33. London: Macmillan, 1964.

———. *Against the Self-Images of the Age: Essays on Ideology and Philosophy.* London: Duckworth, 1971.

McKenzie, Alain. *Le Pavillon des caractères tracés: petit vocabulaire chinois.* Paris: Jean-Jacques Pauvert, 1970.

Malcolm, Norman. *Ludwig Wittgenstein: A Memoir.* With a biographical sketch by Georg Henrik von Wright. London: Oxford University Press, 1958. (Rev. ed., 1966.)

———. 'Is it a Religious Belief that "God exists"?' In *Faith and the Philosophers*, edited by John Hick, pp. 103–10. London: Macmillan, 1964.

Marsden, William. 'On the Traces of the Hindu Language and Literature, extant among the Malays.' *Asiatick Researches* 4 (1795): 221–7.

Marty, Martin E. *Varieties of Unbelief.* New York: Holt, Rinehart & Winston, 1964.

Mathews, R. H. *A Chinese-English Dictionary.* Shanghai: China Inland Mission and Presbyterian Mission Press, 1931.

Mauss, Marcel. Comments on an address by Lucien Lévy-Bruhl on 'La Mentalité primitive'. *Bulletin de la Société française de philosophie* 18, 23ᵉ année, no. 2 (1923): 24–8.

———. 'Essai sur le don: forme et raison de l'échange dans les sociétés archaïques.' *Année sociologique*, n.s., 1 (1925): 30–186.

———. 'Les Techniques du corps.' *Journal de Psychologie* 32 (1935): 271–93.

S

——. *Sociologie et anthropologie*. Paris: Presses Universitaires de France, 1950.

——. *Œuvres*. Edited by Victor Karady. 3 vols. Paris: Editions de Minuit, 1968–9.

Maxwell, William Edward. *The Malay Language, with an introductory Sketch of the Sanskrit Element in Malay*. London: Trübner, 1888.

Mayo, Bernard. 'Belief and Constraint.' *Proceedings of the Aristotelian Society* 64 (1964): 139–56. Reprinted in *Knowledge and Belief*, edited by A. Phillips Griffiths, pp. 147–61. London: Oxford University Press, 1967.

Middelkoop, P. 'About the Translation of the Word *Nachash* into Timorese.' *The Bible Translator* 7 (1956): 130–3.

Monier-Williams, Monier. *A Sanskrit-English Dictionary*. Oxford: Clarendon Press, 1899.

Mounin, Georges, *Les Problèmes théoriques de la traduction*. Paris: Gallimard, 1963.

Müller, F. Max. *The Science of Thought*. London: Longmans Green, 1887.

——. *Contributions to the Science of Mythology*. 2 vols. London: Longmans Green, 1897.

Needham, Rodney. 'A Structural Analysis of Aimol Society.' *Bijdragen tot de Taal-, Land-, en Volkenkunde* 116 (1960): 81–108.

——. *Structure and Sentiment: A Test Case in Social Anthropology*. Chicago: University of Chicago Press, 1962.

——. Introduction to *Primitive Classification*, by Emile Durkheim and Marcel Mauss, pp. vii–xlviii. Chicago: University of Chicago Press, 1963.

——. 'Blood, Thunder, and Mockery of Animals.' *Sociologus* 14 (1964): 136–49.

——. 'Age, Category, and Descent.' *Bijdragen tot de Taal-, Land-en Volkenkunde* 122 (1966): 1–35.

——. 'Right and Left in Nyoro Symbolic Classification.' *Africa* 37 (1967a): 425–51.

——. 'Percussion and Transition.' *Man*, n.s., 2 (1967b): 606–14.

——. 'Gurage Social Classification: Formal Notes on an Unusual System.' *Africa* 39 (1969): 153–66.

——. 'Introduction' to *Rethinking Kinship and Marriage*, edited by Rodney Needham, pp. xiii–cxvii. London: Tavistock, 1971(a).

——. 'Remarks on the Analysis of Kinship and Marriage.' In

Rethinking Kinship and Marriage, pp. 1–34. London: Tavistock, 1971(b).

——, editor. *Rethinking Kinship and Marriage*. A.S.A. Monographs, 11. London: Tavistock, 1971(c).

——. *Right and Left: Essays on Dual Symbolic Classification*. Chicago: University of Chicago Press, forthcoming.

Newman, John Henry. *Sermons, chiefly on the Theory of Religious Belief, preached before the University of Oxford*. London: Rivington, 1843.

——. *Discourses addressed to Mixed Congregations*. London: Longman Brown, Green & Longman, 1849.

——. *An Essay in Aid of a Grammar of Assent*. London: Burnes & Oates, 1881.

Nida, Eugene A. *A Translator's Commentary on Selected Passages*. Mimeographed. New York, 1947.

——. *God's Word in Man's Language*. New York: Harper, 1952.

——. 'Problems in Translating the Scriptures into Shilluk, Anuak, and Nuer.' *The Bible Translator* 6 (1955): 55–63.

——. *Towards a Science of Translating, with Special Reference to Principles and Procedures involved in Bible Translating*. Leiden: Brill, 1964.

Onians, Richard Broxton. *The Origins of European Thought about the Body, the Mind, the Soul, the World, Time, and Fate: New Interpretations of Greek, Roman and kindred evidence, also of some basic Jewish and Christian Beliefs*. Cambridge: At the University Press, 1951.

Onions, C. T., editor. *The Oxford Dictionary of English Etymology*. Oxford: Clarendon Press, 1966.

Onvlee, L. 'Over de Weergave van "Heilig" in het Soembaasch.' *Tijdschrift voor Indische Taal-, Land-, en Volkenkunde* 78 (1938): 124–36.

Pascal, Blaise. *Pensées*. Edited with an introduction and notes by Ch.-M. des Granges. Paris: Garnier, 1964.

Peel, J. D. Y. 'Understanding Alien Belief-Systems.' *British Journal of Sociology* 20 (1969): 69–84.

Pfeiffer, Egon. 'Glaube im Alten Testament: eine grammatikalisch-lexikalische Nachprüfung gegenwärtiger Theorien.' *Zeitschrift für die Alttestamentliche Wissenschaft* 71 (1959): 151–64.

Pieper, Josef. *Über den Glauben*. Munich: Kösel, 1962.

Pitcher, George, editor. *Wittgenstein: The 'Philosophical Investigations'*. London: Macmillan, 1968.

Poerwadarminta, W. J. S. *Kamus Umum Bahasa Indonesia*. Djakarta, 1954.

Pokorny, Julius. *Indogermanisches Etymologisches Wörterbuch*. Bern and Munich, 1948- .

Price, H. H. 'Some Considerations about Belief.' *Proceedings of the Aristotelian Society* 35 (1935): 229–52. Reprinted in *Knowledge and Belief*, edited by A. Phillips Griffiths, pp. 41–59. London: Oxford University Press, 1967.

——. *Belief*. London: Allen & Unwin; New York: Humanities Press, 1969.

Prichard, H. A. 'Knowing and Believing.' Excerpts from *Knowledge and Perception*, by H. A. Prichard (Oxford: Clarendon Press, 1950), reprinted in *Knowledge and Belief*, edited by A. Phillips Griffiths, pp. 60–8. London: Oxford University Press, 1967.

[Radcliffe-] Brown, A. R. *The Andaman Islanders*. Cambridge: At the University Press, 1922.

Radcliffe-Brown, A. R. 'Religion and Society.' *Journal of the Royal Anthropological Institute* 75 (1945): 33–43.

Raglan, Lord. *The Temple and the House*. London: Routledge & Kegan Paul, 1964.

Richards, I. A. *Mencius on the Mind: Experiments in Multiple Definition*. London: Routledge & Kegan Paul, 1932.

——. *How to Read a Page: A Course in Efficient Reading with an Introduction to a Hundred Great Words*. New York: Norton, 1942.

Rose, Henry. *A Philosophicall Essay for the Reunion of Languages: or, The Art of Knowing All by the Mastery of One*. Oxford, 1675.

Royal Anthropological Institute of Great Britain and Ireland. *Notes and Queries on Anthropology*. 6th ed., rev. and rewritten by a committee of the Royal Anthropological Institute of Great Britain and Ireland. London: Routledge & Kegan Paul, 1951.

Russell, Bertrand. *The Analysis of Mind*. London: Allen & Unwin, 1921.

Sartre, Jean-Paul. *L'Imagination*. Paris: Presses Universitaires de France, 1936.

Schlosberg, Harold. 'The Description of Facial Expression in Terms of Two Dimensions.' *Journal of Experimental Psychology* 44 (1952): 229–37.

Schulte Nordholt, H. G. *Culturele Antropologie en Geschiedenis*. Amsterdam: Scheltema & Holkema, 1967.

Sergi, M., translator. *Nop Kuaran ne Yesu Kristo ke Thok Nath: Gospel in Nuer Language*. Rome: Sodality of St. Peter Claver, 1968.

Stern, J. P. *Lichtenberg: A Doctrine of Scattered Occasions*. Bloomington: University of Indiana Press, 1959.

Stewart, Dugald. *Elements of the Philosophy of the Human Mind*. 3 vols. London, 1792–1827.

Stigand, C. H. *A Nuer–English Vocabulary*. Cambridge: At the University Press, 1923.

Swellengrebel, J. L. 'Over de Vertaling van het Woord "Heilige Geest" in enkele Indonesische Talen.' *De Opwekker* 86 (1941): 111–28.

Tertullian. *De Carne Christi*.

Toulmin, Stephen. *The Philosophy of Science: An Introduction*. London: Hutchinson, 1953.

Toulmin, Stephen, Hepburn, Ronald W., and MacIntyre, Alasdair. *Metaphysical Beliefs: Three Essays*. London: SCM Press, 1957.

Urquhart, I. A. N. 'Some Interior Dialects.' *Sarawak Museum Journal* 6 (1955): 193–204.

Verheijen, J. A. J. *Het Hoogste Wezen bij de Manggaraiers*. Studia Instituti Anthropos, vol. 4. Vienna-Mödling: Missiehuis St. Gabriel, 1951.

Vygotsky, Lev Semenovich. *Thought and Language*. Edited and translated by Eugenia Hanfmann and Gertrude Vakar. Cambridge, Mass.: M.I.T. Press, 1955.

Waismann, Friedrich. *The Principles of Linguistic Philosophy*. Edited by R. Harré. London: Macmillan, 1965.

——. *How I See Philosophy*. Edited by R. Harré. London: Macmillan, 1968.

Walter, W. Grey. *Observations on Man, his Frame, his Duty, and his Expectations*. 23rd Eddington Lecture. Cambridge: At the University Press, 1969.

Waterman, G. Henry. 'The Translation of Theological Terms in some of the major Dialects of the Philippines.' *The Bible Translator* 11 (1960): 24–31.

Weiser, Artur. 'Glauben im Alten Testament.' In *Festschrift Georg Beer zum 70. Geburtstage*, edited by Artur Weiser, pp. 88–99. Stuttgart: Kohlhammer, 1935.

Whitehead, Alfred North. *Symbolism: Its Meaning and Effect*. Cambridge: At the University Press, 1927.

——. *The Function of Reason.* Princeton: Princeton University Press, 1929.

Whorf, Benjamin Lee. *Language, Thought, and Reality.* Edited with an introduction by John B. Carroll. Cambridge, Mass.: M.I.T. Press, 1956.

Wilkins, John. *An Essay towards a Real Character and a Philosophical Language.* London, 1668.

Wilkinson, R. J. *A Malay-English Dictionary.* Singapore, 1901.

Williams, Bernard. 'Tertullian's Paradox.' In *New Essays in Philosophical Theology*, edited by Antony Flew and Alasdair MacIntyre, pp. 187–211. London: SCM Press, 1955.

——. 'Deciding to Believe.' In Kiefer & Munitz (1970): 95–111.

Wittgenstein, Ludwig. *Philosophical Investigations.* Translated by G. E. M. Anscombe. (2nd ed., rev., 1958.) Oxford: Blackwell, 1953.

——. *Preliminary Studies for the 'Philosophical Investigations', generally known as The Blue and Brown Books.* Oxford: Blackwell, 1958.

——. *Notebooks 1914–1916.* Oxford: Blackwell, 1961.

——. *Remarks on the Foundations of Mathematics.* Edited by G. H. von Wright, R. Rhees, and G. E. M. Anscombe. Translated by G. E. M. Anscombe. Oxford: Blackwell, 1965.

——. *Lectures and Conversations on Aesthetics, Psychology and Religious Belief.* Compiled from notes taken by Yorick Smythies, Rush Rhees and James Taylor. Edited by Cyril Barrett. Oxford: Blackwell, 1966.

——. *Zettel.* Edited by G. E. M. Anscombe and G. H. von Wright. Translated by G. E. M. Anscombe. Oxford: Blackwell, 1967(a).

——. 'Bemerkungen über Frazers *The Golden Bough*.' Edited by Rush Rhees. *Synthese* 17 (1967b): 233–53.

——. *On Certainty.* Edited by G. E. M. Anscombe and G. H. von Wright. Translated by Denis Paul and G. E. M. Anscombe. Oxford: Blackwell, 1969.

Wouden, F. A. E. van. *Sociale Structuurtypen in de Groote Oost.* Leiden: Ginsberg, 1935.

——. *Types of Social Structure in Eastern Indonesia.* Translated by Rodney Needham. Preface by G. W. Locher. Koninklijk Instituut voor Taal-, Land-, en Volkenkunde Translation Series, 11. The Hague: Nijhoff, 1968.

Wright, G. H. von. 'Georg Christoph Lichtenberg als Philosoph.' *Theoria* 8 (1942): 201–17.

Index